Nathanael West:

An Annotated Bibliography of the Scholarship and Works

Garland Reference Library in the Humanities (Vol. 34)

This Book Is Dedicated
With Love and Appreciation
to My Wife Patti

Copyright © 1976

by Dennis P. Vannatta

All Rights Reserved

Library of Congress Cataloging in Publication Data

Vannatta, Dennis P
   Nathanael West : an annotated bibliography of
the scholarship and works.

   (Garland reference library in the humanities ;
34)
   Includes index.
   1.   West, Nathanael, 1903-1940--Bibliography.
Z8968.38.V35   [PS3545.E8334]   016.813'5'2   75-24093
ISBN 0-8240-9978-8

Printed in the United States of America

Nathanael West:
An Annotated Bibliography of the Scholarship and Works

by

Dennis P. Vannatta

with a foreword by

Jay Martin

Garland Publishing, Inc., New York & London

1976

Contents

CONTENTS

Illustrations

Foreword

In 1931 Nathanael West started a short story titled "The Adventurer." Its theme—the fantasy life of mass-man—was to be West's basic subject in his four novels, though he was never able to complete "The Adventurer" itself. The hero of the tale, Joe Rucker, was once a messenger for the "American Delivery Service" and, en route to his deliveries, frequently stopped at the library. The library is his symbol for the nature of fantasy:

> Take the fortysecond street branch of the Public Library. When I was seventeen... it was a continuous delight. A storehouse of high adventure. Far places. Trackless deserts. Picturesque uniforms. Austere codes. Walled cities to be stormed. Ferocious natives to be outwitted. Heaving decks on which to swing a cutlass. All for a cause—science, sometimes, or comradeship, or country, or fortune, or revenge, or even simply a gallant gesture.

Whenever he entered the library, Joe says, he felt like a dancer, "an intricate figure whose design is joy."

The design of Dennis P. Vannatta's book *Nathanael West: An Annotated Bibliography of Criticism and Works* is joy. To be sure, its basic purpose, one which it certainly accomplishes, is to arrange the commentary on West's work under various subject heads and to discuss the treatment so far accorded West, for the use of future scholars who will wish to advance our understanding of West instead of repeating previous insights. Comment on West has accumulated so rapidly in recent years that it is now time to review the state of research, summarize its main trends, and classify its traditions and basic assumptions.

Vannatta's work does more than this, however, by the very nature of its subject and method. Partially because for a long time so little was definitely known about West's life and because his novels were so little known as to be almost legendary, West came to occupy a special position for critics: his place in the American tradition, his intellectual affiliations,

FOREWORD

his biography, and the sources of his imaginative vision were not so "fixed" in literary history as these were in the cases, say, of Hemingway, Fitzgerald, or Eliot. Even twenty years after his death, West's work had a magical appeal which enticed scores of critics to take critical chances, to guess at sources, to attempt daring psychoanalytical analyses, or to offer esoteric comparisons in order to make West intelligible or to explain the fascination and obvious distinction of his work. Far more than most of his contemporaries did, then, West stirred the imaginations of a later generation of critics.

Vannatta is really drawing the most recent portrait of West. Without precisely intending to do so, he has used the technique of the Cubist collage, organizing a multiplicity of perspectives by others in order to make a composite picture. In his guide we see West from many angles (the biographical, the comparative, the historical/sociological, etc.), and within each of these, from a yet more refined variety of perspectives.

What we have, then, is a scholarly guide to West, a lesson in critical taste and critical controversy from the thirties to the present, and finally, what Joe Rucker called "a storehouse of high adventure"—a record of the excitement which West engendered in earlier critics and now, in Vannatta's work, engenders still.

Turtle Rock Hills   Jay Martin
Irvine, California
26 August 1975

Introduction

When absent-minded Nathanael West drove through that stop sign in El Centro, California, in 1940—killing himself and his wife Eileen—the literary world was not shaken to its foundations. A very few thousand had purchased his four novels, which had inspired only a score of reviews. True, a small but impressive group of fellow writers had recognized his talent—including Edmund Wilson, Malcolm Cowley, George S. Kaufmann, and F. Scott Fitzgerald. But for the bulk of the reading public, Nathanael West did not exist.

Today, I am able to cite over 500 books, articles in periodicals, reviews, theses, and dissertations which concern West in one degree or another. It is not my purpose here to analyze reasons for the West "revival." Those studies cited in chapter three—"The State of the Scholarship on West"—offer a variety of explanations. But do we *need* over 500 books, articles, and so forth on Nathanael West? Obviously, no. One must be struck as much by the repetition of West scholarship as by its variety. Indeed, the scholar in possession of James F. Light's *Nathanael West: An Interpretative Study* and Jay Martin's *Nathanael West: The Art of His Life* would be reasonably well equipped for much of his research on West. Still, so many critical questions remain alive that future work is called for. Is the religious conversion of Miss Lonelyhearts, for example, a viable alternative to contemporary cynicism? Do Miss Lonelyhearts' homosexual tendencies (if such there be) have more than a peripheral impact on the novel? Is *The Day of the Locust* sapped of its vigor by Tod Hackett's lack of involvement, or is it indeed West's finest novel? Are *The Dream Life of Balso Snell* and *A Cool Million* worth reading at all?

If this bibliography does little else, then, I would hope that it would provide scholars with an idea of which Westian lands have been sufficiently explored and mapped and which hold mystery yet.

INTRODUCTION

Some explanation is needed to facilitate use of this bibliography. The Master Checklist (chapter one) is the key to this work. There, all of the scholarship is listed under five headings (books and pamphlets, material in books, articles in periodicals and reviews of the novels, reviews of scholarship, and theses and dissertations). At the end of each item will be found one or more Roman numerals. These refer the reader to subsequent chapters where that work will be annotated. The annotations (up to, but not including, 1975) have been divided into chapters according to the type of scholarship being employed (biography, biographical criticism, source studies, comparative studies, and so forth). If a particular work makes use of more than one type of scholarship, it will be annotated in more than one chapter. Thus, if an item in the Master Checklist ends in the following—"See II, VIII, IX"—the reader would find that item annotated in those chapters. Note that, hereafter, all numbers in brackets refer to Master Checklist item numbers. Also note that a few of the items— mainly references and other works that make brief mention of West—are annotated in the Master Checklist itself. Finally, the annotated chapters are arranged in alphabetical order by the last name of the author, *not* by Master Checklist item number.

I would like to acknowledge my indebtedness to several persons who have helped me throughout the compilation of this bibliography. Most obviously, of course, thanks goes to Professor Jay Martin, who not only was kind enough to read a draft and write a foreword for my study, but who also offered information and encouragement from first to last. Too, without the encouragement of Professor William White this study would probably have never progressed past the rough draft stages. Professor J. Albert Robbins has provided valuable information on the location of manuscripts. I would also like to thank Ms. Brewer and her staff of the Elmer Ellis Library, University of Missouri, Columbia, whose inter-library loan facilities were put under severe strain, I'm afraid, during the researching of this bibliography. And I extend special thanks to Professor Herbert Stappenbeck, whose interest in his students should call for not only gratitude, but emulation.

INTRODUCTION

Finally, several specific sources deserve acknowledgment, including the annual bibliographies published by the Modern Humanities Research Association and the Modern Language Association; *The Year's Work in English Studies; American Literary Scholarship; Dissertation Abstracts International;* James Woodress' *Dissertations in American Literature;* the various checklists compiled by previous West scholars (my annotations are entirely my own); and, I am sure, many other references which I have neglected to mention.

I. Master Checklist of the Scholarship
Concerning Nathanael West

Note: Roman numerals following each item refer to subsequents chapters
where discussions of that item are to be found. Numbers in brackets are
master checklist item numbers. In all subsequent chapters, items will
be listed alphabetically by the last name of the author, *not* by master
checklist item number.

A) Books and Pamphlets Concerning West

1. Comerchero, Victor. *Nathanael West: The Ironic Prophet*. Syracuse:
Syracuse University Press, 1964, 189 pp. See III, V, VIa, VIc, VIe,
VIII, XIc, XIIa, XIIb, XIIc, XIId, XIIe.

2. Hyman, Stanley Edgar. *Nathanael West*. University of Minnesota
Pamphlets on American Writers, No. 21. Minneapolis: University of
Minnesota Press, 1962, 48 pp. See IVc, VII, XIIb, XIIc, XIId, XIIe.

3. Light, James F. *Nathanael West: An Interpretative Study*. Second
edition. Evanston: Northwestern University Press, 1971, 236 pp.
[First edition, 1961, 220 pp.]. See II, III, IVb, V, VIb, VII, X, XIa,
XIIa, XIIb, XIIc, XIId, XIIe.

4. Jackson, Thomas H., ed. *Twentieth Century Interpretations of* Miss
Lonelyhearts. Englewood Cliffs, New Jersey: Prentice-Hall, Incorporated,
1971, 112 pp. The following essays are included:

    5. Thomas H. Jackson, "Introduction," pp. 1-17. See III, IVc, X, XIIc.

    6. James F. Light, "The Christ Dream," pp. 19-38. Taken from his
    Nathanael West: An Interpretative Study; see [3]. See XIIe.

    7. Josephine Herbst, "Nathanael West," pp. 39-45. See also [311],
    will be discussed under that number in subsequent chapters.

    8. Arthur Cohen, "The Possibility of Belief: Nathanael West's
    Holy Fool," pp. 46-48. See also [273], will be discussed under that
    number in subsequent chapters.

    9. Robert Andreach, "Nathanael West's *Miss Lonelyhearts*: Between
    the Dead Pan and the Unborn Christ," pp. 49-60. See also [234],
    will be discussed under that number in subsequent chapters.

    10. Robert I. Edenbaum, "To Kill God and Build a Church: Nathanael
    West's *Miss Lonelyhearts*," pp. 61-69. See II, XIIc.

    11. Stanley Edgar Hyman, "Nathanael West," pp. 70-80. Taken from
    his *Nathanael West*, see [2]. See XIIc.

    12. Edmund L. Volpe, "The Waste Land of Nathanael West," pp. 81-92.

1

Reprinted from *Renascence*, 13 (Winter 1961), 69-77, 112. See
XIc, XIIc.

13. Randall Reid, "No Redeemer, No Promised Land," pp. 93-96.
Taken from his *The Fiction of Nathanael West: No Redeemer, No
Promised Land*, see [66].

14. Josephine Herbst, "*Miss Lonelyhearts*: An Allegory," p. 97.
See also [310], will be discussed under that number in subsequent
chapters.

15. Angel Flores, "Miss Lonelyhearts in the Haunted Castle," p. 98.
See also [286], will be discussed under that number in subsequent
chapters.

16. William Carlos Williams, "Sordid? Good God!" pp. 99-103.
See also [424], will be discussed under that number in subsequent
chapters.

17. Madden, David, ed. *Nathanael West: The Cheaters and the Cheated,
A Collection of Critical Essays*. Deland, Florida: Everett/Edwards,
Incorporated, 1973, 346 pp. A collection of essays selected from those
submitted to a Nathanael West competition sponsored by *The Southern Review*.
Steiner's essay (see [28]) won first prize. All "Confluence of Voices"
sections are collections of quotations from West scholars and acquaintances
directed toward given areas. The following essays are included:

17. David Madden, "Preface," pp. xiii-xiv.

18. David Madden, "Introduction: A Confluence of Voices," pp.
xv-xxiii.

19. Gerald Locklin, "The Man Behind the Novels," pp. 1-16. See
IVc, V.

20. David Madden, "A Confluence of Voices: *The Dream Life of Balso
Snell*," pp. 17-22.

21. Gerald Locklin, "The Journey Into the Microcosm," pp. 23-56.
See III, VIb, XIb, XIIb.

22. John M. Brand, "A Word Is a Word Is a Word," pp. 57-76.
See III, V.

23. David Madden, "A Confluence of Voices: *Miss Lonelyhearts*,"
pp. 77-82.

24. Lawrence W. Distasi, "Nowhere to Throw the Stone," pp. 83-102.
See XIIc.

25. Marcus Smith, "The Crucial Departure: Irony and Point of View,"
pp. 103-110. See III, XIIc.

26. James W. Hickey, "Freudian Criticism," pp. 111-150. See XIIc.

27. David Madden, "A Confluence of Voices: *A Cool Million*," pp. 151-156.

28. T. R. Steiner, "West's Lemuel and the American Dream," pp. 157-170. See also [388], will be discussed under that number in subsequent chapters.

29. David Madden, "A Confluence of Voices: *The Day of the Locust* I," pp. 171-178.

30. Kingsley Widmer, "The Last Masquerade," pp. 179-193. See VII, X, XId.

31. David Madden, "A Confluence of Voices: *The Day of the Locust* II," pp. 195-200.

32. Robert I. Edenbaum, "From American Dream to Pavlovian Nightmare," pp. 201-216. See XIIe.

33. Lavonne Mueller, "Malamud and West: Tyranny of the Dream Dump," pp. 221-234.

34. Max Apple, "History and Case History in Babel's *Red Cavalry* and West's *The Day of the Locust*," pp. 235-248. See XId.

35. Donald T. Torchianna, "The Painter's Eye," pp. 249-282. See VIe, XIIa.

36. James H. Bowden, "No Redactor, No Reward," pp. 283-298. See III, XId, XIId.

37. Warwick Wadlington, "Nathanael West and the Confidence Game," pp. 299-322. See IX.

38. Helen Taylor, "An Annotated Bibliography," pp. 323-341. See II.

39. Malin, Irving. *Nathanael West's Novels*. Carbondale and Edwardsville: Southern Illinois University Press; London and Amsterdam: Feffer and Simons, Incorporated, 1972, 141 pp. See III, XIIa, XIIb, XIIc, XIId, XIIe.

40. Martin, Jay, ed. *Nathanael West: A Collection of Critical Essays*. Englewood Cliffs, New Jersey: Prentice-Hall, Incorporated, 1971, 176 pp. The following essays are included:

40. Jay Martin, "Introduction," pp. 1-10. See II, IVd, XIIa.

41. S. J. Perelman, "Nathanael West: A Portrait," pp. 11-12. See also [356], will be discussed under that number in subsequent chapters.

42. Josephine Herbst, "Nathanael West," pp. 13-26. See also [311], will be discussed under that number in subsequent chapters.

43. Nathanael West, "Through the Hole in the Mundane Millstone,"

3

pp. 29-30. An advertisement for *The Dream Life of Balso Snell*.

44. David Galloway, "A Picaresque Apprenticeship: Nathanael West's *The Dream Life of Balso Snell* and *A Cool Million*," pp. 31-47. See also [291], will be discussed under that number in subsequent chapters.

45. William Carlos Williams, "A New American Writer," pp. 48-49. Originally published in *Il Mare*, 11 (21 January 1931), 4. Translated from Edmundo Dodsworth's Italian by John Erwin and Jay Martin. See VIa, XIIa.

46. Nathanael West, "Some Notes on Violence," pp. 50-51. Reprinted from *Contact*, 1, no. 3 (1932), 132-133.

47. Carter A. Daniel, "Nathanael West's Revisions of *Miss Lonelyhearts*," pp. 52-65. Reprinted from *Studies in Bibliography*, 16 (1963), 232-243. See II.

48. Nathanael West, "Some Notes on *Miss Lonelyhearts*," pp. 66-67. Reprinted from *Contempo*, 3, no. 9 (15 May 1933), 1-2.

49. Angel Flores, "Miss Lonelyhearts in the Haunted Castle," p. 68. Reprinted from *Contempo*, 3, no. 11 (25 July 1933), 1. See also [286], will be discussed under that number in subsequent chapters.

50. Josephine Herbst, "Miss Lonelyhearts: An Allegory," pp. 69-70. See also [310], will be discussed under that number in subsequent chapters.

51 William Carlos Williams, "Sordid? Good God!" pp. 70-73. See also [424], will be discussed under that number in subsequent chapters.

52. Marcus Smith, "Religious Experience in *Miss Lonelyhearts*," pp. 74-90. Reprinted from *Contemporary Literature*, 9, no. 2 (Spring 1968), 172-188. See III, VIc.

53. Edmund L. Volpe, "The Waste Land of Nathanael West," pp. 91-101. See also [12], will be discussed under that number in subsequent chapters.

54. Marc L. Ratner, "'Anywhere Out of This World': Baudelaire and Nathanael West," pp. 102-109. Reprinted from *American Literature*, 31 (January 1960), 456-463. See XIc.

55. Phillipe Soupault, "Introduction to *Mademoiselle Coeur-Brise (Miss Lonelyhearts)*," pp. 110-113. See IVa.

56. Jay Martin, "The Black Hole of Calcoolidge," pp. 114-131. See XIId.

57. Nathanael West, "Bird and Bottle," pp. 132-137. Reprinted from *Pacific Weekly*, 5 (10 November 1936), 329-331.

58. William Carlos Williams, "*The Day of the Locust*," pp. 138-139. Reprinted from *Tomorrow*, 10 (1950), 58-59. See XIIe.

59. Edmund Wilson, "The Boys in the Back Room," pp. 140-143. Reprinted from *Classics and Commercials: A Literary Chronicle of the Forties* (New York: Farrar, Straus and Giroux, 1950), pp. 51-56. See XIIe.

60. Carvel Collins, "Nathanael West's *The Day of the Locust* and *Sanctuary*," pp. 144-146. See also [274], will be discussed under that number in subsequent chapters.

61. W. H. Auden, "West's Disease," pp. 147-163. See also [76], will be discussed under that number in subsequent chapters.

62. Norman Podhoretz, "Nathanael West: A Particular Kind of Joking," pp. 154-160. Reprinted from *Doings and Undoings: The Fifties and After in American Writing* (New York: Farrar, Straus and Giroux, 1964), pp. 65-75. See XIa, XIIb, XIIc.

63. Daniel Aaron, "Late Thoughts on Nathanael West," pp. 161-169. See also [230], will be discussed under that number in subsequent chapters.

64. Martin, Jay. *Nathanael West: The Art of His Life*. New York: Farrar, Straus and Giroux, 1970, 435 pp. See II, III, IVb, V, VIa, VIb, VIc, VId, VII, VIII, IX, X, XIa, XIIb, XIIc.

65. Perry, Robert M. *Nathanael West's* Miss Lonelyhearts: *Introduction and Commentary*. Religious Dimensions in Literature, No. 10. New York: The Seabury Press, 1969, 32 pp. [pamphlet]. Perry summarizes four basic interpretations of the novel: 1) the non-spiritual--the novel is a movement from alienation to an awareness of self; 2) a religious quest--the hero moving through imitation of the prophets to identification with Christ; 3) the hero's examination of the Christian interpretation of life, but ultimate rejection of this; 4) the "broken heart" as a symbol of the universe. This last is the most convincing but is examined in the least detail. See IVc, V, XIIc.

66. Reid, Randall. *The Fiction of Nathanael West: No Redeemer, No Promised Land*. Chicago and London: University of Chicago Press, 1967, 174 pp. See II, III, VIb, VIc, VII, XIb, XIc, XId, XIIa, XIIb, XIIc, XIId, XIIe.

67. Scott, Nathan A., Jr. *Nathanael West: A Critical Essay*. Contemporary Writers in Christian Perspectives. Grand Rapids, Michigan: William B. Eerdmans, 1971, 47 pp. [Pamphlet.] See II, VII, X, XIIb, XIIc, XIId, XIIe.

223. White, William. *Nathanael West: A Comprehensive Bibliography*. Kent, Ohio: The Kent State University Press, 1975, 209 pp. I acquired this item too late to place in its proper position in the number series. It will be discussed under this number [223] throughout. See II.

B) Material Concerning West in Books

68. Aaron, Daniel. *Writers on the Left: Episodes in American Literary Communism.* New York: Harcourt, Brace and World, Incorporated, 1961, pp. 175, 307, 432. See IVb.

69. Abrahams, Roger D. "Androgynes Bound: Nathanael West's *Miss Lonelyhearts." Seven Contemporary Authors: Essays on Cozzens, Miller, West, Golding, Heller, Albee, and Powers,* ed. Thomas B. Whitbread. Austin and London: University of Texas Press, 1966, pp. 49-72. See VIc, XIIc.

70. Allen, Walter. *The Modern Novel in Britain and the United States.* New York: E. P. Dutton and Company, 1964, pp. 167-172. The same discussion is found in [71] and will be discussed under that number in subsequent chapters.

71. Allen, Walter. *Tradition and Dream: A Critical Survey of British and American Fiction From the 1920's to the Present Day.* Middlesex, England: Penguin Books, 1965, pp. 187, 188-190, 190-192. See XIa, XId, XIIa, XIIe.

72. Allen, Walter. *The Urgent West: The American Dream and Modern Man.* New York: E. P. Dutton and Company, Incorporated, 1969, pp. 217-219. See XId.

73. Ames, Stanley Edward, ed. *The 1924 Liber Brunensis.* Providence: Brown University, 1924, p. 142. The Brown University yearbook.

74. Angoff, Allan, ed. *American Writing Today: Its Independence and Vigor.* Washington Square: New York University Press, 1957, pp. 168, 206. See X.

75. Asselineau, Roger. "Edgar Allan Poe." *American Writers: A Collection of Literary Biographies,* ed. Leonard Unger. New York: Charles Scribner's Sons, 1974, p. 425. See XIa.

76. Auden, W. H. "Interlude: West's Disease." *"The Dyer's Hand" and Other Essays.* New York: Random House, 1962, pp. 238-245. See XIIa, XIId.

77. Benét, William Rose. "West, Nathanael." *The Reader's Encyclopedia.* 2nd ed. New York: Thomas Y. Crowell Company, 1965, p. 1083. Contains a dozen lines on West, "an unusual and highly original talent."

78. Bergonzi, Bernard. *The Situation of the Novel.* London: Macmillan and Company, Limited, 1970, pp. 83-84, 95, 98, 104. See VII.

79. Bertoff, Warner. *The Ferment of Realism: American Literature, 1884-1919.* New York: The Free Press; London: Collier-Macmillan Limited, 1965, p. 37. See XIa.

80. Bertoff, Warner. *Fictions and Events: Essays in Criticism and Literary History.* New York: E. P. Dutton and Company, Incorporated,

6

1971, p. 173. See XIIc.

81. Bier, Jesse. *The Rise and Fall of American Humor*. New York, Chicago, San Fransisco: Holt, Rinehart, and Winston, 1968, pp. 210, 230-231, 232, 233, 319, 347n, 356n, 395, 417-418, 421. See VII, VIII, XIa.

82. Bleiler, Everett F., ed. *The Checklist of Fantastic Literature*. Chicago: FAX Collector's Editions, 1972, pp. 283, 316. West's *A Cool Million* is listed.

83. Block, Maxine, ed. *Current Biography: Who's News and Why, 1941*. New York: H. W. Wilson Company, 1941, p. 912. See IVd.

84. Blotner, Joseph. *The Modern American Political Novel, 1900-1960*. Austin and London: University of Texas Press, 1966, pp. 40, 145, 150, 244-247, 322n. See XId, XIId.

85. Bluefarb, Sam. *The Escape Motif in the American Novel: Mark Twain to Richard Wright*. Columbus: Ohio State University Press, 1972, pp. 51, 139. See XIc.

86. Bracey, William. "West, Nathanael." *The Encyclopedia Americana*. International Edition. New York: Americana Corporation, 1964, pp. 633-634. See IVd.

87. Bradbury, Malcolm and David Palmer, eds. *The American Novel in the Nineteen Twenties*. Stratford-upon-Avon Studies #13. London: Edward Arnold; New York: Crane, Russak, 1971. The following essays deal with West:

   88. Malcolm Bradbury, "Style of Life, Style of Art and the American Novel in the Nineteen Twenties," pp. 11-36. See VIa.

   89. Henry Dan Piper, "Social Criticism in the American Novel of the Nineteen Twenties," pp. 59-84. See III, XId.

   90. Brian Way, "Sherwood Anderson," pp. 107-128. See VIa.

   91. Jonathan Raban, "A Surfeit of Commodities: The Novels of Nathanael West," pp. 215-232. See XIIa.

   92. Eric Mottram, "The Hostile Environment and the Revival Artist: A Note on the Twenties," pp. 233-262. See X.

93. Bradbury, M. S. "West, Nathanael." *Webster's New World Companion to English and American Literature*, ed. Arthur Pollard. New York: World Publishing, 1973, pp. 714-715. See IVd.

94. Brown, John. *Panorama de la littérature contemporaine aux Etats-Unis*. Paris: Librairie Gallimard, 1954, pp. 141-142. A brief statement on West, remarking on his lack of fame during his own life and citing the surrealists as a major influence. Lists the four novels.

95. Burgess, Antony. *The Novel Now: A Student's Guide to Contemporary*

Fiction. London: Faber and Faber, 1967, p. 194. See VII.

96. Burke, W. J. and Will D. Howe. *American Authors and Books: 1640 to the Present Day*. 3rd revised ed. (by Irving and Anne Weiss). New York: Crown Publishing, Incorporated, 1972, p. 683. Lists West's dates (incorrectly) and the novels.

97. Caldwell, Erskine. *Call It Experience: The Years of Learning How to Write*. New York: Duell, Sloan and Pearce, 1951, pp. 110-112. See IVa.

98. Coan, Otis W. and Richard G. Lillard. *America in Fiction: An Annotated List of Novels That Interpret Aspects of Life in the United States, Canada, and Mexico*. Palo Alto, California: Pacific Books, Publishers, 1967, p. 113. See XIIe.

99. Coates, Robert M. "Introduction." *Miss Lonelyhearts*, by Nathanael West. New York: The New Classics, 1950, pp. ix-xiv [in 1946, pp. 1-7]. See V, XIIb, XIIc, XIId.

100. Connolly, Cyril. *The Modern Movement: One Hundred Key Books From England, France and America, 1880-1950*. New York: Atheneum, 1966, pp. 73-74. See XIIc.

101. Courtney, Winifred F. *The Reader's Adviser: A Guide to the Best in Literature*. 11th ed., revised and enlarged. New York and London: R. R. Bowker Co., 1968. pp. 490-491. Lists the novels and four studies of West, plus one paragraph on his career and one on his major themes.

102. Cowley, Malcolm. "American Books Abroad." *Literary History of the United States*, eds. Robert Spiller *et al*. New York: The Macmillan Company, 1948. II: 1378.

103. Cowley, Malcolm. *Exile's Return: A Literary Odyssey of the 1920's*. New York: The Viking Press, 1951, pp. 237-240, 284. See XIIc, XIIe.

104. Cowley, Malcolm. *Exile's Return: A Narrative of Ideas*. New York: W. W. Norton and Company, Incorporated, 1934, pp. 231-233. See XIIc.

105. Cowley, Malcolm. "Introduction." *Miss Lonelyhearts*, by Nathanael West. New York: Avon Books, 1959, pp. 11-1v, 96.

106. Driskell, Leon V. and Joan T. Brittain. *The Eternal Crossroads: The Art of Flannery O'Connor*. Lexington: University of Kentucky Press, 1971, pp. 14-16. See VII.

107. [The Editors of *Time*]. "Editor's Preface." *The Day of the Locust*, by Nathanael West. Time Reading Program Special Edition. New York: Time Incorporated, 1965, pp. vii-xii. See III, IVd, XIIa.

108. Fadiman, Clifton and Charles Van Doren, eds. *The American Treasury, 1455-1955*. New York: Harper and Brothers, 1955, p. 971. Includes a brief quote from *Miss Lonelyhearts*, under "On Things in General . . ."

8

109. Fiedler, Leslie A. "The Breakthrough: The American Jewish Novelist and the Fictional Image of the Jew." *Recent American Fiction: Some Critical Views*, ed. Joseph J. Waldmeir. Boston: Houghton Mifflin Company, 1963, pp. 84-109. See IVc, VII, X, XIa, XIIa.

110. Fiedler, Leslie A. "The Dream of the New." *American Dreams, American Nightmares*, ed. David Madden. Carbondale and Edwardsville: Southern Illinois University Press; London and Amsterdam: Feffer and Simons, Incorporated, 1970, pp. 19-27. See XIIa.

111. Fiedler, Leslie A. *Love and Death in the American Novel.* New York: Stein and Day, 1966, pp. 326-328, 485-491. [Revised ed.] See XIIa, XIIc.

112. Fiedler, Leslie. *The Return of the Vanishing American.* New York: Stein and Day, 1968, pp. 144, 147-149, 150. See XId, XIIe.

113. Fiedler, Leslie A. *Waiting For the End.* New York: Dell Publishing Company, 1964, pp. 37, 45, 46, 48, 49, 50, 51, 52, 63, 64, 83, 108, 143, 226. See III, VII, X, XIa, XIIa, XIIc, XIIe.

114. Fitzgerald, F. Scott. "Introduction to *The Great Gatsby*." The Great Gatsby: *A Study*, ed. Frederick J. Hoffman. New York: Charles Scribner's Sons, 1962, pp. 165-168. Reprinted from the 1934 Modern Library edition of the novel. In speaking of the "cowardice" of reviewers, Fitzgerald observes, "Underpaid and overworked, they seem not to care for books, and it has been saddening recently to see young talents in fiction expire from sheer lack of a stage to act on: West, McHugh and many others" (p. 166).

115. Friedman, Melvin J. and Lewis A. Lawson, eds. *The Added Dimension: The Art and Mind of Flannery O'Connor.* New York: Fordham University Press, 1966. The following essays deal with West, at least in passing:

116. Melvin J. Friedman, "Introduction," pp. 1-31. See VII.

117. Frederick J. Hoffman, "The Search For Redemption: Flannery O'Connor's Fiction," pp. 32-48. See XId.

118. Irving Malin, "Flannery O'Connor and the Grotesque," pp. 108-122. See XIb, XIc.

119. Melvin J. Friedman, "Flannery O'Connor's Sacred Objects," pp. 196-208. See VII.

120. Friedrich, Otto. "Ring Lardner." *American Writers: A Collection of Literary Biographies*, ed. Leonard Unger. New York: Charles Scribner's Sons, 1974. II: 436. See XIa.

121. Galloway, David D. *The Absurd Hero in American Fiction.* Revised ed. Austin and London: University of Texas Press, 1970, pp. 69, 93, 95, 135. See XIc, XId, XIe.

122. Gehman, Richard. "Introduction." *The Day of the Locust*, by Nathanael West. New York: The New Classics, 1950, pp. ix-xxiii. See II, IVb, XIa, XIIb.

123. Gerstenberger, Donna and George Kendrick. "Nathanael West." *The American Novel: A Checklist of Twentieth Century Criticism on Novels Written Since 1789. Volume II: Criticism Written 1960-68.* Chicago: The Swallow Press, 1970, pp. 360-362. See II.

124. Gibson, Morgan. "West, Nathanael." *Encyclopedia of World Literature in the Twentieth Century*. New York: Frederick Ungar Publishing Company, 1971. III: 519-520. Contains one paragraph on West's life plus one on each of the novels. Gibson calls *The Day of the Locust* West's most ambitious attempt and concludes, "West's style was brilliantly epigrammatical, nervously metaphorical, bitterly ironic, and expressive of intense though absurd suffering" (p. 519).

125. Goldhurst, William. *F. Scott Fitzgerald and His Contemporaries*. New York and Cleveland: The World Publishing Company, 1963, pp. 226, 236. See IVb.

126. Greenberg, Alvin. "Choice: Ironic Alternatives in the World of the Contemporary American Novel." *American Dreams, American Nightmares*, ed. David Madden. Carbondale and Edwardsville: Southern Illinois University Press; London and Amsterdam: Feffer and Simons, Incorporated, pp. 175-187. See XId.

127. Grigson, Geoffrey, ed. *The Concise Encyclopedia of Modern World Literature*. New York: Hawthorne Books, Incorporated, 1963, p. 483 (portrait on p. 473). See XIIa, XIIb, XIIc.

128. Guttman, Allen. *The Jewish Writer in America: Assimilation and the Crisis of Identity*. New York: Oxford University Press, 1971, pp. 13, 44. Guttman explains that he does not deal with West in his study because West's work does not "deal significantly with the problem of assimilation and the resultant crisis of identity" (p. 13).

129. Harris, Charles B. *Contemporary American Novelists of the Absurd*. New Haven: College and University Press, 1971, pp. 20-21. Harris observes that West is a precursor of the trend of absurdity revealed through form.

130. Hart, James D. "West, Nathanael." *The Oxford Companion to American Literature*. 4th ed. New York: Oxford University Press, 1965, p. 906. Includes a brief biographical sketch and one phrase mention of each novel. He finds *The Day of the Locust* most significant.

131. Hassan, Ihab. *Contemporary American Literature 1945-1972: An Introduction*. New York: Frederick Ungar Publishing Company, 1973, pp. 52, 71, 81. See VII.

132. Hauck, Richard Boyd. *A Cheerful Nihilism: Confidence and "The Absurd" in American Humorous Fiction*. Bloomington: Indiana University Press, 1971, p. 243. See XIa.

133. Haydn, Hiram and Edmund Fuller, eds. *Thesaurus of Book Digests*. New York: Crown Publishers, 1949, p. 493. Under *Miss Lonelyhearts*, a brief synopsis of both that novel and *The Day of the Locust*.

134. Hays, Peter. *The Limping Hero: Grotesques in Literature*. New York: New York University Press, 1971, pp. 84-86. Hays lists Doyle, Pitkin, Tod Hackett and others under "Sterilty Figures" whose grotesqueness symbolizes loss.

135. Heiney, Donald and Lenthiel H. Downs. "Nathanael West (1903-1940)." *Recent American Literature After 1930*. Essentials of Contemporary Literature of the Western World. Woodbury, New York: Barron's Educational Services, Incorporated, 1974. IV: 240-244.

136. Hellman, Lillian. *An Unfinished Woman--a Memoir*. Boston, Toronto: Little, Brown, and Company, 1969, pp. 63, 270. See IVa.

137. Herzberg, Max J. *et al.*, eds. *The Reader's Encyclopedia of American Literature*. New York: Thomas Y. Crowell Company, 1962, p. 1211. See XIIa.

138. Hodgart, Matthew. *Satire*. London: World University Library, 1969, pp. 226-227. See VIa.

139. Hoffman, Frederick J. *The Modern Novel in America, 1900-1950*. Chicago: Henry Regnery Company, 1951, pp. 115n, 129. See XId.

140. Hoffman, Hester R. "West, Nathanael." *The Reader's Adviser*. 10th ed., revised and enlarged. New York: R. R. Bowker Company, 1964, p. 1118. Lists West's novels plus two studies and quotes two paragraphs from Alan Ross's "Introduction" to the *Complete Works*.

141. Hyman, Stanley Edgar. *Flannery O'Connor*. University of Minnesota Pamphlets on American Writers, No. 54. Minneapolis: University of Minnesota Press, 1966, pp. 43, 46. See VII.

142. Hyman, Stanley Edgar. "Nathanael West 1903-1940." *American Writers: A Collection of Literary Biographies*, ed. Leonard Unger. New York: Charles Scribner's Sons, 1974, pp. 285-307. Revised from [2], will be discussed under that number in subsequent chapters.

143. Johansen, Ib. "I. Nathanael West; II. *A Cool Million*." *Six American Novels: From New Deal to New Frontier*, eds. Jens Bogh and Steffen Skovmand. Aarus: Akademisk Boghandel, 1972, pp. 43-81.

144. Kazin, Alfred. *Bright Book of Life: American Novelists and Storytellers from Hemingway to Mailer*. Boston, Toronto: Little, Brown, and Company, 1973, pp. 17-18, 191. See VII.

145. Kearns, G. A. "West, Nathanael." *Cassell's Encyclopedia of World Literature*, Gen. ed. J. Buchanan-Brown. Revised and enlarged. New York: William Morrow and Company, Incorporated, 1973. III: 736. See XIIa.

146. Kernan, Alvin B. "The Mob Tendency: *The Day of the Locust*." *The Plot of Satire*. New Haven and London: Yale University Press, 1965,

pp. 66-80. See VIII.

147. Ketterer, David. *New Worlds for Old: The Apocalyptic Imagination, Science Fiction, and American Literature*. Garden City: Anchor Books, 1974, pp. 4, 9, 35, 208-209. See XIIe.

148. Klein, Marcus, ed. *The American Novel Since World War II*. Greenwich, Connecticut: Fawcett Publications, Incorporated, 1969. The following essays deal with West, at least in passing:

149. Paul Goodman, "Underground Writing, 1960," pp. 186-195. See X.

150. John Hawkes, "Notes on the Wild Goose Chase," pp. 247-251. See also [304], will be discussed under that number in subsequent chapters.

151. William Phillips, "Notes on the New Style," pp. 252-261. See especially p. 252. Brief reference to West. Phillips bemoans the new attitude of "copping out" among contemporary writers and sees this as partial explanation of why they have not found their place in literature, as has West, for instance.

152. Knoll, Robert E., ed. *McAlmon and the Lost Generation: A Self-Portrait*. Lincoln: University of Nebraska Press, 1962, pp. 305, 361n, 381-382. See IVb.

153. Knoll, Robert E. *Robert McAlmon: Expatriate Publisher and Writer*. University of Nebraska Studies, New Series No. 18. Lincoln: University of Nebraska Press, 1957, pp. 18, 84. See IVb.

154. Korges, James. "Erskine Caldwell." *American Writers: A Collection of Literary Biographies*, ed. Leonard Unger. New York: Charles Scribner's Sons, 1974. I: 298. See XId.

155. Kostelanetz, Richard. *The End of Intelligent Writing: Literary Politics in America*. New York: Sheed and Ward, Incorporated, 1973, p. 29. In a diatribe against Norman Podhoretz's *Doings and Undoings*, Kostelanetz lists West among those writers overpraised simply because they are Jewish.

156. Kronenberger, Louis, ed. "West, Nathanael." *Atlantic Brief Lives: A Biographical Companion to the Arts*. Boston, Toronto: Little, Brown, and Company, 1971, p. 862. See IVd.

157. Kunitz, Stanley and Howard Haycraft, eds. "West, Nathanael." New York: The H. W. Wilson Company, 1942, p. 1500. See IVd.

158. Levine, Paul. "Flannery O'Connor: The Soul of the Grotesque." *Minor American Novelists*, ed. Charles Alva Hoyt. Carbondale and Edwardsville: Southern Illinois University Press; London and Amsterdam: Feffer and Simons, Incorporated, 1970, pp. 95-117. See VIa, VIII, XIa, XId.

159. Lewis, R. W. B. "The Aspiring Clown." *Learners and Discerners: A Newer Criticism*, ed. Robert Scholes. Charlottesville: The University

Press of Virginia, 1964, pp. 61-108. See XIc, XId.

160. Lewis, R. W. B. "Days of Wrath and Laughter." *Trials of the Word: Essays in American Literature and the Humanistic Tradition.* New Haven and London: Yale University Press, 1965, pp. 184-236. See IX, XIa, XId, XIIc, XIId.

161. Lewis, R. W. B. "Melville After Moby Dick." *Trials of the Word: Essays in American Literature and the Humanistic Tradition.* New Haven and London: Yale University Press, 1965, pp. 36-76. See VIe.

162. Light, James F. "West, Nathanael." *Encyclopedia Brittanica.* Chicago [*etc*]: Encyclopedia Brittanica, Incorporated, 1967. XXIII: 418. A brief biographical sketch plus one sentence or so on each of the novels. "Stark prose and bizarre imagery" is a trademark of West's style, except for *A Cool Million.*

163. Madden, David, ed. *Proletarian Writers of the Thirties.* Carbondale and Edwardsville: Southern Illinois University Press; London and Amsterdam: Feffer and Simons, Incorporated, 1968. The following essays deal with West, at least in passing:

    163 David Madden, "Introduction," pp. xv-xlii. See XIa.

    164. Leslie Fiedler, "The Two Memories: Reflections on Writers and Writing in the Thirties," pp. 3-25. See VII, XIa.

    165. Marcus Klein, "The Roots of Radicals: Experience in the Thirties," pp. 134-157. See XIIb.

166. Madden, David, ed. *Tough Guy Writers of the Thirties.* Carbondale and Edwardsville: Southern Illinois University Press; London and Amsterdam: Feffer and Simons, Incorporated, 1968. The following essays deal with West, at least in passing:

    167. Thomas Sturak, "Horace McCoy's Objective Lyricism," pp. 137-162. See VII.

    168. E. R. Hagemann, "Focus on 'You Play the Black and the Red Comes Up': 'No Bet'," pp. 163-170. Mentions West in Hollywood writing movie scripts and *The Day of the Locust* as a part of the milieu for Richard Hallas' stories.

    169. Carolyn See, "The Hollywood Novel: The American Dream Cheat," See XIIe.

170. **Magny, Claude-Edmonde**. *The Age of the American Novel: The Film Aesthetic of Fiction Between the Two Wars,* trans. Eleanor Hochman. New York: Frederick Ungar Publishing Company, 1972, pp. 146, 225, 226, 229, 232. See XIa.

171. Mantle, Burns, ed. *The Best Plays of 1938-39 and the Yearbook of Drama in America.* New York: Dodd, Mead and Company, 1939, pp. 427-428. Includes the cast and a brief synopsis of West's *Good Hunting.*

172. Martin, Jay. "Ambrose Bierce." *The Comic Imagination in American Literature*, ed. Louis D. Rubin, Jr. New Brunswick: Rutgers University Press, 1973, pp. 195-206. See XIa.

173. Martin, Jay. "Fitzgerald Recommends Nathanael West For a Guggenheim." *Fitzgerald/Hemingway Annual 1971*, eds. Matthew J. Bruccoli and C. E. Frazer Clark, Jr. Dayton: Microcard Editions, 1971, pp. 302-304. See IVb.

174. May, John R. "Words and Deeds: Apocalyptic Judgment in Faulkner, West, and O'Connor." *Toward a New Earth: Apocalypse in the American Novel*. Notre Dame, London: University of Notre Dame Press, 1972, pp. 34, 40, 92, 114-126, 201, 204-206, 209, 211-214, 217, 220. See VII, X, XIc, XIIc.

175. McKenny, Ruth. *Love Story*. New York: Harcourt, Brace and Company, 1950, pp. 175-176, 195-196. See IVa.

176. Millgate, Michael. *American Social Fiction: James to Cozzens*. Edinburgh and London: Oliver and Boyd, 1964, pp. 154-156, 163-164. See XId, XIIe.

177. Mondadori, Arnoldo, ed. "West, Nathanael." *Dizionario Universale della Letteratura contemporanea*. 1 Edizione: Marzo, 1962, pp. 1148-1149. See IVd.

178. Moore, Harry T. "Preface." *Nathanael West's Novels*, by Irving Malin. Carbondale and Edwardsville: Southern Illinois University Press; London and Amsterdam: Feffer and Simons, Incorporated, 1972, pp. vii-viii. Moore provides a brief biographical sketch of West.

179. Muller, Gilbert H. *Nightmares and Visions: Flannery O'Connor and the Catholic Grotesque*. Athens: University of Georgia Press, 1972, pp. 5, 20-21. See VII, XIa.

180. Murray, Edward. "Nathanael West--the Pictorial Eye in Locust-Land." *The Cinematic Imagination: Writers and the Motion Pctures*. New York: Frederick Ungar Publishing Company, 1972, pp. 206-216. See IVd, V, XIIe.

181. Nathan, Monique. "Avant-propos to Nathanael West, *Romans*." Paris: Editions du Seuil, 1957, pp. 7-12.

182. Nelson, Gerald B. "Lonelyhearts." *Ten Versions of America*. New York: Alfred A. Knopf, 1972, pp. 77-90. See XIIc.

183. Nevius, Blake. "Nathanael West." *The American Novel: Sinclair Lewis to the Present*. Illinois: AHM Publishing Corporation, 1970, pp. 99-100. See II.

184. Nyren, Dorothy, ed. "West, Nathanael (1906-1940)." *A Library of Literary Criticism: Modern American Literature*. 3rd ed. New York: Frederick Ungar Publishing Company, 1964, pp. 514-517. Brief sections from nine reviews and articles about West are reprinted.

185. O'Connor, William Van. *The Grotesque: An American Genre and Other Essays*. Carbondale: Southern Illinois University Press, 1962, pp. 6, 8-9, 12, 18, 21, 55, 56. See XIa, XIIa, XIIc, XIId, XIIe.

186. Olsen, Bruce. "Nathanael West: The Use of Cynicism." *Minor American Novelists*, ed. Charles Alva Hoyt. Carbondale and Edwardsville: Southern Illinois University Press; London and Amsterdam: Feffer and Simons, Incorporated, 1970, pp. 81-94. See IVd, XIIa, XIIb, XIIc, XIIe.

187. Orvell, Miles. *Invisible Parade: The Fiction of Flannery O'Connor*. Philadelphia: Temple University Press, 1972, pp. 21n, 51-52, 58, 73, 83n. See VII.

188. Parkes, David L. "West, Nathanael." *Twentieth Century Writing: A Reader's Guide to Contemporary Literature*, eds. Kenneth Richardson and R. Clive Willis. London [etc.]: Newnes Books, 1969, p. 642. See XIa.

189. Parry, Idris. "Kafka, Gogol, and Nathanael West." *Kafka: A Collection of Critical Essays*, ed. Ronald Gray. Englewood Cliffs, New Jersey: Prentice-Hall, Incorporated, 1962, pp. 85-90. See XId.

190. Powell, Lawrence Clark. "*The Day of the Locust*: Nathanael West." *California Classics: The Creative Literature of the Golden State*. Los Angeles: The Ward Ritchie Press, 1971, pp. 344-356. See II, III, V, XId, XIIb.

191. Pritchett, V. S. "*Miss Lonelyhearts*." *The Living Novel and Later Appreciations*. New York: Random House, 1968, pp. 276-282. See XIIa, XIIa, XIIc, XIIe.

192. Raban, Jonathan. "A Surfeit of Commodities: The Novels of Nathanael West." *The American Novel and the Nineteen Twenties*. Stratford-upon-Avon Studies #13. eds. Malcolm Bradbury and David Palmer. London: Edward Arnold; New York: Crane, Russak, 1971, pp. 215-232. Listed also as [91], will be discussed under that number in subsequent chapters.

193. Ramsaye, Terry, ed. "West, Nathaniel [sic]." *International Motion Picture Almanac* [1939-40]. New York: The Quigley Publishing Company, 1939, p. 673. See II.

194. Ross, Alan. "The Dead Center: An Introduction to Nathanael West." *The Complete Works of Nathanael West*. New York: Farrar, Straus and Cudahy, 1957, pp. vii-xxii. See X, XIIb, XIIc, XIId, XIIe.

195. Ross, Alan. "Einführung." *Schreiben Sie Miss Lonelyhearts*. Zurich: Diogenes Verlag, 1961, pp. 5-10; Frankfurt am Main, Hamburg: Fischer Bucherei, 1963, pp. 5-11. Translated from [194].

196. Ross, Alan. "An Introduction to Nathanael West." *Miss Lonelyhearts*. London: The Grey Walls Press, 1949, pp. 7-25. Reprinted in revised form in [194].

197. [Ross, Alan]. "West, Nathanael." *The Concise Encyclopedia of Modern World Literature*, ed. Geoffrey Grigson. New York: Hawthorne Books,

Books, Incorporated, 1963, p. 483 (portrait, p. 473). See XIIa, XIIc, XIId, XIIe.

198. Rubin, Louis D., Jr. *The Curious Death of the Novel: Essays in American Literature*. Baton Rouge: Louisiana State University Press, 1967, p. 21. "As for Mailer [Norman], he seems to have learned early in his career that if one can't produce a war novel as good as Hemingway's, or as Hollywood novel as good as . . . Nathanael West's, . . . then the best thing to do in order to maintain one's sanity is to go around writing articles attacking those of one's contemporaries who are also trying to do those things."

199. Salzman, Jack, ed. *Years of Protest: A Collection of American Writings of the 1930's*. New York: Pegasus, 1967, p. 406. Reprints "Miss Lonelyhearts and the Dead Pan" from *Contact*, 1932. Salzman's note (p. 406) observes, "Although all of West's work was published in the thirties, it took a new generation to accept his harsh and surrealistic view of contemporary life."

200. Schulberg, Budd. "Introduction." *The Day of the Locust*, by Nathanael West. Time Reading Program Special Edition. New York: Time Incorporated, 1965, pp. xiii-xxiii. See IVa.

201. Schulberg, Budd. "The Writer and Hollywood." *Writing in America*, eds. John Fisher and Robert B. Silvers. New Brunswick: Rutgers University Press, 1960, pp. 95-107. See IVa.

202. Schulz, Max F. *Black Humor of the Sixties: A Pluralistic Definition of Man and His World*. Athens: Ohio University Press, 1973, pp. 12, 17, 113. See XIa, XId.

203. Schulz, Max F. *Radical Sophistication: Studies in Contemporary Jewish-American Novelists*. Athens: Ohio University Press, 1969, pp. 36-55, 170, 179, 185. See V, XIIb, XIIc, XIId, XIIe.

204. Scott, Nathan A., Jr. *Modern Literature and the Religious Frontier*. New York: Harper and Brothers, 1958, p. 74. See XIa.

205. Spiller, Robert *et al.*, eds. *Literary History of the United States*. New York: The Macmillan Company, 1948. III: 151. Mentions West among recent American authors.

206. Spiller, Robert *et al.*, eds. *Literary History of the United States*. 3rd ed., revised. New York: The Macmillan Company; London: Collier-Macmillan, Limited, 1963, p. 1378. Speaks of the French publication of neglected American novels: "for example, the fantastic *Miss Lonelyhearts*, by Nathanael West."

207. Stephens, Martha. *The Question of Flannery O'Connor*. Baton Rouge: Louisiana State University Press, 1973, pp. 49, 96. See VII.

208. Straumann, Heinrich. *American Literature in the Twentieth Century*. 3rd ed., revised. New York: Harper and Row, 1965, pp. 78-79. [Originally

published by Hutchinson's University Library, London, 1951. See XIIa.

209. Swingewood, Alan. "Alienation, Reification, and the Novel: Sartre, Camus, Nathanael West." *The Sociology of Literature*, by Diana T. Laurenson and Alan Swingewood. New York: Schocken Books, 1972, pp. 207-248. See XIa, XIIa, XIIc.

210. Symons, Julian. *Critical Occasions*. London: Hamish Hamilton, 1966, pp. 99-105. See III, V, XIIa, XIIb, XIIc, XIId, XIIe.

211. Tiusanen, Antero. "Suomentanut." *Vastaathan kirjeeseeni, Miss Lonelyhearts*. Porvoo, Helsinki: Werner Soderstrom Osakeyhtio, 1966, pp. 7-12.

212. Walker, Franklin. *A Literary History of Southern California*. Chronicles of California Series. Berkeley and Los Angeles: University of California Press, 1950, p. 259. See XIa.

213. Ward, A. C. "West, Nathanael." *Longman Companion to Twentieth Century Literature*. London: Longman Group Limited, 1970, p. 565. See IVd.

214. Weaver, Mike. *William Carlos Williams: The American Background*. Cambridge: At the University Press, 1971, pp. 134-136, 145, 216. See VIc.

215. Weber, Brom. "The Mode of 'Black Humor!." *The Comic Imagination in American Literature*, ed. Louis Rubin. New Brunswick: Rutgers University Press, 1973, pp. 361-371. See VIa.

216. Weber, Brom. "Sherwood Anderson." *American Writers: A Collection of Literary Biographies*, ed. Leonard Unger. New York: Charles Scribner's Sons, 1974. I: 97, 107. See VIa. 217.

217. Weber, J. Sherwood, ed. *Good Reading: A Guide for Serious Readers*. By the Committee on College Reading. New York: Weybright and Talley, 1969, p. 132. A one-sentence summary of *Miss Lonelyhearts*; lists West's dates as 1906-1940.

218. Wells, Walter. *Tycoons and Locusts: A Regional Look at Hollywood Fiction of the 1930's*. Carbondale and Edwardsville: Southern Illinois University Press; London and Amsterdam: Feffer and Simon, Incorporated, 1973, pp. 11, 39, 49-70, 71-73, 80, 84, 87, 94, 95, 100, 101, 107, 109, 110, 117, 118, 119, 125, 56, 62, 103, 122. See XIa, XIIe.

219. Whitbread, Thomas B. "Introduction." *Seven Contemporary American Authors: Essays on Cozzens, Miller, West, Golding, Heller, Albee, and Powers*, ed. Thomas B. Whitbread. Austin and London: University of Texas Press, 1966. See XIIc.

220. [White, William]. "The Complete Works of Nathanael West." *Best Masterplots, 1954-1962*, ed. Frank N. Magill. New York: Salem Press, 1963, pp. 103-106. Also found in *Masterplots: 1958 Annual*, pp. 55-59. See III, VIII.

221. [White, William]. *"Miss Lonelyhearts."* *Masterpieces of World Literature in Digest Form.* 3rd Series, ed. Frank N. Magill. New York: Harper and Brothers, 1960, pp. 664-667. See XIIc.

222. White, William. "Nathanael West." *Cyclopedia of World Authors*, eds. Frank N. Magill and Dayton Kohler. New York: Harper and Brothers, 1958, pp. 1144-1145. A one-page biographical sketch with critical comments on the novels interspersed. Also lists a dozen studies of West.

223. White, William. *Nathanael West: A Comprehensive Bibliography.* Kent, Ohio: The Kent State University Press, 1975. See II.

224. Widmer, Kingsley. "The Sweet Savage Prophecies of Nathanael West." *The Thirties: Fiction, Poetry, Drama*, ed. Warren French. Deland, Florida: Everett/Edwards, Incorporated, 1967, pp. 97-106. See VII, XIIa, XIIb, XIIc, XIId, XIIe.

225. Wiggins, Robert A. "Ambrose Bierce." *American Writers: A Collection of Literary Biographies*, ed. Leonard Unger. New York: Charles Scribner's Sons, 1974. I: 190, 211. See XIa.

226. Williams, William Carlos. *The Autobiography of William Carlos Williams.* New York: A New Directions Book, 1967, pp. 270, 301-302. See IVa, XIIe.

227. Williams, William Carlos. *The Selected Letters of William Carlos Williams*, ed. John C. Thirwall. New York: McDowell, Obolensky, 1957, pp. 125, 126, 128. See IVa.

228. Wilson, Edmund. *A Literary Chronicle: 1920-1950.* New York: Doubleday and Company, Incorporated, 1956, pp. 241, 242n, 245-248, 249, 358. See VIa, XIa, XIc, XIIb, XIIc.

229. Woodress, James. "Nathanael West (1903-1940)." *American Fiction, 1900-1950: A Guide to Information Sources.* Detroit: Gale Research Company, 1974. I: 205-208. See II.

18

C) Articles in Periodicals and Reviews
of the Novels

230. Aaron, Daniel. "Late Thoughts on Nathanael West." *The Massachusetts Review*, 6, no. 2 (Winter-Spring 1965), 307-317. Aaron concludes his essay by reprinting S. J. Perelman's "Nathanael West: A Portrait." See VIc, X.

231. Aaron, Daniel. "'The Truly Monstrous': A Note on Nathanael West." *Partisan Review*, 14, no. 1 (1947), 98-106. See III, IVd, XIIa.

232. Aaron, Daniel. "Writing For Apocalypse." *The Hudson Review*, 3 (Winter 1951), 634-636. See XId.

233. Alter, Robert. "The Apocalyptic Temper." *Commentary*, 41, no. 6 (June 1966), 61-66. See XId.

234. Andreach, Robert. "Nathanael West's *Miss Lonelyhearts*: Between the Dead Pan and the Unborn Christ." *Modern Fiction Studies*, 12, no. 2 (Summer 1966), 251-261. See IX, XIIc.

235. Angell, Richard C. [Review of two new editions.] *New Mexico Quarterly*, 33, no. 2 (Summer 1963), 237-238. See XIIa.

236. Anon. "Books and Reviews." *New Outlook*, 162 (July 1933), 55, 58-59. See XIIc. [Review of *Miss Lonelyhearts*.]

237. Anon. "Brief Review." *New Masses*, 12 (August 21, 1934), 25. See XIId. [Review of *A Cool Million*.]

238. Anon. "The Great Despiser." *Time*, 69 (17 June 1957), 102-106. See XIIa. [Review of the *Complete Works*.]

239. Anon. "In the Jungle." *Review of Reviews*, 90 (August 1934), 6-7. See XIId. [Review of *A Cool Million*.]

240. Anon. "Is a Nathanael West Revival Under Way?" *College English*, 18, no. 8 (May 1957), 430. A brief note mentioning the publication of West's *Complete Works* and Harvey Breit's interview of S. J. Perelman in *The New York Times Book Review* (24 March 1957).

241. Anon. "'Miss Lonelyhearts' and Some Other Recent Works of Fiction." *The New York Times Book Review* (23 April 1933), p. 6. See XIIc. [Review of *Miss Lonelyhearts*.]

242. Anon. "'My Sister Eileen' Killed in Accident." *The New York Times* (23 December 1940), p. 23. See IVd.

243. Anon. "Nathanael West." *The Publisher's Weekly*, 138 (28 December 1940), 2326. See IVd.

244. Anon. "Nathanael West." *Times Literary Supplement*, 57 (24 January 1958), 44. See III, IVd, XIIa, XIIb, XIIc, XIId, XIIe.

245. Anon. "Neglected Novelist." *Newsweek*, 36 (4 September 1950), 77-78. See XIIe. [Review of *The Day of the Locust*.]

246. Anon. "The Reviewer." *Times Literary Supplement* (28 February 1958), 115. [Review of the *Complete Works*.]

247. Anon. "Rubbing Off the Sheen." *Newsweek*, 49 (13 May 1957), 126-127. See XIIa. [Review of West's *Complete Works*.]

248. Anon. "Scenario Writer and Wife Killed in Auto Collision." *The Los Angeles Times* (23 December 1940). Section C, p. 1. See IVd.

249. Anon. "Shorter Notices." *The Nation*, 139 (25 July 1934), 112. See XIId. [Review of *A Cool Million*.]

250. Anon. "Truly Monstrous." *Time*, 33 (19 June 1939), 84. See XIIe. [Review of *The Day of the Locust*.]

251. Balke, Betty Tevis. "Some Judeo-Christian Themes Seen Through the Eyes of J. D. Salinger and Nathanael West." *Cresset*, 31, no. 7 (1968), 14-18. See IVc, XIc.

252. Bellamy, W. J. "Nathanael West." *The Cambridge Quarterly*, 4, no. 1 (Winter 1968-69), 95-106. See XIIa. [Review of West's *Complete Works*.]

253. Berolzheimer, Hobart H. [Review of West's *Complete Works*.] *Library Journal*, 82 (1 June 1957), 1539. See XIIa.

254. Bittner, William, "A la recherche d'un écrivain perdu." *Les Langues Modernes*, 54 (July-August 1960), 274-282. See II, XIIa, XIId, XIIe.

255. Bittner, William. "Catching Up With Nathanael West." *The Nation*, 184, no. 18 (4 May 1957), 394-396. See XIIa, XIIb, XIIc, XIId. [Review of West's *Complete Works*.]

256. Britten, Florence Haxton. "Grotesquely Beautiful Novel." *The New York Herald Tribune Books* (30 April 1933), 6. See XIIc. [Review of *Miss Lonelyhearts*.]

257. Britten, Florence Haxton. "New Novels From Far and Near." *The New York Herald Tribune Books* (21 May 1939), 7. See XIIe. [Review of *The Day of the Locust*.]

258. Britten, Florence Haxton. "Youth Against Age in Recent Leading Fiction." *The New York Herald Tribune Books*, 10 (1 July 1934), 8-9. See XIId. [Review of *A Cool Million*.]

259. Brown, Bob. "Go West, Young Writer!" *Contempo*, 3 (25 July 1933), 4-5. A review of *Miss Lonelyhearts*--"West, through labor, gives birth to neither wobbly-necked incubator book nor colicy trilogy. *Miss Lonelyhearts* is no stillborn bastard. West's creative gusto blows life into clay lungs" (p. 5).

20

260. Brown, Daniel R. "The War Within Nathanael West: Naturalism and Existentialism." *Modern Fiction Studies*, 20, no. 2 (Summer 1974), 181-202. See IX.

261. Buckley, Tom. "'The Day of the Locust': Hollywood, by West, by Hollywood." *The New York Times Magazine* (2 June 1974), 10-14, 50-58, 68-73. A review of the movie version of the novel. Interspersed between comments on the movie are discussions of West's life and troubles as a writer. Many photographs of Hollywood and the movie are included. Although little critical comment on the novel is made, the essay interestly evokes the texture of Hollywood.

262. Buddingh, C. "Nathanael West." *Tirade*, 8 (1964), 506-514.

263. Burke, Tom. "The Day of the Day of the Locust." *Esquire*, 82 (September 1974), 120-126, 174-175. A review of the movie version of the novel, containing many photographs. Burke comments that West "perceived, even in the Thirties, when he wrote his books, that no other culture in all the aeons had invented movies because no other culture had so needed the opulent, perpetually replaceable illusions; that the illusions would work; that the industry that produced them would attract staggering multitudes of psychotically vain and avaricious, the monumentally self-serving, who would finally destroy it" (p. 122).

264. Bush, C. W. "This Stupendous Fabric: the Metaphysics of Order in Melville's *Pierre* and Nathanael West's *Miss Lonelyhearts*." *Journal of American Studies*, 1, no. 2 (October 1967), 269-274. See XIc, XIIc.

265. Cladwell, Erskine. [Ad for *Miss Lonelyhearts*.] *Contempo*, 3 (25 July 1933), 7. See XIIc.

266. Carlisle, Henry. "The Comic Imagination." *The American Scholar*, 28 (Winter 1958-59), 96-108. See III, XIa.

267. Chamberlain, John. "Books of the Times." *The New York Times* (19 June 1934), p. 17. See XIId. [Review of *A Cool Million*.]

268. Cheney, Brainard. "Miss O'Connor Creates Unusual Humor Out of Ordinary Sin." *The Sewanee Review*, 71, no. 4 (Autumn 1963), 644-652. See XIa.

269. Christie, Erling. "*Miss Lonelyhearts*." *Tendenser og Profiler*. Oslo: Ashehong, 1955, pp. 131-144.

270. Coates, Robert M. [Ad for *Miss Lonelyhearts*.] *Contempo*, 3 (25 July 1933), 7. See XIIc.

271. Coates, Robert M. "The Four Novels of Nathanael West, That Fierce, Humane Moralist." *The New York Herald Tribune Book Review*, 33 (9 May 1957), 4. See XIIa. [Review of West's *Complete Works*.]

272. Coates, Robert M. "Messiah of the Lonelyheart." *The New Yorker*, 9 (15 April 1933), 59. See XIIc. [Review of *Miss Lonelyhearts*.]

273. Cohen, Arthur. "Nathanael West's Holy Fool." *The Commonweal*, 64, no. 10 (8 June 1956), 276-278. See VIc.

274. Collins, Carvel. "Nathanael West's *The Day of the Locust* and *Sanctuary.*" *Faulkner Studies*, 2, no. 2 (Summer 1953), 23-24. See XIe.

275. Cowley, Malcolm. "It's the Telling That Counts." *The New York Times Book Review* (12 May 1957), 4-5. See XIIa. [Review of West's *Complete Works*.]

276. Cramer, Carter M. "The World of Nathanael West: A Critical Interpretation." *The Emporia State Research Studies*, 19, no. 4 (June 1971), 5-71. [Revised from his Master's thesis.] See II, III, VIII, X, XIIb, XIIc, XIId, XIIe.

277, D[avies], H[ugh] S[ykes]. "American Periodicals." *The Criterion*, 11 (July 1932), 772-775. See XIIc.

278. Donovan, Alan. "Nathanael West and the Surrealistic Muse." *Kentucky Review*, 2, no. 1 (1968), 82-95. See VIa.

279. Edenbaum, Robert I. "Dada and Surrealism in the United States: A Literary Instance." *Arts in Society*, 5, no. 1 (1968), 114-125. See VIa, VIb, VII, XId.

280. Edenbaum, Robert I. "A Surfeit of Shoddy: Nathanael West's *A Cool Million.*" *Southern Humanities Review*, 2, no. 4 (Fall 1968), 427-439. See X, XId.

281. Engle, Paul. "The Exciting Prose of Nathanael West." *The Chicago Sunday Tribune* (12 May 1957). Section 4, p. 3. See XIIa. [Review of West's *Complete Works*.]

282. Fadiman, Clifton. "Books." *The New Yorker*, 15 (20 May 1939), 78-80. See XIIe. [Review of *The Day of the Locust*.]

283. Fiedler, Leslie A. [on *A Cool Million*.] *The American Scholar*, 25 (Autumn 1956), 478.

284. Fiedler, Leslie A. "Master of Dreams." *Partisan Review*, 34, no. 3 (Summer 1967), 339-356. See X.

285. Flavin, Robert J. "Animal Imagery in the Works of Nathanael West." *Thoth*, 6, no. 2 (Spring 1965), 25-30. See XIIa.

286. Flores, Angel. "Miss Lonelyhearts in the Haunted Castle." *Contempo*, 3, no. 11 (25 July 1933), 1. See VIc.

287. Frank, Mike. "The Passion of *Miss Lonelyhearts* According to Nathanael West." *Studies in Short Fiction*, 10, no. 1 (Winter 1973), 67-73. See III, XIIc.

288. Friedman, Robert. "Nathaniel [*sic*] West's 'Day of the Locust'." *Daily Worker* (23 November 1950), p. 11. See XIIe. [Review.]

289. G., V. N. *"The Dream Life of Balso Snell,"* *Contempo*, 1 (21 August 1931), 3. See XIIb.

290. Galloway, David, D. "Nathanael West's Dream Dump." *Critique: Studies in Modern Fiction*, 6, no. 3 (Winter 1963-64), 46-64. See V, VIa, XId, XIIe.

291. Galloway, David D. "A Picaresque Apprenticeship: Nathanael West's *The Dream Life of Balso Snell* and *A Cool Million*." *Wisconsin Studies in Contemporary Literature*, 5, no. 2 (Summer 1964), 110-126. See XIId.

292. Gannett, Lewis. "Books and Things." *The New York Herald Tribune* (21 June 1934), p. 19. See XIId. [Review of *A Cool Million*.]

293. Geha, Richard, Jr. *"Miss Lonelyhearts*: A Dual Mission of Mercy." *Hartford Studies in Literature*, 3 (1971), 116-131. See XIIc.

294. Gehman, Richard B. "My Favorite Forgotten Book." *Tomorrow*, 8, no. 7 (March 1949), 61-62. See III, IVc, XIIe. [Review of *The Day of the Locust*.]

295. Gehman, Richard B. "Nathanael West: A Novelist Apart." *The Atlantic Monthly*, 186, no. 3 (September 1950), 69-72. Condensed from the New Directions Press edition of *The Day of the Locust*, "Introduction," 1950. See IVd, XIa, XIIb, XIIe.

296. Gilmore, Thomas B., Jr. "The Dark Night of the Cave: A Rejoinder to Kernan." *Satire Newsletter*, 2, no. 2 (Spring 1965), 95-100. See VIII.

297. Graham, John. "Struggling Upward: *The Minister's Charge* and *A Cool Million*." *Canadian Review of American Studies*, 4 (1974), 184-196. See V, XId.

298. Greiner, Don. "Strange Laughter: The Comedy of John Hawkes." *The Southwest Review*, 56, no. 4 (Autumn 1971), 318-327. See VII.

299. Hammett, Dashiell. [Ad for *Miss Lonelyhearts*.] *Contempo*, 3 (25 July 1933), 7. See XIIc.

300. Hand, Nancy Walker. "A Novel in the Form of a Comic Strip: Nathanael West's *Miss Lonelyhearts*." *The Serif*, 5, no. 2 (June 1968), 14-21. See VIc, XIIc.

301. Hassan, Ihab H. "Love in the Modern American Novel: Expense of Spirit and Waste of Shame." *Western Humanities Review*, 14, no. 2 (Spring 1960), 149-161. See IX.

302. Hawkes, John. "Flannery O'Connor's Devil." *The Sewanee Review*, 70, no. 3 (Summer 1962), 395-407. See XIa.

303. Hawkes, John. "John Hawkes on His Novels [an interview with John Graham]." *The Massachusetts Review*, 7 (Summer 1966), 449-461. See XIIa.

23

304. Hawkes, John. "Notes on the Wild Goose Chase," in a symposium with
D. J. Hughes and Ihab Hassan--"Fiction Today." *The Massachusetts Review*,
3 (Summer 1962), 784-788. See XIa.

305. Hayes, E. Nelson. "Recent Fiction." *The Progressive*, 21 (June
1957), 35-39. See XIIa. [Review of West's *Complete Works*.]

306. Hayes, Richard. "Dear Miss Lonelyhearts." *The Commonweal*, 67
(25 October 1957), 98. In a review of Howard Teichmann's stage adaption
of *Miss Lonelyhearts* (directed by Alan Schneider, starring Pat O'Brien
and Fritz Weaver), Hayes concludes that the play is a failure. "Mr.
Teichmann has made the error of assuming that the paraphernalia of actuality
has any objective existence in West's work: he fails to see that, for
this novelist, incident, character, personality, ostensible satire are
but the necessary rubbish of illusion."

307. Henkle, Roger B. "Pynchon's Tapestries on the Western Wall."
Modern Fiction Studies, 17, no. 2 (Summer 1971), 207-220. See VII.

308. Herbst, Josephine. [Ad for *Miss Lonelyhearts*.] *Contempo*, 3
(25 July 1933), 7. See XIIc.

309. Herbst, Josephine. "Hunter of Doves." *Botteghe Oscure*. Quaderno
13 (1954), 310-344. A short story with the main character--Noel Bartram--
patterned after West. "He was dead. Now he seemed in peril of a double
death for the work which should have left his image clear was to be, it
seemed, the exact medium that would forever blur him" (p. 310).

310. Herbst, Josephine. *"Miss Lonelyhearts*: An Allegory." *Contempo*,
3, no. 11 (25 July 1933), 4. See XIIc.

311. Herbst, Josephine. "Nathanael West." *The Kenyon Review*, 23
(Autumn 1961), 611-630. See II, XIa.

312. Hogan, William. "Nathanael West, Symbol of the Literary 1930's."
The San Fransisco Chronicle (22 May 1957), p. 23. See XIIa. [Review of
West's *Complete Works*.]

313. Hollis, C. Carroll. "Nathanael West and Surrealist Violence."
Fresco, 7, no. 5 (1957), 5-13. See III, IVd, VId, XIa, XIc, XIIb, XIIc.

314. Hollis, C. Carroll. "Nathanael West and the 'Lonely Crowd'."
Thought, 33 (Autumn 1958), 398-416. See VId, XIc, XIIb, XIIc.

315. Hollis, C. Carroll. "Nathanael West: Diagnostician of the Lonely
Crowd." *Fresco*, 8, no. 1 (1957), 5-21. See II, IVc, V, XIId, XIIe.

316. Hough, Graham. "New Novels." *Encounter*, 53 (February 1958),
84-87. See XIIa. [Review of West's *Complete Works*.]

317. Jacobs, Robert G. "Nathanael West: The Christology of Unbelief."
Iowa English Yearbook, 9 (Fall 1964), 68-74. See XIIc.

318. Kanters, Robert. "Nathanael West perdu et retrouvé." *Figaro Littéraire*, 12 (August 1961), 2. Sii XIa.

319. Kraus, W. Keith. "Communication: Mr. Kraus to Mr. White on N. West." *American Notes & Queries*, 6, no. 8 (April 1968), 128. See II. (In connection with this, see [321] and [419].)

320. Kraus, W. Keith. "Nathanael West: A Further Bibliographical Note." *The Serif*, 4, no. 1 (1967), 32. See II.

321. Kraus, W. Keith. "An Uncited Nathanael West Story." *American Notes & Queries*, 5, no. 10 (June 1967), 163-164. See II. (For a reply, see [419].)

322. Levart, Herman H. [Letter concerning (376).] *The Western Review*, 20 (Spring 1956), 254-255. Levart accuses Schneider (see [376]) of almost complete plagiarism of his own Master's thesis and the work of other scholars--a charge that the editors of *The Western Review* in effect support. For Schneider's reply, see [377].

323. Levin, Meyer. "The Candid Cameraman." *Esquire*, 6 (December 1936), 133-142. [Review of the movie "The President's Mystery," whose script West helped write. However, no mention of West is included.]

324. Lewis, R. W. B. "Hart Crane and the Clown Tradition." *The Massachusetts Review*, 4 (Summer 1963), 745-767. See XIc.

325. Liebling, A. J. "Shed a Tear for Mr. West." *The New York World Telegram* (24 June 1933), p. 14. [Review of *Miss Lonelyhearts*.]

326. Light, James F. "Genius on Campus: Nathanael West at Brown." *Contact*, 3 (1959), 97-111. Later revised and included in [3].

327. Light, James F. "*Miss Lonelyhearts*: The Imagery of Nightmare." *American Quarterly*, 3, no. 4 (Winter 1956), 316-328. See IX, XIIc. Later revised and included in [3].

328. Light, James F. "Nathanael West." *Prairie Schooner*, 31, no. 3 (Fall 1957), 279-283. See XIIb, XIId, XIIe. [Review of West's *Complete Works*.]

329. Light, James F. "Nathanael West and the Ravaging Locust." *American Quarterly*, 12, no. 1 (Spring 1960), 44-54. Later revised and included in [3].

330. Light, James F. "Nathanael West, 'Balso Snell', and the Mundane Millstone." *Modern Fiction Studies*, 4 (1958), 319-328. Later revised and included in [3].

331. Light, James F. "Violence, Dreams, and Dostoevsky: The Art of Nathanael West." *College English*, 19, no. 5 (February 1958), 208-213. Revised and included in [3].

332. Light, James F. [Letter.] *The New York Times Book Review* (11 August

25

1957), p. 21. Light requests any information about West available for his new study.

333. Linberg-Seyersted, Brita. "Three Variations of the American Success Story: The Careers of Luke Larkin, Lemuel Barker, and Lemuel Pitkin." *English Studies*, 53, no. 2 (April 1972), 125-141. See VIII, X, XIId.

334. Lokke, V. L. "A Side Glance at Medusa: Hollywood, the Literature Boys, and Nathanael West." *Southwest Review*, 46, no. 1 (Winter 1961), 35-45. See XIIe.

335. Lorch, Thomas M. "The Inverted Structure of *Balso Snell*." *Studies in Short Fiction*, 4, no. 1 (Fall 1966), 33-41. See XIb, XIIb.

336. Lorch, Thomas M. "Religion and Art in *Miss Lonelyhearts*." *Renascence*, 20, no. 1 (Autumn 1967), 11-17. See VIc, XIIc.

337. Lorch, Thomas M. "West's *Miss Lonelyhearts*: Skepticism Mitigated?" *Renascence*, 18, no. 2 (Winter 1966), 99-109. See VIc.

338. Lund, Mary Graham. "Backwards-Forwards in Forbidden Lands." *Western World Review*, 3, no. 1 (Spring 1968), 21-27. See IVd, XIa.

339. Markfield, Wallace. "From the Underbelly." *The New Leader*, 33 (27 November 1950), 25. See XIIe. [Review of *The Day of the Locust*.]

340. Marsh, Fred T. "*A Cool Million* and Other Recent Works of Fiction." *The New York Times Book Review* (1 July 1934), p. 6. See XIId.

341. Matthews, T. S. "A Gallery of New Novels." *The New Republic*, 79 (18 July 1934), 271-272. See XId. [Review of *A Cool Million*.]

342. Matthews, T. S. "Novels--A Fortnight's Grist." *The New Republic*, 74 (26 April 1933), 314-315. See XIIc. [Review of *Miss Lonelyhearts*.]

343. McDonald, Dwight. "No Art and No Box Office." *Encounter*, 13, no. 1 (July 1959), 51-55. A highly unfavorable review of the movie, *Lonelyhearts*. However, McDonald remarks, "I greatly admire West's novel, which seems to me a meticulously pure expression of our special American sort of agony, the horror of aloneness, and of our type of corruption, that of mass culture. It is a prose poem . . ." (p. 52).

344. McLaughlin, Richard. "West of Hollywood." *Theatre Arts*, 35 (August 1951), 46-47, 93. See IVd, XIa, XIIb, XIId, XIIe.

345. Milburn, George. "The Hollywood Nobody Knows." *The Saturday Review of Literature*, 20, no. 4 (20 May 1939), 14-15. See XIIc, XIIe. [Review of *The Day of the Locust*.]

346. Mjoberg, Joran. "Nathanael West: En ironisk papetiker." *Bonniers Litterara Magasin*, 25 (1956), 133-137. [In Swedish.]

347. Mott, Frank Luther. [Review of *Miss Lonelyhearts*.] *Journalism Quarterly*, 10 (June 1933), 170-171. See XIIc.

348. Nichols, James W. "Nathanael West, Sinclair Lewis, Alexander Pope and Satiric Contrasts." *Satire Newsletter*, 5, no. 2 (Spring 1968), 119-122. See XIa, XIe.

350. Ooi, Kogi. "Nathanael West Saihyota." *Eigo Studies*, 119 (1974), 404-405.

351. Orvell, Miles D. "The Messianic Sexuality of 'Miss Lonelyhearts'." *Studies in Short Fiction*, 10, no. 2 (Spring 1973), 159-167. See VIc, XIIc.

352. Pearce, Richard. "'Pylon', 'Awake and Sing!' and the Apocalyptic Imagination of the 30's." *Criticism*, 13, no. 2 (Spring 1971), 131-142. See XId.

353. Peden, William. "Nathanael West." *The Virginia Quarterly Review*, 33, no. 3 (Summer 1957), 468-472. See XIIa, XIIb, XIIc, XIId, XIIe. [Review of West's *Complete Works*.]

354. Peden, William. "Pilgrimage to Destruction." *The New York Times* (27 September 1959), p. 5. Peden calls James Purdy's *Malcolm* an example of Fielding's "comic epic in prose," like West's novels.

355. Perelman, S. J. "Good-bye, Broadway, Hello, Mr. Square." *The Saturday Evening Post*, 237 (23 May 1964), 94-96. See IVa.

356. Perelman, S. J. "Nathanael West: A Portrait." *Contempo*, 3 (25 July 1933), 1, 4. See IVa.

357. Petrullo, Helen B. "Clichés and Three Political Satires of the Thirties." *Satire Newsletter*, 8, no. 2 (Spring 1971), 109-117. See XId.

358. Phillips, Robert S. "F [*sic*] and The Day of the Locust." *Fitzgerald Newsletter*, 15 (Fall 1961), 68-69. See XId.

359. Pinsker, Sanford. "Charles Dickens and Nathanael West: Great Expectations Unfulfilled." *Topic*, 18 (1969), 40-52. See VIII, XIc, XId.

360. Pisk, George M. "The Graveyard of Dreams: A Study of Nathanael West's Last Novel, *The Day of the Locust.*" *The South Central Bulletin*, 27, no. 4 (Winter 1967), 64-72. See V, IX, X, XIIe.

361. Popkin, Henry. "Nathanael West," *Times Literary Supplement*, 57 (11 April 1958), 195. See III.

362. Popkin, Henry. "The Taming of Nathanael West." *The New Republic*, 137 (21 October 1957), 19-20. A review of Howard Teichmann's stage adaption of *Miss Lonelyhearts*. "What West's savage, violent, grotesque book required was a savage, violent, grotesque adaption and production. . . . But his own drama gets watered down in Teichmann's play. It is watered down, humanized, buried in a natural world West never made" (p. 19).

363. Quinton, Anthony. "The Complete Works of Nathanael West." *The London Magazine*, 5, no. 5 (May 1958), 72-75. See III.

364. Ratner, Marc L. "Rebellion of Wrath and Laughter: Styron's *Set This House on Fire.*" *The Southern Review*, 7 (October 1971), 1007-1020. See VII.

365. Raven, Simon. "Sub-Men and Super Women." *Spectator*, 199 (6 December 1957), 810. See XIIa.

366. Reynolds, Quentin. "When 'Pep' Was a Ghost." *Brown Alumni Monthly*, 58 (December 1957), 8-9 (portrait on p. 9). See IVa.

367. Richardson, Robert D. "*Miss Lonelyhearts.*" *The University Review*, 33, no. 2 (December 1966), 151-157. See XIc, XIIb, XIIc.

368. Richmond, Lee J. "A Time to Mourn and a Time to Dance: Horace McCoy's *They Shoot Horses, Don't They.*" *Twentieth Century Literature*, 17, no. 2 (April 1971), 91-100. See XIa.

369. Rosenfield, Isaac. "Faulkner and Contemporaries." *Partisan Review*, 18, no. 1 (January-February 1951), 106-114. See XIIa.

370. Russell, Ralph. "He Might Have Been a Major Novelist." *The Reporter*, 16 (30 May 1957), 45-46. See XIIa. [Review of West's *Complete Works.*]

371. S., G. "The New Books." *The Saturday Review of Literature*, 10 (30 June 1934), 785. See XIId. [Review of *A Cool Million.*]

372. Salomon, Louis B. "California Grotesque." *The Nation*, 149 (15 July 1939, 78-79. See XIIe. [Review of *The Day of the Locust.*]

373. Sanders, David. [Review of West's *Complete Works.*] *Books Abroad*, 31 (1957), 376-377. See XIIa.

374. Sanford, John. "Nathanael West." *The Screen Writer*, 2 (December 1946), 10-13. See IVa.

375. Sasahara, Akira. "The World of *Miss Lonelyhearts.*" *Essays and Studies in English Language and Literature*, 53-54 (1968), 109-130. [In Japenese.]

376. Schneider, Cyril M. "The Individuality of Nathanael West." *The Western Review*, 20, no. 1 (Autumn 1955), 7-28. See V, VIc, X, XIa, XIIa, XIIb, XIIe.

377. Schneider, Cyril M. [Letter.] *The Western Review*, 20 (Spring 1956), 255-256. A reply to [322].

378. Schoenewald, Richard L. "No Second Act." *The Commonweal*, 66 (10 May 1957), 162-163. See XIIa. [Review of West's *Complete Works.*]

379. Schrank, Joseph. "Pep." *The New York Times Book Review* (9 June 1957), p. 30. See IVa.

380. Schulberg, Budd Wilson. "Literature of the Film: The Hollywood

Novel." *Films*, 1, no. 2 (Spring 1940), 68-78. See XIIe.

381. Schwartz, Edward Greenfield. "The Novels of Nathanael West." *Accent*, 17 (Autumn 1957), 251-262. See III, IVd, VIe, XIIb, XIIc, XIId.

382. Seymour-Smith, Martin. "Prophet of Black Humor." *Spectator*, 221 (19 July 1968), 94-95. See III, IVd, XIIa, XIIc, XIId, XIIe.

383. Shepard, Douglas. "Nathanael West Rewrites Horatio Alger." *Satire Newsletter*, 3, no. 1 (Fall 1965), 13-28. See VId, XId.

384. Simonson, Harold P. "California, Nathanael West, and the Journey's End." *The Closed Frontier: Studies in American Literary Tragedy*. New York [*etc.*]: Holt, Rinehart and Winston, Incorporated, 1970, pp. 99-124. See XIc, XId, XIIa, XIIe.

385. Skerrett, Joseph Taylor, Jr. "Dostoievsky, Nathanael West, and Some Contemporary American Fiction." *The University of Dayton Review*, 4, no. 1 (Winter 1967), 23-36. See VII, XIa, XIc, XIIa.

386. Smith, Roger H. "Complete Works of Nathanael West." *The Saturday Review of Literature*, 40 (11 May 1957), 13-14. See X, XIIa, XIIe.

387. Solberg, S. E. "The Novels of Nathaniel [*sic*] West--A Sargasso of the Imagination." *The English Language and Literature*, 14 (October 1963), 125-146. See III, X.

388. Steiner, T. R. "West's Lemuel and the American Dream." *The Southern Review*, 7, no. 4 (October 1971), 994-1006. See XIId.

389. Swan, Michael. "New Novels." *The New Statesman and Nation*, 38 (6 August 1949), 153-154. See XIIc. [Review of *Miss Lonelyhearts*.]

390. Thale, Mary. "The Moviegoer of the 1950's." *Twentieth Century Literature*, 14, no. 2 (July 1968), 84-89. See XIc.

391. Tibbetts, A. M. "Nathanael West's *The Dream Life of Balso Snell*." *Studies in Short Fiction*, 2, no. 2 (Winter 1965), 105-112. See XIIb.

392. Tibbetts, A. M. "The Strange Half-World of Nathanael West." *Prairie Schooner*, 34, no. 1 (Spring 1960), 8-14. See VIII, XIIa, XIIc, XIIe.

393. Troy, William. "Four Newer Novelists." *The Nation*, 136 (14 June 1933), 672-673. See XIIc. [Review of *Miss Lonelyhearts*.]

394. Van Gelder, Robert. "A Tragic Chorus." *The New York Times Book Review*, 44 (21 May 1939), 6-7. See XIIe. [Review of *The Day of the Locust*.]

395. Van Voorhees, Archibald. "The Happy Mortician." *The Saturday Review of Literature*, 40 (11 May 1957), 13. In a review of West's *Complete Works*, the author comments on West's growing popularity and concludes with a brief biographical sketch.

396. White, William. "Belated Fame." *The Detroit Free Press Sunday Magazine* (26 May 1957), p. 5. [Review of West's *Complete Works.*]

397. White, William. "Bibliography of Nathanael West." *The Book Collector*, 11 (Autumn 1962), 351. See II.

398. White, William. "Ernest Hemingway and Nathanael West: How Well-Known Is Your Collector's Item?" *American Book Collector*, 14 (May 1964), 29. See III.

399. White, William. "Fate and Nathanael West: A 1970 Note." *Literary Sketches*, 10, no. 10 (October 1970), 6-7. See III.

400. White, William. "'Go West!' Notes From a Bibliographer." *American Book Collector*, 19, no. 5 (1969), 7-10. SEE II, III.

401. White, William. "How Forgotten Was Nathanael West?" *American Book Collector*, 8, no. 4 (1958), 13-17. See II, III, IVd.

402. White, William. "*Miss Lonelyhearts*: You've Read the Book, Now See the Movie." *American Book Collector*, 24 (November-December 1973), 31-32. See II.

403. White, William. "More Books On Nathanael West." *American Book Collector*, 22, no. 6 (1972), 37. See II.

404. White, William. "Nathanael West." *Times Literary Supplement*, 57 (21 February 1958), 101. See III.

405. White, William. "Nathanael West." *Times Literary Supplement*, 57 (9 May 1958), 255. See III.

406. White, William. "Nathanael West: A Bibliography." *Studies in Bibliography*, 11 (1958), 207-224. See II.

407. White, William. "Nathanael West: A Bibliography Addenda (1957-1964), 5-18. See II.

408. White, William. "Nathanael West: A Working Checklist." *Bulletin of Bibliography*, 29, no. 4 (1972), 140-143. See II.

409. White, William. "Nathanael West: Further Bibliographical Notes." *The Serif*, 2, no. 3 (September 1965), 28-31. See II.

410. White, William. "Nathanael West: More By and About." *American Book Collector*, 22 (September 1971), 6. See II.

411. White, William. "Nathanael West's 'A Cool Million'." *American Notes & Queries*, 8, no. 8 (April 1970), 120. See II.

412. White, William. "Nathanael West's 'Balso Snell' in Cloth." *The Papers of the Bibliographical Society of America*, 60, no. 4 (1966), 474-476. See II.

413. White, William. "Notes on Hemingway, West, Tolkien, and Wise." *American Book Collector*, 18, nos. 5&6 (1968), 30-31. See III.

414. White, William. "A Novelist Ahead of His Time: Nathanael West." *Orient/West*, 6 (January 1961), 55-64. See II, III, IVc, XIIb, XIIc, XIId.

415. White, William. "The Plastered Duchess." *Brown Alumni Monthly*, 40, no. 7 (April 1960), 22. See II.

416. White, William. [Review of *Miss Lonelyhearts and The Day of the Locust*.] *Bulletin of Bibliography*, 23, no. 10 (January-April 1963), 223. See II.

417. White, William. [Review of Vol. 2 of *Studies in Bibliography*.] *Bulletin of Bibliography*, 22, no. 5 (January-April 1958), 104. See II.

418. White, William. "Some Uncollected Authors XXXII: Nathanael West, 1903?--1940." *The Book Collector*, 11 (1962), 206-210. See II, IVd.

419. White, William. "'Uncited West Story': A Dissent." *American Notes & Queries*, 6, no. 5 (January 1968), 72-73. See II.

420. White, William. "Unpublished Faulkner: Reply to a Nathanael West Questionnaire." *American Book Collector*, 17, no. 1 (September 1966), 27. See IVb.

421. Widmer, Kingsley. "The Hollywood Image." *Coastlines*, 5, no. 1 (1961), 17-27. See XId.

422. Williams, David. "A Lancashire Boyhood." *The Manchester Guardian* (3 December 1957), 4. See XIIa. [Review of West's *Complete Works*.]

423. Williams, William Carlos. "The Contact Story." *Contact*, 1 (1958), 75-77. See IVa.

424. Williams, William Carlos. "Sordid? Good God!" *Contempo*, 3, no. 11 (25 July 1933), pp. 5. 8. See XIIa.

425. Wilson, Edmund. [Ad for *Miss Lonelyhearts*.] *Contempo*, 3, no. 11 (25 July 1933), 7. See XIIa, XIIc.

426. Wilson, Edmund. "Hollywood Dance of Death." *The New Republic*, 99 (26 July 1939), 339-340. [Review of *The Day of the Locust*. Most of the comment made here is also found in (228).]

427. Wilson, T. C. "American Humor." *The Saturday Review of Literature*, 9 (13 May 1933), 589. See XIIc. [Review of *Miss Lonelyhearts*.]

428. [Your Reviewer.] "Nathanael West." *Times Literary Supplement*, 57 (28 February 1958), 115. See II.

429. Zimmer, Dieter E. "Nathanael West, oder Warnungen vorm Tag der Heuschrechen." *Neue Rundschau*, 83 (1972), 287-302. See IVc, XIIa.

430. Zoltnick, Joan. "The Medium Is the Message, Or Is It? A Study of Nathanael West's Comic Strip Novel." *Journal of Popular Culture*, 5, no. 1 (Summer 1971), 236-240. See VIc.

D) Reviews of Scholarly Works
Concerning West

Note. Since the emphasis of these reviews is on the scholarly work itself
and not on West, I have not felt it necessary to annotate the following.

1) Reviews of James F. Light's *Nathanael West: An Interpretative Study*:

431. Anon. *Antiquarian Bookman*, 28 (7 August 1961), 459.

432. Anon. *The Virginia Quarterly Review*, 37 (Autumn 1961), 136.

433. Ashmead, John. *American Literature*, 18 (1962), 189.

434. B., V. A. "The Bizarre Mr. West." *The Chicago Daily News* (3 June
1961).

435. Bellman, Samuel I. "Nathanael West's Bitter Life of Cynicism,
Failure Analyzed." *The Los Angeles Times* (13 August 1961). Section C,
p. 8.

436. Conroy, Jack. "Nightmare World of Nathanael West." *The Chicago
Sun-Times* (13 August 1961).

437. Gorn, Lester. "World of West." *The San Francisco Examiner* (9 June
1961).

438. Kostelanetz, Richard. *Arizona Quarterly* (1962).

439. Lid, R. W. *The San Francisco Chronicle* (23 July 1961), p. 20.

440. Wermuth, Paul C. *Library Journal*, 86 (15 September 1961), 2946.

441. White, William. "Nathanael West." *American Book Collector*, 12
(October 1961), 4.

442. White, William. *Bulletin of Bibliography*, 23 (1961), 126.

2) Reviews of Stanley Edgar Hyman's *Nathanael West*:

443. Angell, Richard C. *New Mexico Quarterly*, 33 (1963), 237.

444. Malin, Irving. *Books Abroad*, 38 (1964), 70.

445. White, William. "Nathanael West-iana." *American Book Collector*,
13 (February 1963), 7.

3) Reviews of Victor Comerchero's *Nathanael West: The Ironic Prophet*:

446. Bernard, Kenneth. *Western Humanities Review*, 20 (1966), 170-171.

447. Davis, Robert. *Books Abroad*, 29 (1965), 452.

448. Lancour, Harold. *Library Journal*, 90 (1965), 648.

449. Lee, Brian. *Notes & Queries*, 17 (1970), 79-80.

450. Light, James F. *American Literature*, 37 (1965), 222.

451. Ruhe, Edward L. *Midcontinent American Studies Journal*, 7 (1966), 61-63.

452. Stafford, William T. *American Literary Scholarship: An Annual/1964*, ed. James Woodress. Durham, North Carolina: Duke University Press, 1966, p. 178.

4) Review of Roger D. Abrahams' "Androgynes Bound: Nathanael West's *Miss Lonelyhearts*" (see [69]):

453. Locklin, Gerald. *Studies in Short Fiction*, 5 (Summer 1968), 404.

5) Reviews of Randall Reid's *Nathanael West: No Redeemer, No Promised Land:*

454. Anon. *Prairie Schooner*, 42 (1968), 365.

455. Bush, Clive. *Journal of American Studies*, 3 (1969), 157-158.

456. Eisinger, Chester. *English Language Notes*, 6 (1968), 148-151.

457. Gado, Frank. *Studia Neophilologeia*, 41 (1969), 203-204.

458. Green, James L. *American Literature Abstracts*, 2 (1969), 339.

459. Gross, Barry. *Studies in the Novel*, 1 (1969), 377-378.

460. Janssens, G. A. M. *Neophilologus*, 53 (1969), 238-239.

461. Jones, Joel M. *American Literature Abstracts*, 4 (1968), 94-96.

462. Lee, Brian. *Notes and Queries*, 17 (1970), 79-80.

463. Light, James F. *American Literature*, 40 (1968), 421.

464. Lund, Mary G. *Per/Se*, 3 (1968), 79.

465. Pops, Martin. *Criticism*, 10 (1968), 367.

6) Reviews of Jay Martin's *Nathanael West: The Art of His Life*:

466. Bedient, Calvin. "In Dreams Begin." *Partisan Review*, 38 (1971), 345-349.

467. Cassill, R. V. "The Dossier on Nathanael West." *Book World* (5 July 1970), p. 3.

468. Darrack, Brad. "A Great Dispiser." *Time*, 96 (17 August 1970), 64-65.

469. Dupee, F. W. *Catholic World*, 212 (November 1970), 110.

470. Gado, Frank. *American Literature*, 33 (1971), 298-299.

471. Howe, Irving. "That Rare and Marvelous Figure--An Original." *The New York Times Book Review* (12 July 1970), 1, 40.

472. Light, James F. *Satire Newsletter*, 8 (1970), 65-68.

473. Malin, Irving. "Late to Honor." *The Catholic World*, 212 (November 1970), 110.

474. Maloff, Saul. "Beware of 'Literature Boys'." *The Commonweal*, 93 (1970), 96-98.

475. Samuels, Charles Thomas. "Suicide as Rhetoric." *The New Republic*, 162 (23 May 1970), 23-24.

476. Schorer, Mark. "Nathan Weinstein: The Cheated." *The Atlantic Monthly*, 226 (October 1970), 127-130.

477. Sissman, L. E. "West." *The New Yorker* (10 October 1970), pp. 185-191.

478. Swados, Harvey. "*Nathanael West: The Art of His Life*." *The Saturday Review of Literature*, 53 (27 June 1970), 28-29.

479. Wakefield, Dan. "Mister Lonelyhearts." *The American Scholar*, 39 (1970), 524-526.

E)   Theses and Dissertations Concerning West

480. Brand, John. *Fiction as Decreation: The Novels of Nathanael West*. Texas Christian University, 1969, 215 pp. Ph. D. dissertation. (See *Dissertation Abstracts International*, 30 [1970]: 3449A.)

481. Briggs, Arlen J. *Nathanael West and Surrealism*. University of Oregon, 1972, 237 pp. Ph. D. dissertation. (See *Dissertation Abstracts International*, 33 [1974]: 6901A-02A.)

482. Brown, Daniel. *Nathanael West: The War Within*. Wayne State University, 1969, 189 pp. Ph. D. dissertation. (See *Dissertation Abstracts International*, 32 [1971]: 2676A.)

483. Comerchero, Victor. *Nathanael West: The Tuning Fork*. University of Iowa, 1961, 248 pp. (See *Dissertation Abstracts*, 22 [1962]: 2791.)

484. Cramer, Carter M. *The World of Nathanael West: A Critical Interpretation*. Kansas State Teachers College at Emporia, 1971. Masters Thesis (See [276]).

485. Frizot, Daniel. *The Clown Figure in Louis-Ferdinand Céline and Nathanael West, or the Tragi-comic in Modern Fiction*. Purdue University, 1973, 252 pp. Ph. D. dissertation. (See *Dissertation Abstracts International*, 34 [1974]: 5908A-09A.)

486. Houston, James D. *Three Variations of Grotesquerie in Twentieth Century American Fiction*. Stanford University, 1962. Masters Thesis.

487. Keyes, J. M. *Nathanael West: A Technical View*. University of Toronto, 1972. Ph. D. dissertation.

488. Krupat, Arnold. *The Saintly Hero: A Study of the Saintly Hero in Some Contemporary American Novels*. Columbia University, 1966. Ph. D. dissertation. (See *Dissertation Abstracts*, 28 [1967]: 2251A.)

489. Kugelmas, Harold. *The Search For Identity: The Development of the Protean Model of Self in Contemporary American Fiction*. University of Oregon, 1972. (See *Dissertation Abstracts International*, 34 [1973]: 1285A.)

490. Levart, Herman H. *Nathanael West: A Study of His Fiction*. Columbia University, 1952, 58 pp. Masters Thesis.

491. Light, James F. *Nathanael West: A Critical Study, With Some Biographical Material*. Syracuse University, 1953, 255 pp. Ph. D. dissertation. (See [3].)

492. Locklin, Gerald. *A Critical Study of the Novels of Nathanael West*. University of Arizona, 1964, 301 pp. Ph. D. dissertation. (See *Dissertation Abstracts*, 25 [1964]: 3576-3577.)

493. Lokke, Virgil L. *The Literary Image of Hollywood*. Iowa State University, 1954. Ph. D. dissertation. (See *Dissertation Abstracts*, 15 [1955]: 2210.)

494. Lorch, Thomas M. *The Peculiar Half-World of Nathanael West*. Yale University, 1964, 269 pp. Ph. D. dissertation. (See *Dissertation Abstracts*, 26 [1965]: 2218.)

495. Mann, Nora. *The Novels of Nathanael West*. University of Missouri, Columbia, 1968, 181 pp. Ph. D. dissertation. (See *Dissertation Abstracts*, 29 [1969]: 2716A.)

496. Michaels, Lloyd I. *A Particular Kind of Joking: Nathanael West and Burlesque*. State University of New York at Buffalo, 1972, 191 pp. Ph. D. dissertation. (See *Dissertation Abstracts International*, 33 [1973]: 188A-89A.)

497. Petrullo, Helen B. *Satire and Freedom: Sinclair Lewis, Nathanael West, and James Thurber*. Syracuse University, 1967, 219 pp. Ph. D. dissertation. (See *Dissertation Abstracts*, 28 [1967]: 1445A.)

498. Pisk, George M. *A Fire in Dreamland: A Suggested Unifying Principle in the Works of Nathanael West*. University of Texas, 1959, 134 pp. Masters Thesis.

499. Reid, Randall C. *Nathanael West: No Redeemer, No Promised Land*. Stanford University, 1967, 208 pp. Ph. D. dissertation. (See *Dissertation Abstracts*, 27 [1967]: 2159A.) Also, see [66].

500. Robinson, David E. *Unaccomodated Man: The Estranged World in Contemporary American Fiction*. Duke University, 1971, 297 pp. Ph. D. dissertation. (See *Dissertation Abstracts International*, 32 [1972]: 5803A.)

501. Schneider, Cyril M. *Nathanael West: A Study of His Work*. New York University, 1953, 74 pp. Masters Thesis.

502. Schoenewolf, Carroll R. *The Novels of Nathanael West*. University of Oklahoma, 1973. Ph. D. dissertation. (See *Dissertation Abstracts International*, 34 [1974]: 1934A.)

503. Smith, Marcus. *The Art and Influence of Nathanael West*. University of Wisconsin, Madison, 1964, 318 pp. Ph. D. dissertation. (See *Dissertation Abstracts*, 25 [1965]: 4155-56.)

504. Wadlington, Warwick. *The Theme of the Confidence Game in Certain American Writers*. Tulane University, 1967, 268 pp. Ph. D. dissertation. (See *Dissertation Abstracts*, 28 [1968]: 3691A.)

505. Wexelblatt, Robert. *Disintegration in the Works of F. Scott Fitzgerald and Nathanael West*. Brandeis University, 1973, 294 pp. Ph. D. dissertation. (See *Dissertation Abstracts International*, 34 [1974]: 4296A.)

506. Zaidman, Laura M. *Nathanael West: The Varieties of Religious Experience*. Florida State University, Tallahassee, 1972.

507. Zoltnick, Joan. *Nathanael West: A Study of the Paradox of Art*. New York University, 1969, 148 pp. Ph. D. dissertation. (See *Dissertation Abstracts International*, 30 [1970]: 3482A-83A.)

II. Bibliographical Studies

Works discussed in this chapter make admittedly a heterogenous group, partially because "bibliography" is not consistently defined, even by bibliographers. Included here are almost any scholarly discussions of West and his works (save biographical statements) which do not attempt a critical evaluation: i.e. checklists, formal bibliographical descriptions and partial descriptions of certain editions (mainly for book collectors), discussions of the revisions of a particular novel, attribution studies, and sales figures on the various editions of West's novels. Even though bibliographers rather consistently tend to ignore twentieth century writers, it is a measure of the magnitude of the West "revival" that--despite the almost total lack of bibliographical studies of West prior to the late 1950's--we are able to list such a number today.

254. Bittner, William. "A la recherche d'un ecrivain perdu." *Les Langues Modernes*, 54 (July-August 1960), 274-282. Bittner devotes almost two pages to recounting the publishing history of the novels.

276. Cramer, Carter M. "The World of Nathanael West: A Critical Interpretation." *The Emporia State Research Studies*, 19, no. 4 (June 1971), 5-71. Cramer's revised Master's thesis concludes with a brief unannotated bibliography.

47. Daniel, Carter A. "West's Revisions of *Miss Lonelyhearts*." *Nathanael West: A Collection of Critical Essays*, ed. Jay Martin. Englewood Cliffs, New Jersey: Prentice-Hall, Incorporated, 1971, pp. 52-65. Daniel examines revisions of five early chapters of the novel published before the novel's publication. Among the more interesting changes discussed are the change in the hero's name (from Thomas Matlock to Miss Lonelyhearts) and from first to third person narrative. Says Daniel, "The sardonically matter-of-fact, seemingly objective narration is a valuable stylistic asset, since to maintain the continual element of surprise there must be only limited insight into Miss Lonelyheart's thoughts" (p. 53). Daniel concludes that the final versions of the revised chapters are less diffuse than the earlier ones. Most of the essay is composed of a two column juxtaposition of earlier and later versions with comment between--probably the finest discussion of this particular subject.

10. Edenbaum, Robert I. "To Kill God and Build a Church: Nathanael West's *Miss Lonelyhearts*." *Twentieth Century Interpretations of* Miss Lonelyhearts, ed. Thomas H. Jackson. Englewood Cliffs, New Jersey: Prentice-Hall, Incorporated, 1971, pp. 61-69. Included is a discussion of changes between *Contact* and *Contempo* segments of *Miss Lonelyhearts* and the final version (see also [47]). "The differences between versions indicate not only that West's conception of his characters changed and coalesced, but that he gradually came to take himself, his writing, and the world more seriously" (p. 62). Edenbaum finds that the revisions make more distinct the differences between the attitudes of Shrike and Miss Lonelyhearts.

122. Gehman, Richard. "Introduction." *The Day of the Locust.* New York:

The New Classics, 1950, pp. ix-xxiii. Included are brief comments on the revisions of the novel.

123. Gerstenberger, Donna and George Hendrick. "Nathanael West." *The American Novel: A Checklist of Twentieth Century Criticism on Novels Written Since 1789. Volume II: Criticism Written 1960-68.* Chicago: The Swallow Press, 1970, pp. 360-362. A selected, unannotated checklist of criticism and bibliographical studies.

311. Herbst, Josephine. "Nathanael West." *The Kenyon Review,* 23 (Autumn 1961), 611-630. Herbst comments on last minute revisions of *Miss Lonelyhearts.*

315. Hollis, C. Carroll. "Nathanael West: Diagnostician of the Lonely Crowd." *Fresco,* 8, no. 1 (1957), 5-21. Included in the notes following the essay is a list of sales figures on the novels.

4. Jackson, Thomas H., ed. *Twentieth Century Interpretations of* Miss Lonelyhearts. Englewood Cliffs, New Jersey: Prentice-Hall, Incorporated, 1971. The book ends with a chronology of West's life and works juxtaposed to a chronology of important publications and events of the age. There follows a nine item annotated bibliography.

320. Kraus, W. Keith. "Nathanael West: A Further Bibliographical Note." *The Serif,* 4, no. 1 (1967), 32. Kraus comments on William White's omission of the movie "Lonelyhearts" from his bibliographical studies of West and also comments briefly on a few reviews of the movie.

321. Kraus, W. Keith. "An Uncited Nathanael West Story." *American Notes and Queries,* 5, no. 10 (June 1967), 163-164. Kraus claims that West's first use of his name change did not occur at the publication of *The Dream Life of Balso Snell,* as commonly assumed, but two years before in a previously uncited story--"A Barefaced Lie," *Overland Monthly,* 87 (July 1929), 210, 219. He claims that the story was later incorporated into a tale in *A Cool Million.* States Kraus, "In transition, the story takes on the note of violence that distinguishes West's later work" (p. 163). For a dissent by William White, see [419].

319. Kraus, W. Keith. "Communication: Mr. Kraus to Mr. White on N. West." *American Notes and Queries,* 6, no. 8 (April 1968), 128. A rejoinder to William White's rejoinder (see [419]). Kraus cites further evidence to support his claim that "A Barefaced Lie" is indeed a West story, including brief examinations of facets of "subject matter, setting, and method" (p. 128).

3. Light, James F. *Nathanael West: An Interpretative Study.* 2nd ed. Evanston, Illinois: Northwestern University Press, 1971. In the "Forward" to his study, Light describes and evaluates the book-length studies of West published since the first edition of this work. Discussed in depth are the works of Hyman, Comerchero, Reid, and Martin.

38. Taylor, Helen. "An Annotated Bibliography." *Nathanael West: The Cheaters and the Cheated, a Collection of Critical Essays,* ed. David Madden. Deland, Florida: Everett/Edwards, Incorporated, 1973, pp. 323-41.

After listing West's works, Taylor lists books, chapters in books, and articles in periodicals on West, most items annotated. The latter two categories are highly selective. Taylor begins her essay with a brief prose overview of the direction which most West criticism seems to be taking and then cites areas where more work needs to be done.

40. Martin, Jay, ed. *Nathanael West: A Collection of Critical Essays.* Englewood Cliffs, New Jersey: Prentice-Hall, Incorporated, 1971. The book ends with a selected checklist of books and articles (the articles annotated) dealing with West (pp. 175-176).

64. Martin, Jay. *Nathanael West: The Art of His Life.* New York: Farrar, Straus and Giroux, 1970. A great deal of bibliographical information is included in Martin's biography, as one might imagine, but certain sections might be particularly helpful. For discussions of the revisions of *Miss Lonelyhearts* (from the early *Contact* episode on) see pp. 150 and following. Martin also includes an early section of *The Day of the Locust,* originally published in *Pacific Weekly,* November 16, 1936 (see p. 347). For bibliographical information on the individual novels, see the following: *The Dream Life of Balso Snell,* p. 124; *Miss Lonelyhearts,* p. 176; *A Cool Million,* pp. 244-245; *The Day of the Locust,* pp. 324, 340-344.

183. Nevius, Blake. "Nathanael West." *The American Novel: Sinclair Lewis to the Present.* Illinois: AHM Publishing, Incorporated, 1970, pp. 99-100. An unannotated, selective checklist in three sections: 1) bibliographical studies; 2) biographical and critical books and 3) biographical and critical essays.

190. Powell, Lawrence Clark. *"The Day of the Locust:* Nathanael West." *California Classics: The Creative Literature of the Golden State.* Los Angeles: The Ward Ritchie Press, 1971, pp. 344-56, 359. Contains some information on the sales of West's novels.

193. Ramsaye, Terry, ed. "West, Nathaniel [sic]." *International Motion Picture Almanac* [1939-40]. New York: The Quigley Publishing Company, 1939, p. 673. Lists five screenplays and collaborations by West from 1935-38.

66. Reid, Randall. *The Fiction of Nathanael West: No Redeemer, No Promised Land.* Chicago: University of Chicago Press, 1967. Reid's study concludes with a brief selected and unannotated checklist of West criticism, and he also lists relevant background reading.

67. Scott, Nathan A., Jr. *Nathanael West: A Critical Essay,* Contemporary Writers in Christian Perspective. Grand Rapids, Michigan: William B. Eerdmans, 1971. Contains some information on the sales of West's novels.

397. White, William. "Bibliography of Nathanael West." *The Book Collector,* 11 (Autumn 1962), p. 351. Here White comments on a new reprint of *Miss Lonelyhearts* and *A Cool Million* (Penguin Books, 1962). White finds errors in the editors' identification of the first English publication of the two novels and also finds error in copyright information and biographical data.

400. White, William. "'Go West!' Notes From a Bibliographer." *American Book Collector*, 19, no. 5 (1969): 7-10. White comments on the book-length studies of Light, Hyman, Comerchero, and Reid. Also included is a largely unannotated list of articles on West. White concludes with formal bibliographical descriptions of five new translations and two new editions of West's novels.

401. White, William. "How Forgotten Was Nathanael West?" *American Book Collector*, 8 no. 4 (1958), 13-17. White briefly mentions West's published short fiction, plus scripts written in Hollywood (p. 9). White also cites one play by West, *Good Hunting*, with Joseph Schrank (1938).

402. White, William. "*Miss Lonelyhearts*: You've Read the Book, Now See the Movie." *American Book Collector*, 24 (November-December 1973), 31-32. White discusses his purchase of a film pressbook of *Miss Lonelyhearts*, plus several of Hemingway's. White describes the pressbook and the relation between it and the movie ("Lonelyhearts") and concludes that the film "does not improve with age" (p. 32).

403. White, William. "More Books on Nathanael West." *American Book Collector*, 22, no. 6 (1972), 37. Briefly discusses five new books on West.

406. White, William. "Nathanael West: A Bibliography." *Studies in Bibliography*, 11 (1958), 207-224. This is the first formal bibliography dealing with West attempted, to my knowledge. White lists West's works, plus articles and reviews on West. It is interesting that no book-length works on West had been written as late as this. The bibliography contains some errors, which White corrects in subsequent checklists.

407. White, William. "Nathanael West: A Bibliography, Addenda (1957-1964)." *The Serif*, 2, no. 1 (1965), 5-18. White begins with comments on West's increased popularity since the publication of his (White's) 1958 checklist. In addition to giving information on the sales of various editions of West's novels, White gives bibliographical descriptions of various editions he has examined, plus listing translations which he has not personally examined. He also locates a copy of *The Dream Life of Balso Snell* in boards which he had previously cited but not found. He concludes with a partially annotated checklist of essays, reviews, etc. published since his last bibliography.

223. White, William. *Nathanael West: A Comprehensive Bibliography. Kent, Ohio: The Kent State University Press*, 1975. White's bibliography furnishes complete bibliographical descriptions of the editions of West's novels, including reproductions of title pages, lists West' publications in periodicals, his plays, movie scripts, works published in books or anthologies. Also included is an exhaustive checklist of biographical and critical material about West (mostly unannotated). White's study ends with over sixty pages of unpublished writings by West: stories, essays, and poems from college days and later.

408. White, William. "Nathanael West: A Working Checklist." *Bulletin of Bibliography*, 29, no. 4 (1972), 140-143. After listing West's works (no full bibliographical descriptions this time), White provides an

42

annotated list of essential items (books, chapters of books, and articles in periodicals) "those who are working on the author of *Miss Lonelyhearts* will find it necessary to consult" (p. 140).

409. White, William. "Nathanael West: Further Bibliographical Notes." *The Serif*, 2, no. 3 (September 1965), 28-31. Here White discusses and describes variants in editions of *Miss Lonelyhearts*, *A Cool Million*, and *The Day of the Locust* and lists six new essays and reviews dealing with West.

410. White, William. "Nathanael West: More By and About." *American Book Collector*, 22, (September 1971), 6. White lists and comments on three previously uncited pieces by West and two new books on West.

411. White, William. "Nathanael West's 'A Cool Million'." *American Notes and Queries*, 8, no. 8 (April 1970), 120. White describes two variant bindings of *A Cool Million* and inquires into the source of the variation--second or third impressions, *etc.*?

412. White, William. "Nathanael West's 'Balso Snell' in Cloth." *The Papers of the Bibliographical Society of America*, 60, no. 4 (1966), 474-476. White provides a detailed bibliographical description of copies one to fifteen of the first edition of *The Dream Life of Balso Snell* and then corrects a previous assumption he had made about a first edition copy of that novel.

414. White, William. "A Novelist Ahead of His Time: Nathanael West." *Orient/West*, 6 (January 1961), 55-64. The essay includes a two page summary of the scholarship on West.

415. White, William. "The Plastered Duchess." *Brown Alumni Monthly*, 40, no. 7 (April 1960), 22. In a letter to the editor White comments on the authorship and contents of a bawdy 1924 Brown play, *The Plastered Duchess*.

416. White, William. [Review of *Miss Lonelyhearts* and *The Day of the Locust*]. *The Bulletin of Bibliography*, 23, no. 10 (January-April 1963), 223. In a review of the New Directions reissue of the two novels, White identifies the plates that the new issues were made from and concludes that West's reputation will rest ultimately upon those two novels.

417. White, William. [Review of Volume III of *Studies in Bibliography*]. *Bulletin of Bibliography*, 22, no. 5 (January-April 1958), 104. White cites and corrects errors in his 1958 bibliography on West (see [406]).

418. White, William. "Some Uncollected Authors XXXII: Nathanael West, 1903?-1940." *The Book Collector*, 11 (1962), 206-210. White comments on the desirability and possibility of finding first edition copies of West's novels. The essay ends with a formal bibliographical description of each of the novels, plus the *Complete Works*.

419. White, William. "'Uncited West Story': A Dissent." *American Notes and Queries*, 6, no. 5 (January 1968), 72-73. White informs Keith Kraus (see [321]) that "A Barefaced Lie" had already been cited by White in his 1958 bibliography (see [406]). White feels that insufficient evidence

exists to infer that the N. West of the story and Nathanael West are one
and the same.

229. Woodress, James. "Nathanael West (1903-1940)." *American Fiction,
1900-1950: A Guide to Information Sources.* Detroit: Gale Research
Company, 1974. I, 205-208 (see also pp. 28,29). After a one paragraph
biographical sketch, Woodress lists some of the bibliographical and
manuscript sources available to West scholars, lists West's works and a few
of the reprints, lists biographies and reminiscences, and summarizes
the major critical works dealing with West.

428. [Your Reviewer]. "Nathanael West." *Times Literary Supplement*, 57
(28 February 1958), 115. The reviewer acknowledges several mistakes made
in earlier comments on West, pointed out by William White in a previous
letter (see [404]).

III. The State of the Scholarship on West

Essays, reviews, and books dealing with Nathanael West are remark-
ably consistent in the pattern that their introductions take. Almost
without exception, the author of such a work will remark on West's
obscurity during his lifetime, then observe the striking rise in the
amount of critical comment on West of late. I suppose that all such
introductions could technically be considered "State of the Scholarship"
statements; but included in this chapter are only those works or sections
of works which make some more substantial effort at defining the common
critical stance toward West or a particular work at a given time.

231. Aaron, Daniel. "'The Truly Monstrous': A Note on Nathanael West."
Partisan Review, 14, no. 1 (1947), 98-106. Aaron begins by noting West's
lack of fame during his lifetime, and at the time of the writing of his
article, Aaron notes that *Miss Lonelyhearts* "has neither been popular
among those who enjoy bad novels nor known to enough people who like good
ones" (p. 98).

244. Anon. "Nathanael West." *Times Literary Supplement*, 57 (24 January
1958), 44. The anonymous author cites West's virtual disregard, except
for Edmund Wilson, during his life. Though West was "obviously part of
the stream" of fiction in the 1930's, his bleak pessimism reduced his
audience, claims the author.

36. Bowden, James H. "No Redactor, No Reward." *Nathanael West: The
Cheaters and the Cheated, A Collection of Critical Essays*, ed. David
Madden. Deland, Florida: Everett/Edwards, Incorporated, 1973, pp.283-98.
Bowden begins by summarizing the critical view of West and concludes that
critics consistently hedge from according him a significant place in lit-
erature.

22. Brand, John M. "A Word Is a Word Is a Word." *Nathanael West: The
Cheaters and the Cheated, A Collection of Critical Essays*, ed. David
Madden. Deland, Florida: Everett/Edwards, Incorporated, 1973, pp. 57-76.
A more specialized "State of the Scholarship" statement. Brand mentions
several salient articles and books which ignore West's Jewishness, and
Brand maintains that West can only be interpreted in light of his
Jewish legacy.

266. Carlisle, Henry. "The Comic Tradition." *The American Scholar*,
28 (Winter 1958-59), 96-108. Says Carlisle, "One case in point [of American
humor which has been left unassayed] is the late Nathanael West. The
welcome publication two years ago of his novels in a single volume . . .
does not appear to have substantially improved the public fortunes of
one of the best and most durable satirical novelists of the late 1930's"
(p. 102).

1. Comerchero, Victor. *Nathanael West: The Ironic Prophet*. Syracuse:
Syracuse University Press, 1964. In his forward, Victor Comerchero cites
West's lack of recognition previously while maintaining that he wishes to
"rectify West's critical imbalance" (p. xii). After supporting his point

by citing the meager sales figures for the novels, Comerchero finds the source of the lack of interest in West's "unmitigated pessimism" (p. 2).

276. Cramer, Carter M. "The World of Nathanael West: A Critical Interpretation." *The Emporia State Research Studies*, 19, no. 4 (June 1971), 5-71. Cramer begins each section devoted to an entire novel with a cross-section of the criticism concerning that novel.

107. [The Editors of *Time*]. "Editors' Preface." *The Day of the Locust*, by Nathanael West, Time Reading Program Special Edition. New York: Time Incorporated, 1965, pp. vii-xii. The editors comment on West's neglect and believe that he was ignored because "no standard of popular literature was applicable there [in his works]" (p. vii).

113. Fiedler, Leslie A. *Waiting For the End*. New York: Dell Publishing Company, 1964, pp. 45-46. Fiedler claims that West was more influential during the forties and fifties than many more famous writers of the thirties, but his reputation, once small, is now "overbalanced" (p. 45).

287. Frank, Mike. "The Passion of *Miss Lonelyhearts* According to Nathanael West." *Studies in Short Fiction*, 10, no. 1 (Winter 1973), 67-73. Frank begins with an overview of the dominant themes in the criticism of the novel: 1) Miss Lonelyhearts is warped or 2) the world is warped. He sees Hyman (see [2]) as combining the two views.

294. Gehman, Richard. "My Favorite Forgotten Book." *Tomorrow*, 8, no. 7 (March 1949), 61-62. Begins by noting the critical reception (generally lack of) of *The Day of the Locust*.

313. Hollis, C. Carroll. "Nathanael West and Surrealist Violence." *Fresco*, 7 no. 5 (1957), 5-13. The first page serves as a "State of the Scholarship" statement. He concludes, "At long last this publication of West's complete fiction will bring him the dubious and belated fame as the master of the novel of selected violence" (p. 6).

5. Jackson, Thomas H. "Introduction." *Twentieth Century Interpretations of* Miss Lonelyhearts. Englewood Cliffs, New Jersey: Prentice-Hall, Incorporated, 1971, pp. 1-17. Jackson begins with a brief overview of the criticism of the novel and concludes that so many interpretations are possible and at least partially valid because critics are able to pick out any one disorder the West finds in society and see it as the central one. Jackson feels that the effect is more of a collage of ills.

3. Light, James F. *Nathanael West: An Interpretative Study*. 2nd ed. Evanston: Northwestern University Press, 1971. Note the following sections for discussions of the critical receptions of each of the novels: *Miss Lonelyhearts*, pp. 106-110; *A Cool Million*, pp. 139-140; *The Day of the* Locust, pp. 193-196.

21. Locklin, Gerald. "The Journey Into the Microcosm." *Nathanael West: The Cheaters and the Cheated, A Collection of Critical Essays*, ed. David Madden. Deland, Florida: Everett/Edwards, Incorporated, 1973, pp. 23-56. Locklin summarizes the current state of scholarship concerning *The Dream*

Life of Balso Snell, quoting from various points of view.

39. Malin, Irving. *Nathanael West's Novels*. Carbondale and Edwardsville: Southern Illinois University Press, London and Amsterdam: Feffer and Simons, Incorporated, 1972. Malin provides an overview of the critical views of the source of West's discontent. He largely discounts the psychological interpretation.

64. Martin, Jay. *Nathanael West: The Art of His Life*. New York: Farrar, Straus and Giroux, 1970. For discussions of the critical receptions of the individual novels, see the following passages: *Miss Lonelyhearts*, pp. 191-192; *A Cool Million*, pp. 246-247; *The Day of the Locust*, pp. 337-340.

89. Piper, Henry Dan. "Social Criticism in the American Novel of the Nineteen Twenties." *The American Novel in the Nineteen Twenties*, eds. Malcolm Bradbury and David Palmer. Stratford-upon-Avon Studies # 13. London: Edward Arnold, New York: Crane, Russak, 1971, pp. 59-84. Piper notes with interest that Alfred Kazin in *On Native Grounds* fails to even mention West.

361. Popkin, Henry. "Nathanael West." *Times Literary Supplement*, 57 (11 April 1958), 195. In a letter commenting on the January 24th review of the *Complete Works*, Popkin claims that the West revival began much earlier than either the *TLS* reviewer or William White (see [405]) imply. Popkin states that West received attention in Europe as early as 1946 and "corrects" several mistakes allegedly made by White in dating the publications of West's novels. Too, he disagrees with the reviewer's and Alan Ross's view of West as a "footloose sophisticate."

190. Powell, Lawrence Clark. *"The Day of the Locust*: Nathanael West." *California Classics: The Creative Literature of The Golden State*. Los Angeles: The Ward Ritchie Press, 1971, pp. 344-56. Contains some information on the reception of West's novels, particularly *Miss Lonelyhearts*.

363. Quinton, Anthony. "The Complete Works of Nathanael West." *The London Magazine*, 5, no. 5 (May 1958), 72-75. Quinton claims that the two prevailing views of West--1) the American assumption that West is an astute political analyst and 2) the British belief that West is little more than an immature sensationalist--are both incomplete. He believes, rather, that the novels cannot be understood in political terms. *Miss Lonelyhearts*, for instance, is not an attack on media hypocrisy or even the times, nor even an attack on Shrike, who is likeable enough after all; but it is instead an attack on the entire universe which, for man, is constructed like "a highly ingenious torture chamber" (p. 73). Therefore, West's theme is metaphysical, not political: "an organized response to the condition of humanity" (p. 74). Quinton concludes that the British simply underrate West's achievement, although it is correct to say that West never completely "found himself"(p. 74).

66. Reid, Randall. *The Fiction of Nathanael West: No Redeemer, No Promised Land*. Chicago and London: The University of Chicago Press, 1967. Reid begins by commenting on the abundance (*over*abundance) of criticism on West as opposed to decades earlier.

381. Schwartz, Edward Greenfield. "The Novels of Nathanael West." *Accent*,
17 (Autumn 1957), 251-262. Schwartz opens with a discussion of West's
lack of popularity among proletarian writers and critics of the 1930's.
"Lacking dogma, hope, and idealism, West's novels seemed anachronistic
in a decade dominated by proletarian fiction" (p. 251).

382. Seymour-Smith, Martin. "Prophet of Black Humor." *Spectator*, 221
(19 July 1968), 94-95. Seymour-Smith claims that West was long ignored
because the modern American novel was and is self-consciously Jewish, and
West disavowed Judaism.

52. Smith, Marcus. "Religious Experience in *Miss Lonelyhearts*." *Nathanael
West: A Collection of Critical Essays*. Englewood Cliffs, New Jersey:
Prentice-Hall, Incorporated, 1971, pp. 74-90. Smith summarizes the two
prevailing views of Miss Lonelyhearts: either he is a tragic saint (James
Light's view) or he is a psychotic fool (Arthur Cohen)..Smith claims
that the two in modern society are really one and the same.

387. Solberg, S.E. "The Novels of Nathaniel [sic] West--A Sargasso of
the Imagination." *The English Language and Literature*, 14 (October 1963),
125-146. Solberg maintains that the primary reason for West's lack of
popularity in his own time was that his style was too European and surrealistic, which did not become popular until the fifties and sixties in the
works of Malamud, Burroughs, and Kerouac.

209. Swingewood, Alan. "Alienation, Reification, and the Novel: Satre,
Camus, and Nathanael West." *The Sociology of Literature*, by Diana T.
Laurenson and Alan Swingewood. New York: Schocken Books, 1972, pp.
207-248. Swingewood explains that West was neglected because he refused to
follow the two dominant literary modes of the thirties--exterior realism
or interior realism (Proust and Joyce).

210. Symons, Julian. *Critical Occasions*. London: Hamish Hamilton, 1966,
pp. 99-105. Symons begins by commenting on West's anonymity during his
life and then cites relevant exceptions (particularly Wilson). Symons
claims that West was neglected--not because he was out of the mainstream
(he was decidedly a part of it)--but because of his extreme pessimism.
"It is this nihilistic pessimism, this sense that all social institutions
are shams and that the act of love is merely 'the incandescence that
precedes being more lonely than ever', that plays a large part in earning
respect for West today" (p. 100).

220. White, William. "The Complete Works of Nathanael West." *Best
Masterplots, 1954-1964*, eds. Frank N. Magill and Dayton Kohler. New York:
Salem Press, Incorporated, 1964, pp. 103-106. Includes comments on West's
reputation and the acceptance of the novels during his life.

398. White, William. "Ernest Hemingway and Nathanael West: How Well-
Known Is Your Collector's Item?" *American Book Collector*, 14 (May 1964),
29. Here White writes under the theme that casual mention of an author is
a sign of increased renown, and he cites a case of casual mention of West
in a *Time* article.

399. White, William. "Fate and Nathanael West: A 1970 Note." *Literary*

Sketches, 10, no. 10 (October 1970), 6-7. A note on the irony of West's neglect during his own lifetime as contrasted to the present popularity. Also contains some side comments on the number of books sold by West, his earnings, etc.

400. White, William. "'Go West!' Notes From a Bibliographer." *American Book Collector*, 19, no. 5 (1969), 7-10. White cites the drastic change in West's popularity since the issue of White's first bibliography (1958).

401. White, William. "How Forgotten Was Nathanael West?" *American Book Collector*, 8 no. 4 (1958), 13-17. White begins with a *New York Times* clipping on West's death; he sees this error filled account as being emblematic of West's one-time obscurity.

404. White, William. "Nathanael West." *Times Literary Supplement*, 57 (21 February 1958), 101. After commenting on an earlier review of the *Complete Works* in *Times Literary Supplement* (January 24, 1958), White corrects some errors in the biographical information. He also claims that the West revival began in 1950 at the publication of *The Day of the Locust* and *Miss Lonelyhearts* by New Directions.

405. White, William. "Nathanael West." *Times Literary Supplement*, 57 (9 May 1958), 255. In a reply to Henry Popkin's letter (see [361]) White says that his facts (cited by Popkin as being in error) are correct.

413. White, William. "Notes on Hemingway, West, Tolkien and Wise." *American Book Collector*, 18, nos. 5&6 (1968), 30-31. White comments on the tremendous rise in interest in West. Four books, over 100 articles, and numerous reprints of the novels published since White's 1958 bibliography.

414. White, William. "A Novelist Ahead of His Time: Nathanael West." *Orient/West*, 6 (January 1961), 55-64. The first two pages of the essay comprise an attempt to explain West's obscurity during his life with White quoting from several scholars and West himself. White concludes simply that West was ahead of his time.

IV. Biographical Studies

The large number of scholars who have made biographical statements
in one form or another about Nathanael West attests to his being an interesting man as well as an interesting writer (the two often only coin-
cidentally join in one individual). So many scholars have contributed in
varying degrees to the portrait of West that I have found it necessary to
divide this chapter into four sections: A) reminiscences or anecdotes
by those who knew him personally; B) what I consider "substantive" additions
to our picture of West; C) works which summarize or interpret existing
information to some length (generally over two-three pages); and D) works
such as anthologies or references which may offer a brief biographical
sketch but do not offer new insight into the man, either by way of adding
information or interpreting existing data (as those in section C) might).

A) Reminiscences

97. Caldwell, Erskine. *Call It Experience: The Years of Learning How
to Write*. New York: Duell, Sloan, and Pearce, 1951, pp. 110-112.
Caldwell tells of staying at a New York hotel managed by West, with reminiscences of West's reaction to the poor reviews of *The Dream Life of Balso
Snell*--not embittered, but puzzled by the lack of understanding. Caldwell
also recalls something of West's frustrations while writing *Miss Lonelyhearts*.

136. Hellman, Lillian. *An Unfinished Woman--A Memoir*. Boston, Toronto:
Little, Brown and Company, 1969, pp. 63, 270. An interesting picture of
Dashiel Hammett staying in a New York hotel which West managed (and man-
aged to run down, according to Hellman). Hellman calls *The Day of the
Locust* "the only good book about Hollywood ever written" (p. 270).

311. Herbst, Josephine. "Nathanael West." *The Kenyon Review*, 23
(Autumn 1961), 611-630. An interesting, colorfully written reminiscence
of Herbst's first, and subsequent, meeting with West.

175. McKenny, Ruth. *Love Story*. New York: Harcourt, Brace and Company,
1950, pp. 175-176, 195-196. McKenny reprints part of a letter from her
sister announcing her engagement to West (pp. 175-176). She also recounts
the news of West's death and says of him, "He left three remarkable works
of fiction--and the memory of literary promise as true and as important
as any of his generation" (p. 195).

355. Perelman, S. J. "Good-bye, Broadway, Hello, Mr. Square." *The
Saturday Evening Post*, 237 (23 May 1964), 94-96. The only mention of
West was how he "would rangle us a couple of rooms at minimal rates"
(p. 96), while Perelman was low on funds in New York.

356. Perelman, S. J. "Nathanael West: A Portrait." *Contempo*, 3,
no. 11 (25 July 1933), 1, 4. A tongue-in-cheek portrait--"I love his
sudden impish smile, the twinkle of those alert green eyes, and the print
of his cloven hoof in the shrubbery" (p. 4).

366. Reynolds, Quentin. "When 'Pep' Was a Ghost." *Brown Alumni Monthly*, 58 (December 1957), pp. 8-9. A reminiscence by a friend at Brown who wishes to "contradict the growing legend" about the presumably tragic, cynical West. Reynolds offers a few anecdotes of West's days at Brown, mostly showing his wit and good humor. Most interesting is Reynolds' account of a speech he gave at Spring Day which West wrote for him. Included in the satirical speech were elements that later found their way into *The Dream Life of Balso Snell*--the wooden horse, Saint Puce, Maloney the Areopagite, etc.

374. Sanford, John. "Nathanael West." *The Screen Writer*, 2 (December 1946), 10-13. A poignant reminiscence of West, a close friend of Sanford's, who would "never have written a line if it hadn't been for him" (p. 10). The essay mostly concerns their boyhood days in New York City.

379. Schrank, Joseph. "Pep." *The New York Times Book Review* (9 June 1957), p. 30. In a letter to the editor, Schrank explains the source of West's nickname, "Pep". According to West, it was given to him because of his lazy, shuffling walk.

200. Schulberg, Budd. "Introduction." *The Day of the Locust*, by Nathanael West, Time Reading Program Special Edition. New York: Time Incorporated, 1965, pp. xiii-xxiii. Included is an anecdotal account of West's days in Hollywood with fellow screen writers who gathered around Stanley Rose's bookshop. Also included is an interesting discussion of West's involvement (or lack of) in the political ferment of the day.

201. Schulberg, Budd. "The Writer and Hollywood." *Writing in America*, eds. John Fisher and Robert B. Silvers. New Brunswick, New Jersey: Rutgers University Press, 1960, pp. 95-107. Schulberg includes West among those writers he "bumped into" in Hollywood and describes West as having had a "pictorial mind" (p. 97).

55. Soupalt, Phillipe. "Introduction to *Mademoiselle Coeur-Brise*." *Nathanael West: A Collection of Critical Essays*. Englewood Cliffs, New Jersey: Prentice-Hall, Incorporated, 1971, pp. 110-113. Describes West as Soupalt knew him in New York City. "Nathanael West was probably (a polite way of speaking) the one writer of his generation . . . who has most willingly accepted the knowledge that he is an American" (p. 112). West had "that deep laughter that rises from the entrails and transforms a smile into a grimace" (p. 112). An interesting feature of the essay (though admittedly irrelevant to this discussion) is Soupalt's diatribe against the American journalistic tradition of the advice column.

226. Williams, William Carlos. *The Autobiography of William Carlos Williams*. New York: A New Directions Book, pp. 301-302. Williams describes West visiting the Erwinna, Pennsylvania, area and admiring the countryside. He also gives a brief sketch of his acquaintance with West-- "a talent as fine as any of his day" (p. 302).

423. Williams, William Carlos. "The Contact Story." *Contact*, 1 (1958), 75-77. A brief account of the history of *Contact* and West's suggestion to reissue the magazine after it had lapsed.

227. Williams, William Carlos. *The Selected Letters of William Carlos Williams*, ed. John C. Thirwall. New York: McDowell, Obolensky, 1957, pp. 125, 126, 128. In a letter of 14 July 1932 to West, Williams asks West to back him in a proposed delay of a Communist number of *Contact*. In a letter of June 1932 to Ezra Pound, Williams mentions Pound's concern that *Contact* was to be merely a "mouthpiece" for West (p. 126). In a letter of 2 August 1932, Williams wishes to talk to West about the third issue of *Contact* and the need, above all, to make it interesting to the reader (p. 128).

B) Substantive Additions to the West Portrait

68. Aaron, Daniel. *Writers on the Left: Episodes in American Literary Communism*. New York: Harcourt, Brace and World, Incorporated, 1961, pp. 175, 307, 432. Aaron mentions West--"the most talented writer of them all" (p. 307)--speaking at a SanFrancisco writers' conference, 13 November 1936, on "Makers of Mass Neuroses."

122. Gehman, Richard. "Introduction." *The Day of the Locust*, by Nathanael West. New York: The New Classics, 1950, pp. ix-xxiii. Contains some anecdotes about West amidst a brief biographical description, probably the best such statement published up unto that time.

125. Goldhurst, William. *F. Scott Fitzgerald and His Contemporaries*. New York and Cleveland: The World Publishing Company, 1963, pp. 226, 236. Goldhurst mentions that Fitzgerald often gave help to younger writers, including West. He reprints a letter from West to Fitzgerald thanking him for a letter of recommendation to the Guggenheim committee (5 April 1939).

152. Knoll, Robert E., ed. *McAlmon and the Lost Generation: A Self-Portrait*. Lincoln: The University of Nebraska Press, 1962, pp. 305, 361n, 381-382. Reported is part of a personal conversation McAlmon had with Ezra Pound, where McAlmon states that he is relieved that he had nothing to do with the publication of *The Dream Life of Balso Snell*. However, McAlmon did call *Miss Lonelyhearts* "a brilliant production" (p. 305). The note on p. 361 discusses McAlmon's relationship to the *Contact* editions published by West and William Carlos Williams. A brief biographical sketch of West is furnished at the end (pp. 381-382).

153. Knoll, Robert E. *Robert McAlmon: Expatriate Publisher and Writer*. University of Nebraska Studies, New Series No. 18. Lincoln: The University of Nebraska Press, 1957, pp. 18, 84. Discussed is McAlmon's relationship to Contact Editions (however, he had no connection with the publication of *The Dream Life of Balso Snell*). Also includes some information on the number of copies of *The Dream Life of Balso Snell* to be printed (p. 84).

3. Light, James F. *Nathanael West: An Interpretative Study*. 2nd ed. Evanston: Northwestern University Press, 1971. Light's critical biography was the best biographical statement on West until the publication of Jay Martin's *Nathanael West: The Art of His Life* (see [64]) and is still well worth our while. Light's biographical material centers almost

entirely on West's college years and after. Discussed in detail are West's
main interests at college: athletics; "a life of the hard-drinking,
hard-petting, adolescent Bohemian in the Scott Fitzgerald tradition"
(p. 13); fraternity life and politics; and even the academic life, to a
slight degree. Light spices his work with many quotations from friends
and acquaintances of West. The reader might also find of particular interest Light's discussion of West's reading interests (pp. 24-31).

173. Martin, Jay. "Fitzgerald Recommends Nathanael West For a Guggenheim." *The Fitzgerald/Hemingway Annual 1971*, eds. Matthew J. Bruccoli and
C. E. Frazer Clark, Jr. Dayton: Microcard Editions, 1971, pp. 302-304.
Martin reproduces a letter (West to Fitzgerald) asking for a recommendation
to the Guggenheim committee, plus Fitzgerald's letter to the committee--
"In my opinion, Nathanael West is a potential leader in the field of prose
fiction" (p. 304). West's proposal was for a novel about the morality of
the college generation of 1924. According to Martin, West also solicited
(and received) letters from Malcolm Cowley, Edmund Wilson, and George S.
Kaufmann, all of whom responded favorably. West's request, however, was
denied.

64. Martin, Jay. *Nathanael West: The Art of His Life*. New York:
Farrar, Straus, and Giroux, 1970. Interest in West the man culminated
in this fine biography by Martin. The extensive list of acknowledgments
and multitude of concluding notes attest to the thoroughness of the
scholarship here. This scrupulously factual account traces West's
alienation back to family roots in Russia, West's tendency toward violence to his days in New York City as a youth, and his propensity to
satire to his school days at DeWitt Clinton High School. It would be
absurd to attempt to summarize the biography here, but it might be helpful to direct the reader to particularly useful sections, especially
accounts that might be difficult to find in other sources. Of interest
is Martin's description of West's complex nature: stemming as he believes
from "the contrast between intellectual and emotional life, between
his passive ability to understand experience and his lack of capacity
for deeply active involvement in it" (p. 94). Other discussions are
valuable for their focus on West's literary experiences most often
ignored in favor of focussing exclusively on the novels: for instance,
West's efforts on *Contact* magazine (pp. 143-150); West's working
with S. J. Perelman on the play *Even Stephen* (never produced); discussion of West's application for a Guggenheim for a proposed autobiographical novel (pp. 252-254); and several discussions of West as
a Hollywood script writer (see pp. 276-281, 281-289, 358-359, *etc.*).
Also valuable is an appendix which lists and gives plot summaries of
West's movie scripts (see pp. 401-406).

420. White, William. "Unpublished Faulkner: Reply to a Nathanael West
Questionnaire." *American Book Collector*, 17, no. 1 (September 1966), 27.
White reproduces a questionnaire a student writing a work on West sent to
Faulkner, plus Faulkner's answers. As White maintains, the answers tell
us more about Faulkner than about West.

C) Biographical Summaries or Reinterpretations
of West's Life

251. Balke, Betty Tevis. "Some Judeo-Christian Themes Seen Through the
Eyes of J. D. Salinger and Nathanael West." *Cresset*, 31, no. 7 (1968),
14-18. Balke compares West's and Salinger's lives to see how they "responded to their Jewishness" (p. 14).

109. Fiedler, Leslie A. "The Breakthrough: The American Jewish Novelist
and the Fictional Image of the Jew." *Recent American Fiction: Some
Critical Views*, ed. Joseph J. Waldmeir. Boston: Houghton Mifflin Company,
1963, pp. 84-109. Fiedler concludes his discussion of West by commenting
on the importance of his Jewishness.

294. Gehman, Richard B. "My Favorite Forgotten Book." *Tomorrow*, 8,
no. 7 (March 1949), 61-62. Contains a brief biographical sketch made
largely from personal interviews.

315. Hollis, C. Carroll. "Nathanael West: Diagnostician of the Lonely
Crowd." *Fresco*, 8, no. 1 (1957), 5-21. Hollis claims that West's death,
like his life, was symbolic--"It was part of society's gradual but compulsive suicide" (p. 19).

2. Hyman, Stanley Edgar. *Nathanael West*. Pamphlets on American Writers,
no. 21. Minneapolis: University of Minnesota Press, 1962. Hyman devotes
a six page summary to West's life.

5. Jackson, Thomas H. "Introduction." *Twentieth Century Interpretations
of* Miss Lonelyhearts, ed. Thomas H. Jackson. Englewood Cliffs, New Jersey:
Prentice-Hall, Incorporated, 1971, pp. 1-17. Jackson ends his introduction
with a four page summary of West's life.

19. Locklin, Gerald. "The Man Behind the Novels." *Nathanael West: The
Cheaters and the Cheated, A Collection of Critical Essays*, ed. David
Madden. Deland, Florida: Everett/Edwards, Incorporated, 1973, pp. 1-16.
Calling West "surely the most underrated and unjustly neglected American
writer since Herman Melville" (p. 1), Locklin begins his essay with a
sketch of West's activities, primarily from his college graduation on. Most
of the essay is an attempt--not merely to render facts about West--but
to establish the personality and character of the man. Locklin's chief
contribution, in my estimation, is to indicate that West himself was a
striking contrast--in his amiability, *etc.*--to the picture that the readers
may reconstruct from the novels. Locklin concludes, therefore, that
"West's criticism of life cannot be dismissed as the histrionics of a
cantankerous misanthrope" (p. 5). Locklin cautions that we should not
confuse amiability with happiness, however, and he traces the source of
West's inner conflict to his chronic lack of financial and artistic security, plus the problem with his Jewish heritage. Locklin mentions West's
reading habits and also reproduces his "Christmass Poem" from his early
days as a writer. Much of Locklin's information comes from Light's
study (see [3]).

65. Perry, Robert M. *Nathanael West's* Miss Lonelyhearts: *Introduction
and Commentary*. New York: Seabury Press, 1969. Perry begins with a

five page biographical sketch.

414. White, William. "A Novelist Ahead of His Time: Nathanael West." *Orient/West*, 6 (January 1961), 55-64. Most of the article is an account of West's life, primarily from college days on, with interpolated comments on the novels. White also reprints the *New York Times* obituary notice and cites the several errors as being emblematic of West's fate.

429. Zimmer, Dieter E. "Nathanael West, oder Warnungen vorm Tag der Heuschrechen." *Neue Rundschau* , 83 (1972), 287-302 [in German]. Included in the essay is a sketch of West's life and career, including some family history.

D) Briefer Sketches

231. Aaron, Daniel. "'The Truly Monstrous': A Note on Nathanael West." *Partisan Review*, 14, no. 1 (1947), 98-106. Aaron gives all the information he can find on West in two paragraphs.

242. Anon. "'My Sister Eileen' Killed in Accident." *The New York Times* (23 December 1940), p. 23. This obituary, typically, has more comment on West's wife that on him (Nathaniel [sic]). Cites West for writing a number of screen plays, three novels (no mention of *The Dream Life of Balso Snell*) and "several plays in collaboration with Joseph Schrank."

243. Anon. "Nathanael West." *The Publisher's Weekly*, 138 (December 28, 1940), 2326. Obituary notice, in one brief paragraph lists the novels and one screenplay--*Advice to the Lovelorn*.

244. Anon. "Nathanael West." *Times Literary Supplement*, 57 (24 January 1958), 44. A brief synopsis of West's life, containing some errors.

248. Anon. "Screen Writer and Wife Killed in Auto Collision." *The Los Angeles Times* (23 December 1940), Section C, p. 1. Obituary notice. Lists West as "Prominent scenario writer . . . .. Among his books were "Cool Million," "Miss Lonely Hearts," and "The Day of the Locust," said by critics to have been among the outstanding satirical books concerning Hollywood" (p. 1).

83. Block, Maxine, ed. "West, Nathanael." *Current Biography: Who's News and Why, 1941*. New York: H. W. Wilson Company, 1941, p. 912. A nine line obituary, four about West's wife. Lists the date of West's birth as 1906 and fails to list *The Dream Life of Balso Snell* among the novels.

86. Bracey, William. "West, Nathanael." *The Encyclopedia Americana*. International Ed. New York: American Corporation, 1964, pp. 633-634. In a brief sketch listing West's dates and works, the author concludes, "Nathanael West's originality, striking imagery, precision of language, and unique talent for poetic phrase and satire make him significant as an American novelist" (p. 634).

93. Bradbury, M.S. "West, Nathanael." *Webster's New World Companion to English and American Literature*, ed. Arthur Pollard. New York: World Publishing, 1973, pp. 714-715. In a two page summary of West's life and art, Bradbury calls West "undoubtedly a remarkable artist, though a most uneven one" (p. 714). He finds *The Day of the Locust* West's finest novel.

107. [The Editors of *Time*]. "Editors' Preface." *The Day of the Locust*, by Nathanael West. Time Reading Program Special Edition. New York: Time Incorporated, 1965, pp. vii-xii. The last two pages comprise a brief biographical sketch.

295. Gehman, Richard B. "Nathanael West: A Novelist Apart." *The Atlantic Monthly*, 186, no. 3 (September 1950), 69-72. Comprises a brief biographical sketch.

313. Hollis, C. Carroll. "Nathanael West and Surrealist Violence." *Fresco*, 7, no. 5 (1957), pp. 5-13. Contains some biographical information, particularly concerning West's years in Paris.

156. Kronenberger, Louis, ed. "West, Nathanael." *Atlantic Brief Lives: A Biographical Companion to the Arts*. Boston, Toronto: Little, Brown, and Company, 1971, p. 862. A brief biographical sketch containing some errors.

157. Kunitz, Stanley and Howard Haycraft. "West, Nathanael." *Twentieth Century Authors*. New York: The H.W. Wilson Company, 1942, p. 1500. A short biographical sketch complete with the usual errors. The First Supplement in 1955 (p. 1069) adds references to Edmund Wilson's articles and reviews on West.

338. Lund, Mary Graham. "Backwards-Forwards in Forbidden Lands." *Western World Review*, 3, no. 1 (Spring 1968), pp. 21-27. Lund inaccurately reports that West completed *The Dream Life of Balso Snell* in Paris.

40. Martin, Jay, ed. "Introduction." *Nathanael West: A Collection of Critical Essays*. Englewood Cliffs, New Jersey: Prentice-Hall, Incorporated, 1971, pp. 1-10. Martin begins his introduction with a brief overview of West's life and personality. The book ends with a chronology of the important dates in West's life.

344. McLaughlin, Richard. "West of Hollywood." *Theatre Arts*, 35 (August 1951), pp. 46-47, 93. Provides some scant information on West's life, much incorrect.

177. Mondadori, Arnoldo, ed. "West, Nathanael." *Dizionario Universale della Letteratura contemporanea*. 1 Edizione: Marzo 1962, 1148-1149 [in Italian]. A half-page summary of West's life and works, also lists a half-dozen studies of West.

180. Murray, Edward. "Nathanael West--The Pictorial Eye in Locust Land." *The Cinematic Imagination: Writers and the Motion Pictures*. New York: Frederick Ungar Publishing Company, 1972, pp. 206-216. Includes a discussion of West's career in Hollywood between the publishing of *Miss*

Lonelyhearts and *The Day of the Locust* (pp. 211-213).

186. Olsen, Bruce. "Nathanael West: The Use of Cynicism." *Minor American Novelists*, ed. Charles Alva Hoyt. Carbondale and Edwardsville: Southern Illinois University Press; London and Amsterdam: Feffer and Simons, Incorporated, 1970, pp. 81-94. In brief commentary on West the man, Olsen remarks, "Everything about West suggested the role-player, the wearer of masks, though none of them definitively" (p. 82).

381. Schwartz, Edward Greenfield. "The Novels of Nathanael West." *Accent*, 17 (Autumn 1957), 251-262. Includes a brief sketch of West's life.

382. Seymour-Smith, Martin. "Prophet of Black Humor." *Spectator*, 221 (19 July 1968), 94-95. Contains some biographical information.

213. Ward, A. C. "West, Nathanael." *Longman Companion to Twentieth Century Literature*. London: Longman Group, Limited, 1970, p. 565. In a brief biographical sketch, Ward gives West's dates and lists three novels (not *A Cool Million*).

401. White, William. "How Forgotten Was Nathanael West?" *The American Book Collector*, 8, no. 4 (1958), 13-17. Contains a brief biographical sketch, including some errors.

418. White, William. "Some Uncollected Authors XXXII: Nathanael West, 1903?-1940." *Book Collector*, 11 (1962), 206-210. Contains a three page summary of West's life.

V. Biographical Criticism

Where one might have been taken aback by the large amount of bibliographical information dealing with West, one is equally surprised at the
meager output of biographical criticism--especially considering that West
worked for several years as a rather obscure artist in Hollywood, as did
Tod Hackett, hero of *The Day of the Locust*. Very likely, part of the
reason is the disfavor biographical criticism often suffers as a residue
from the New Critical influence. At any rate, a few critics have incorporated facts or surmises about West's life as support for their
interpretations of the works.

22. Brand, John M. "A Word Is a Word Is a Word." *Nathanael West: The
Cheaters and the Cheated, A Collection of Critical Essays*, ed. David
Madden. Deland, Florida: Everett/Edwards, Incorporated, 1973, pp. 57-76.
Brand's essay is an exploration of West's "essential Jewishness" (p. 58),
which Brand finds relevant despite frequent ridicule of the Jew in West's
writings. Brand finds West's themes reflecting several major Jewish
concerns: "the word as liberàting act (*The Dream Life of Balso Snell*),
the New Covenant and the heart's renewal (*Miss Lonelyhearts*), the mission
of the Suffering Servant (*A Cool Million*), and the Day of the Lord and
the reconstitution of creation (*The Day of the Locust*)" (p. 58). The
major portion of the work deals with an examination of the Jewish elements
in *The Dream Life of Balso Snell*: particularly important is the signi-
ficance of the spoken word as an act partaking of connection with the
divine world, an act potentially prophetic and liberating. Brand concludes
that West's vision is reductive. I find this one of the finer essays
dealing with West's Jewish influence.

99. Coates, Robert M. "Introduction." *Miss Lonelyhearts*, by Nathanael
West. New York: The New Classics, 1950, pp. ix-xiv. Coates surmises
that the pervasive pessimism in West's works has its roots in West's
having reached manhood between the wars.

1. Comerchero, Victor. *Nathanael West: The Ironic Prophet*. Syracuse:
Syracuse University Press, 1964. Chapter 2 of Comerchero's study--
"The Author Reveals Himself"-- explores self-revelation in West's works.
Comments Comerchero, "Individually, each of West's characters remains a
caricature; cumulatively, they create an engrossing picture of a 'type',
of a collective man who has been created in West's own image" (p. 8).
This type Comerchero dubs the 'Westian man'. However, this self-revelation
is rarely merely autobiographical. Rather, the characters reveal West's
intensity and obsessions. Comerchero divides the characters in West's
novels into those who are aware of life (the Westian man: Snell, Miss
Lonelyhearts, Tod, Shrike, *etc.*) and those who are not (Betty, Faye,
Lemuel Pitkin). Most of the major characters, like West himself, were
tortured by introspection. Comerchero concludes that the fate of West's
characters fails to engage one, "and sometimes it strikes one as comic"
(p. 12).

290. Galloway, David D. "Nathanael West's Dream Dump." *Critique: Studies in Modern Fiction*, 6, no. 3 (Winter 1963-64), 46-64. Galloway claims that West's observations as a hotel manager had a profound influence on his vision as seen in the first three novels. All culminates in West's vision of Hollywood as found in *The Day of the Locust*. States Galloway, "In the prolapsed world which West chronicled the dream inevitably metamorphozed into nightmare, and it was logical that the white heat of his creative energies should at last be turned on the dream capital of Hollywood, where dreams were sealed in cans and marketed to the world" (p. 46). Galloway concludes, "He found in Hollywood both an instant symbolism and a microcosm of his favorite subjects: the ignoble lie, the world of illusion, the surrealistic incongruities of the American experience" (p. 47).

297. Graham, John. "Struggling Upward: *The Minister's Charge* and *A Cool Million*." *Canadian Review of American Studies*, 4 (1974), 184-196. Graham reads West's interest in the American success ethic as being partly a result of his upbringing (parents trying to mold him around the work ethic) and partly a result of his reaction to the success ethic encouraged at Brown.

315. Hollis, C. Carroll. "Nathanael West: Diagnostician of the Lonely Crowd." *Fresco*, 8, no. 1 (1957), 5-21. Hollis claims that Tod Hackett in *The Day of the Locust* "is clearly West's alter ego" (p. 13). Hackett, like West, "is more tolerantly amused than spiritually distressed at his forced encounters with its [Hollywood's] habituées" (p. 13), except for the throngs that have come there to die. Hollis concludes, in *The Day of the Locust*, "West is presenting symbolically his terrifying vision of a world without faith" (p. 19).

3. Light, James F. *Nathanael West: An Interpretative Study*. 2nd ed. Evanston: Northwestern University Press, 1971. Included is a fine discussion of West and Judaism, particularly as a background for writing *The Day of the Locust*. Concludes Light, "The reason West's novels are involved in the Quest is a rejection of a heritage, both familial and racial, that burdened West just as Joyce's heritage weighed on that great nay sayer" (p. 148). Light also claims that West's final novel is indebted to his days as a screenwriter more than any of the rest of his writing, particularly in the use of pictorially dramatized short scenes (see especially 144-148, 190).

19. Locklin, Gerald. "The Journey Into the Microcosm." *Nathanael West: The Cheaters and the Cheated, A Collection of Critical Essays*, ed. David Madden. Deland, Florida: Everett/Edwards, Incorporated, 1973, pp. 1-16. Locklin traces psychological stress evident in West's works to a chronic lack of financial and artistic security.

64. Martin, Jay. *Nathanael West: The Art of His Life*. Farrar, Straus and Giroux, 1970. Many discussions apply here, but of particular importance are discussions of the biographical backgrounds to *The Dream Life of Balso Snell* and *Miss Lonelyhearts* (see Chapter Six) and *The Day of the Locust* (see pp. 265 *et passim* and 303 *et passim*).

180. Murray, Edward. "Nathanael West--the Pictorial Eye in Locust-Land." *The Cinematic Imagination: Writers and the Motion Pictures*. New York: Frederick Ungar Publishing Company, 1972, pp. 206-216. Murray opens with a summary of West's life in Hollywood and comments on his attitude toward working there. He finds the chief feature of West's style--partly due to the Hollywood influence--to be its pictorial quality.

65. Perry, Robert M. *Nathanael West's* Miss Lonelyhearts: *Introduction and Commentary*. New York: Seabury Press, 1969. Perry describes *Miss Lonelyhearts* as having its source in a social evening with S. J. Perelman where West read clippings from an advice column (p. 11).

360. Pisk, George M. "The Graveyard of Dreams: A Study of Nathanael West's Last Novel, *The Day of the Locust*." *The South Central Bulletin*, 27, no. 4 (Winter 1967), 64-72. Pisk briefly traces the resemblance between Tod Hackett and West.

190. Powell, Lawrence Clark. "*The Day of the Locust*: Nathanael West." *California Classics: The Creative Literature of the Golden State*. Los Angeles: The Ward Ritchie Press, 1971, pp. 344-356, 359. Powell tries to show how West developed as a writer by tracing him through various stages in his life.

376. Schneider, Cyril M. "The Individuality of Nathanael West." *The Western Review*, 20, no. 1 (Autumn 1955), 7-28. Schneider traces the fear of the mob in *The Day of the Locust* to an earlier story, "Western Union Boy," and eventually to an incident in West's life.

203. Schulz, Max F. *Radical Sophistication: Studies in Contemporary Jewish-American Novelists*. Athens, Ohio: Ohio University Press, 1969, pp. 36-55, 179, 185. Schulz claims that West, more than other Jewish-American writers, could not remain content in "suspension between heavenly aspirations and earthly limitations" (p. 36), and his work, therefore, represents a search for absolutes.

210. Symons, Julian. *Critical Occasions*. London: Hamish Hamilton, 1966, pp. 99-105. Symons claims that the main problem with West is his insisting on turning all subjects which would cause him pain to confront into a joke.

VI. Source Studies

Anyone who has read Richard Altick's *The Art of Literary Research* is familiar with the pitfalls of source studies. Merely finding a common theme or philosophy is almost never adequate grounds for arguing that one author's work is the source of another's. Nor can even similar plots, scenes or characters be considered more than "circumstantial" evidence of the source of a particular work or idea. Yet source studies are a fascinating and--even when largely without adequate support--a useful exercise; and a good many scholars have attempted to trace the sources of West's ideas. However, a problem arises in the very act of classification, for many of the works included here could as well fall under "Comparative Criticism" or even "Studies in the History of Ideas." Part of the problem is that not all scholars make as distinct as one would wish the difference between citing the source of a technique, motif, or idea of West's and merely observing a parallel. Granted that the classification itself is rather ambiguous then, I believe that the works listed here are best described as "possible" source studies.

For ease of use, I have further broken down these studies into five sub-groups: A) those dealing with the West canon in general, those dealing with B) *The Dream Life of Balso Snell*, C) *Miss Lonelyhearts*, D) *A Cool Million*, and E) *The Day of the Locust*.

A) General Source Studies

1. Comerchero, Victor. *Nathanael West: The Ironic Prophet*. Syracuse: Syracuse University Press, 1964. Comerchero discusses two major influences on West--Baudelaire and Freud (pp. 167-168).

278. Donovan, Alan. "Nathanael West and the Surrealistic Muse." *Kentucky Review*, 2, no. 1 (1968), 82-95. Donovan examines West's use of surrealistic (dream-like) images and techniques. He concludes that West's use is emblematic of contemporary literature in general. After defining surrealism, Donovan shows how West was indebted to this movement and calls *The Dream Life of Balso Snell* "one of the few purely surrealistic American novels" (p. 84). However, all of West's novels make use of "surreal imagery to illumine the real" (p. 84). Also examined here is how the surreal imagery arises out of West's major theme of "blasted dreams." After examining the image patterns in the four novels, Donovan concludes that the greatest problem is the distance this creates between the reader and the characters (i.e. the images may be unintelligible to the "uninitiated" reader). Too, "The surreal tone of the novel . . . renders unlikely any feeling for its characters as people" (p. 93).

279. Edenbaum, Robert I. "Dada and Surrealism in the United States: A Literary Instance." *Arts in Society*, 5, no. 1 (1968), 114-125. States Edenbaum, "West was probably more influenced by dada and surrealism than any other writer [American] in the twenties and thirties" (p. 114). Edenbaum explains that, while Americans took off for war during World War I, their European counterparts among the intellectuals were revolting against the older generation. West, he concludes, was a product of the

European attitude. Edenbaum offers an in-depth explanation of the roots of dadaism and surrealism in what is one of the finest essays on the subject to be found.

290. Galloway, David D. "Nathanael West's Dream Dump." *Critique: Studies in Modern Fiction*, 6, no. 3 (Winter 1963-64), 46-64. Galloway traces West's comic techniques to the French symbolists and dadaists.

138. Hodgart, Matthew. *Satire*. London: World University Library, 1969, pp. 226-227. Hodgart sees West as a direct descendant from Voltaire (particularly *Candide*). "West writes in an extremely economical and lucid style; his blend of irony and compassion, his outraged moral sense and fascination with absurd details, places him in line of the great satirists")p. 227).

158. Levine, Paul. "Flannery O'Connor: The Soul of the Grotesque." *Minor American Novelists*, ed. Charles Alva Hoyt. Carbondale and Edwardsville: Southern Illinois University Press; London and Amsterdam: Feffer and Simons, Incorporated, 1970, pp. 95-117. Levine maintains that Hollywood and S. J. Perelman "seemed to have influenced West's weakness for slapstick black humor and his fascination with the mythology of popular culture" (p. 97).

64. Martin, Jay. *Nathanael West: The Art of His Life*. New York: Farrar, Straus and Giroux, 1970. See Chapter Four for a discussion of West's literary influences while at Brown. Martin maintains that the German expressionists were as great an influence on West as the French surrealists. Particularly influential was Kafka (see pp. 82-83). Martin also maintains that West was not necessarily a dadaist, though he shared some of their views (pp. 46-47). West shared in the tradition of Mencken, Ring Lardner, Sherwood Anderson, and Theodore Drieser, admiring all but the latter. Also examined is the influence of Dostoevsky (despite West's claim that the tighter French novels were the ideal in literature) (see p. 115).

90. Way, Brian. "Sherwood Anderson." *The American Novel in the Nineteen Twenties*. Stratford-upon-Avon Studies # 13. London: Edward Arnold; New York: Crane, Russak, 1971, pp. 107-128. Way calls Anderson a "vital influence" on West, among others.

215. Weber, Brom. "The Mode of 'Black Humor'." *The Comic Imagination in American Literature*, ed. Louis Rubin. New Brunswick, New Jersey: Rutgers University Press, 1973, pp. 361-371. Weber says that West was the only writer to come out of the dada-surrealist school of the twenties to write a sustained piece of black humor (*The Dream Life of Balso Snell*, which he calls an "extraordinarily good first novel" (p. 367). Weber concludes that West took his intellectual stimulus from Europe rather than America, although he does cite a number of American authors from the late nineteenth and early twentieth centuries who preceded West as "deliberate practitioners of black humor" (p. 370).

216. Weber, Brom "Sherwood Anderson." *American Writers: A Collection of Literary Biographies*, ed. Leonard Unger. New York: Charles Scribner's

Sons, 1974. I, pp. 97, 107. Lists West among those many writers influenced by Anderson. More specifically, Weber sees West writing in the wasteland theme first employed by Anderson in *Winesburg, Ohio*.

45. Williams, William Carlos. "A New American Writer." *Nathanael West: A Collections of Critical Essays*, ed. Jay Martin. Englewood Cliffs, New Jersey: Prentice-Hall, Incorporated, 1971, pp. 48-49. Here Williams claims that West takes his idiom from newspapers reporters.

228. Wilson, Edmund. "The Boys in the Back Room." *A Literary Chronicle: 1920-1950*. New York: Doubleday and Company, Incorporated, 1956, pp. 241, 242n, 245-248, 249, 358. Wilson cites the influence of "post-war Frenchmen who had specialized, with a certain procosity, in the delirious and diabolic fantasy that descended from Rimbaud and Lautreamont" (p. 245).

B) *The Dream Life of Balso Snell*

279. Edenbaum, Robert I. "Dada and Surrealism in the United States: A Literary Instance." *Arts in Society*, 5, no. 1 (1968), 114-125. Edenbaum examines *The Dream Life of Balso Snell* as a dada protest against writing books. Says Edenbaum, "The book is little more than a series of parodies and literary clichés, more often than not merely facetious, but at its heart is the dada aim of trying to rouse the beligerence of the audience, to engage its passions through enraging it" (p. 120).

3. Light, James F. *Nathanael West: An Interpretative Study*. 2nd ed. Evanston: Northwestern University Press, 1971. Among the influences on West, Light lists Joyce, Freud, dada and surrealism. Of particular importance for *The Dream Life of Balso Snell* is Cabell's *Jurgen* and Huysman's *La Bas* and *En Route*. From the former West takes "aspects of his mannered tone and his questing plot" (p. 59), and from the latter he gained a familiarity with mystics. All those sources discussed influenced West, but all were also targets of satire. (See pp. 40-65 in particular).

21. Locklin, Gerald. "The Man Behind the Novels." *Nathanael West: The Cheaters and the Cheated, A Collection of Critical Essays*, ed. David Madden. Deland, Florida: Everett/Edwards, Incorporated, 1973, pp. 23-56. A good analysis of West's indebtedness to, yet difference from, Dostoevsky. Chief differences are in West's philosophical cynicism and imagistic style. Locklin claims that *The Dream Life of Balso Snell* is ultimately a rejection, not merely of art, but of life itself. This spirit of rejection stems in part from the dada influence. (See pp. 53 *et passim*).

64. Martin, Jay. *Nathanael West: The Art of His Life*. New York: Farrar, Straus, and Giroux, 1970. Martin tells us, among other things, that the source of Balso Snell's name is a basketball coach at Brown during West's college days there.

66. Reid, Randall. *The Fiction of Nathanael West: No Redeemer, No Promised Land*. Chicago and London: University of Chicago Press, 1967. Reid discusses Huysman's *La Bas* and *En Route* as sources for West's

knowledge of mysticism as displayed in *The Dream Life of Balso Snell*.
He also sees Aldous Huxley's *Antic Hay* as the source for part of Beagle
Darwin's playlet.

C) *Miss Lonelyhearts*

230. Aaron, Daniel. "Late Thoughts on Nathanael West." *The Massachusetts Review*, 6, no. 2 (Winter-Spring 1965), 307-317. Aaron describes
in detail West's reliance on William James' *The Varieties of Religious
Experience*. He claims that the theme of the novel is one of spiritual,
not economic, deprivation. Thus, *Miss Lonelyhearts* "enforces rather
the conclusion of William James than that of Karl Marx" (p. 312).

69. Abrahams, Roger D. "Androgynes Bound: Nathanael West's *Miss
Lonelyhearts*." *Seven Contemporary American Authors: Essays on Cozzens,
Miller, West, Golding, Heller, Albee, and Powers*, ed. Thomas B. Whitbread.
Austin and London: University of Texas Press, 1966, pp. 49-72. Abrahams
sees the novel developing from three basic sources (under the influence
of the surrealists and symbolists): allegory, satire and the psychological novel (pp. 53-54).

273. Cohen, Arthur. "Nathanael West's Holy Fool." *The Commonweal*,
64, no. 10 (8 June 1956), 276-78. Cohen compares West to Dostoevsky,
particularly in the importance of tone over style in each author's canon.
Like Dostoevsky's characters, West's force a close scrutiny of most
sacred beliefs, test them by life's standards, and often fall victim to
their very insistence on testing those beliefs. Like Dostoevsky, West was
concerned with creating the "Holy Fool"--the perfect sinner and perfect
saint. Dostoevsky was prophetic--describing the coming destruction of
man's spirit; West described what had already happened. Cohen concludes
that *Miss Lonelyhearts* was the most optimistic of the novels, because
there the anguish was the most intolerable. He says that, in the end,
West could not accept Dostoevsky's universal solution: "the fidelity
of inwardness and attentiveness of love" (p. 278).

1. Comerchero, Victor. *Nathanael West: The Ironic Prophet*. Syracuse:
Syracuse University Press, 1964. Comerchero traces the influence of
Jessie Weston on *Miss Lonelyhearts*, particularly the search for the
holy grail (pp. 86-92).

286. Flores, Angel. "Miss Lonelyhearts in the Haunted Castle." *Contempo*,
3, no. 11 (25 July 1933), 1. Flores cites West's indebtedness to Dos-
toevsky--"In *Miss Lonelyhearts* do appear the hairshirts worn by Fyodor's
heroes, and the air rings with anti-Christian catapults, bloody guffaws
and mystical quavers" (p. 1). Flores also traces to Cocteau (and more
importantly to Dali, Chirico and surrealism) the "peculiar nightmare
quality, that pervasive uncanniness" in West. The essay ends with a comparison to West's comtemporaries who dullily follow realism.

300. Hand, Nancy Walker. "A Novel in the Form of a Comic Strip:
Nathanael West's *Miss Lonelyhearts*." *The Serif*, 5, no. 2 (June 1968),
14-21. Hand deals in most thorough fashion with the novel's indebtedness

to the comic strip form. The most obvious similarity is in the episodic structure which creates "an impression of disorder, of chaos and un-predictability, which reflects West's view of man's life" (p. 14). Other parallels are the use of violence, the tendency to escape into dreams, and the condensation of form. Miss Lonelyhearts is the unsuc-cessful hero in the comic strip sense, but the ending of the novel under-cuts this by having him ultimately fail, unlike the comic strip hero, who manages to succeed despite his bungling. Finally, like the comic strip, the novel is unified by a "simple idea"--in this case, the Christ dream.

336. Lorch, Thomas M. "Religion and Art in *Miss Lonelyhearts*." Renascence, 20, no. 1 (Autumn 1967), 11-17. Lorch claims that West relies on the philosophy of Dostoevsky, particularly the Father Zossima section of *The Brothers Karamazov*, to support the importance of the Christian philos-opher. Miss Lonelyhearts "Goes to his death in the fullness of Christian faith, charity, and hope" (p. 13).

337. Lorch, Thomas M. "West's *Miss Lonelyhearts*: Skepticism Mitigated?" *Renascence*, 18, no. 2 (Winter 1966), 99-109. Lorch traces the patterns of religious development as found in James' *The Varieties of Religious Experience* and Starbuck's *Psychology of Religion* and parallels that to *Miss Lonelyhearts*. Most of the discussion centers on West's indebtedness to James. Like James, West denies the existence of a supernatural being but acknowledges the power of religion in the lives of men. Too, Lorch describes the similarity of Miss Lonelyhearts' experience to the route to mystical awareness as described by St. John of the Cross--in *Dark Night of the Soul* and *Ascent of Mount Carmel*--and Jacques Maritain in *The Degrees of Knowledge* (see 106 *et passim*). Demanded here is freedom from physical desires and withdrawal from the world--a process Miss Lonelyhearts experiences. Withdrawal always involves suffering, and, therefore, Lorch believes that the skepticism of James is undercut by the positive force of mystical belief.

64. Martin, Jay. *Nathanael West: The Art of His Life*. New York: Farrar, Straus and Giroux, 1970. In commenting on West's short story "The Imposter" Martin comments, "West would later base the character of Miss Lonelyhearts on psychoanalytical case studies, and Beano's case also has classic psychotic outlines, which fitted in with the Paris scene, the surrealist interest in the insane, the modern interest in the artist-figure, and West's personal scorn for the phony artist" (p. 90). Other sources for *Miss Lonelyhearts* discussed by Martin are actual letters sent to newspapers, James' *The Varieties of Religious Experience*, and the first chapter of Freud's *Civilization and Its Discontents* (1930). Martin concludes from Freud that Miss Lonelyhearts is "fixated at the oral level of development, unable fully to distinguish between flesh and spirit" (p. 190). See also pp. 186-187.

351. Orvell, Miles D. "The Messianic Sexuality of 'Miss Lonelyhearts'." *Studies in Short Fiction*, 10, no. 2 (Spring 1973), 159-167. In a close examination of "Miss Lonelyhearts on a Field Trip" Orvell concludes that West may have been inspired by the view of Christ found in Eliot and Weston, and he also traces the theme, in part, to *The Dream Life of*

Balso Snell. Too, Orvell sees West as sharing Whitman's view of America heading toward an "impoverishing materialism" (p. 167); but for West, no optimism, no hope of regeneration is possible.

66. Reid, Randall. *The Fiction of Nathanael West: No Redeemer, No Promised Land.* Chicago and London: The University of Chicago Press, 1967. Reid examines in great detail West's indebtedness to James' *The Varieties of Religious Experience* (pp. 44-50). Also examined is Dostoevsky as a source for *Miss Lonelyhearts.* "Both Raskolnikov and Miss Lonelyhearts respond to external reality as though it were an apparition or a revelation" (p. 55). Huxley's *Antic Hay* is another possible source. Reid sees Huxley's Coleman as a predecessor of Shrike. Another source examined by Reid is Baudelaire--"Both Baudelaire and Dostoevsky repeatedly analyse the evils of egoism, the voluptuous pleasure of remorse, the stupidity of liberal utopianism, and the sin of ennui" (p. 64). Also cited are Rimbaud (kaleidescopic technique) and Huysmans (from whom West borrowed his form, but also parodied). A final discussion concerns West's use of Freud. Reid claims that West used Freud as an artistic matrix for myth, not as a believer. He concludes, "The world of *Miss Lonelyhearts* is a waste land. Its psychology owes far more to regenerative myths than to Freud and far more to ascetic and apocalyptic Christianity than to Jessie L. Weston. The world confirms the saint's anguished vision of this life. It reaches but to dust" (p. 84).

376. Schneider, Cyril M. "The Individuality of Nathanael West." *The Western Review*, 20, no. 1 (Autumn 1955), 7-28. Schneider examines West's reliance on Starbuck's *Psychology of Religion* and Eliot's *The Waste Land.* He also finds John Bunyan a major influence; however, in Bunyan, Christian awakes, but the relevance of the dream is not impaired, while for West the Christ dream is a monstrous irony.

52. Smith, Marcus. "Religious Experience in *Miss Lonelyhearts.*" *Nathanael West: A Collection of Critical Essays*, ed. Jay Martin. Englewood Cliffs, New Jersey: Prentice-Hall, Incorporated, 1971, pp. 74-90. Smith bases his discussion on West's cited sources: James' *The Varieties of Religious Experience* and Starbuck's *The Psychology of Religion.* James is the more important source, finds Smith. He explicates the novel following West's suggestions in "Some Notes on *Miss Lonelyhearts.*" He concludes that James would say that whatever experience produces an effect on us is real, so to with religious experience; applying a simple pragmatic evaluation to experience, religious experience for Miss Lonelyhearts is a failure. "Miss Lonelyhearts' religious experience does not help him to cope with reality" (p. 90).

214. Weaver, Mike. *William Carlos Williams: The American Background.* Cambridge: At the University Press, 1971, pp. 134-136, 145, 216. Weaver discusses *Miss Lonelyhearts* in a context of Williams' fondness for newspapers as a source for literary inspiration, particularly in their use of language. Also discussed is West's desire to make the novel in the form of a comic strip--"In this way West combined the radical techniques of the popular arts with the naturalistic tradition of John Dos Passos, James T. Farrell, and the early Edward Dahlberg" (p. 135). Weaver claims that West used case histories in the novel for their literal, not symbolic,

content.

430. Zoltnick, Joan. "The Medium Is the Message, Or Is It? A Study of Nathanael West's Comic Strip Novel." *Journal of Popular Culture*, 5, no. 1 (Summer 1971), 236-240. Zoltnick claims that West's idea for a comic strip novel (*Miss Lonelyhearts*) may have come from the collage novels of Max Ernst and Hogarth's satires. Besides the residual effects remaining in the novel that West himself cited, Zoltnick observes that "communication is largely through action and gesture; which not infrequently creates the effect of pictorial pantomime" (p. 237). She notes also West's use of compressed dialogue, a comic strip feature. She claims that West's use of the comic strip is ironic because a major theme of the novel is the breakdown in communication, particularly of the mass media. After examining some prominent themes in history of comic strips, Zoltnick concludes, "If Miss Lonelyhearts' spiritual and sexual failure is an emblem of the inability of the American male to assert himself in our culture and if West diagnoses this failure as emblematic of a sick society, it is ironic that he should make this diagnosis in the style of a comic strip which reflects and reinforces this sickness it calls normality" (p. 239).

D) *A Cool Million*

313. Hollis, C. Carroll. "Nathanael West and Surrealist Violence." *Fresco*, 7, no. 5 (1957), 5-13. Hollis claims that S.J. Perelman "must be assumed responsible for the initial form, style, and tone of this new departure [*A Cool Million*] for West" (p. 12).

314. Hollis, C. Carroll. "Nathanael West and the 'Lonely Crowd'." *Thought*, 33, (Autumn 1958), 398-416. See [313] for same discussion on S. J. Perelman as a source for *A Cool Million*. Here see p. 404 in particular.

64. Martin, Jay. *Nathanael West: The Art of His Life*. New York: Farrar, Straus, and Giroux, 1970. For a discussion of Horatio Alger, Hitler's *Mein Kampf*, and West's days at Brown as background material for *A Cool Million*, see pp. 236 *et passim*.

383. Shepard, Douglas. "Nathanael West Rewrites Horatio Alger." *Satire Newsletter*, 3, no. 1 (Fall 1965), 13-28. An in-depth examination of West's use of Alger as a source for *A Cool Million*. Says Shepard, "Clearly the satirical thrust of the plot line depends on its inverting the usual Alger rags-to-riches-through-honest-effort-pattern" (p. 13). Also parodied is Alger's style. Most of the essay is taken up with a two column juxtaposition of passages from Alger and West.

E) *The Day of the Locust*

1. Comerchero, Victor. *Nathanael West: The Ironic Prophet*. Syracuse: Syracuse University Press, 1964. Comerchero finds the influence of Eliot, particularly *The Waste Land*, heavy on *The Day of the Locust*.

161. Lewis, R.W.B. "Melville After *Moby Dick*." *Trials of the Word: Essays in American Literature and the Humanistic Tradition*. New Haven and London: Yale University Press, 1965, pp. 184-236. Lewis sees the type of satire as found in Melville's *The Confidence Man* (rather than that of Voltaire's *Candide*) as the predecessor of *The Day of the Locust* because the protagonist is the creator, not merely the victim, of satire. However, he does not go into much detail to support his claim. See p. 63.

381. Schwartz, Edward Greenfield. "The Novels of Nathanael West." *Accent*, 17 (Autumn 1957), 251-262. Schwartz discounts one possible source for *The Day of the Locust* and offers another in its place. Of the charge that West was a surrealist, Schwartz comments, "Unlike the surrealists (and the dadaists), West had no program. His pessimism didn't lead to nihilism or to an intense hatred of the rational world. On the contrary, his pose is that of the objective observer who merely records the horror" (p. 258). Schwartz also finds that, although West spoke of a dislike for the naturalists--in *The Day of the Locust*, "He shares some of the attitudes of the naturalists, particularly Stephen Crane's horror and sadness at the sight of 'the truly monstrous'" (p. 259). Schwartz concludes that West's true inspiration in the novel was the paintings of Magnasco, not surrealism.

35. Torchianna, Donald T. "The Painter's Eye." *Nathanael West: The Cheaters and the Cheated, A Collection of Critical Essays*, ed. David Madden. Deland, Florida: Everett/Edwards, Incorporated, 1973, pp. 249-282. Torchianna examines the influence of a variety of painters on West's handling of materials in *The Day of the Locust*. The hard, objective perspective of the novel comes from Tod Hackett's having the central role. Examined in the essay is "Tod's own persistent reference to his acknowledged masters, painters preoccupied, indeed obsessed, with the fantastic and the bizarre as they mysteriously define human life during its seemingly recurrent frenzies of the spirit" (p. 251). Important to Tod's vision is the influence of several painters' ways of viewing life, among them Goya (sex and violence), Daumier (performer/audience relationship), and Magnasco (the fanatics). Also explored is the possible influence of Rosa, Guardi, and Desiderio in their imaginary landscapes. From Guardi comes "the imaginary view, often an architectural *capriccio*, a pastoral scene containing incongruous pieces of architecture and equally incongruous figures" (p. 272). From Desiderio comes the motif of saintly martyrdom against the backdrop of the saintly city. West, Tod, and the painters all have one thing in common, concludes Torchianna. All treat "repulsive" subjects with a combination of revulsion and joy.

70

VII. Influence Studies

One test of an author's stature lies in the weight of his influence on fellow writers and subsequent generations. The number and variety of writers influenced by West in the scant three-and-one-half decades since his death is impressive, but the list is almost startling when one considers the relative obscurity of West's name during his life and for over a decade after his death.

78. Bergonzi, Bernard. *The Situation of the Novel*. London: Macmillan and Company, Limited, 1970, pp. 83-84, 95, 98, 104. Bergonzi discusses West as a predecessor of the "comic-apocalyptic" school: Barth, Heller, Southern, and others. He finds that West's work is often absurd, but almost never funny. Bergonzi finds that Ralph Ellison is also influenced by West, but he and West are distinguished from the previously mentioned authors by those authors' almost inhuman coldness. West, on the other hand, is always grounded in human values. Bergonzi compares the dismemberment of Benny Profane in Pynchon's *V* to Lemuel Pitkin's dismemberment in *A Cool Million*. He also claims that Evelyn Waugh's *A Handful of Dust* recalls West's work.

81. Bier, Jesse. *The Rise and Fall of American Humor*. New York, Chicago, and San Francisco: Holt, Rinehart, and Winston, 1968, pp. 347n, 356n. Bier cites West as an influence on Joseph Heller's *Catch-22* (p. 347n). Too, he calls James Purdy's sardonicism "pseudo-Nathanael West" in "dime-novel style" (p. 356n).

95. Burgess, Anthony. *The Novel Now: A Student's Guide to Contemporary Fiction*. London: Faber and Faber, 1967, p. 194. "Perhaps a prototype of the contemporary Jewish-American author is that important novelist of the nineteen-thirties, Nathanael West, whose *Miss Lonelyhearts* and *The Day of the Locust* are full of the anguish of rejected humanity and the debasing of true values (love and beauty) by the gods of money which America worships" (p. 194).

106. Driskell, Leon V. and Joan T. Brittain. *The Eternal Crossroads: The Art of Flannery O'Connor*. Lexington: University of Kentucky Press, 1971, pp. 14-16. The authors conclude--after examining West's influence on O'Connor--that his influence is superficial at the most. "Although West's influence on Miss O'Connor was neither pervasive nor deep, one should observe that, despite his Jewish origins, his books dramatize an essentially Christian quest" (p. 15) as do O'Connor's. The authors also compare O'Connor's *Wise Blood* to *Miss Lonelyhearts* and find the ending of West's novel to be more optimistic than do most critics. They place great importance on the fact that, although Miss Lonelyhearts is lost, Betty has been "initiated" into a more realistic, more balanced view of the world, thus better able to survive in the modern world.

279. Edenbaum, Robert I. "Dada and Surrealism in the United States: A Literary Instance." *Arts in Society*, 5, no. 1 (1968), 114-125. Edenbaum finds West and the entire movement of surrealism and dadaism to be a

precursor of "black humor" today. He concludes that all share in the attempt to achieve order.

109. Fiedler, Leslie A. "The Breakthrough: The American Jewish Novelist and the Fictional Image of the Jew." *Recent American Fiction: Some Critical Views*, ed. Joseph J. Waldmeir. Boston: Houghton Mifflin Company, 1963, pp. 84-109. Fiedler says that Bellow's Augie March is a descendant of the *shlemiels* of West and Henry Roth.

164. Fiedler, Leslie A. "The Two Memories: Reflections on Writers and Writing in the Thirties." *Proletarian Writers of the Thirties*, David Madden. Carbondale and Edwardsville: Southern Illinois University Press; London and Amsterdam: Feffer and Simons, Incorporated, 1968, pp. 3-25. Fiedler sees West as one of the key figures of the thirties, especially since he is so influential today. Fiedler finds West particularly influential on Jeremy Larner, whose *Drive, He Said* derives its vision from *Miss Lonelyhearts* and *The Day of the Locust* (p. 8).

113. Fiedler, Leslie A. *Waiting For the End*. New York: Dell Publishing Company, 1964, pp. 37, 45, 46, 48, 49, 50-52, 63-64, 83, 108, 143, 226. Fiedler claims that the center of the literary generation of the last few decades is a group of urban Jewish writers following the example of West and Daniel Fuchs.

119. Friedman, Melvin J. "Flannery O'Connor's Sacred Objects." *The Added Dimension: The Art and Mind of Flannery O'Connor*, eds. Melvin J. Friedman and Lewis A. Lawson. New York: Fordham University Press, 1966, pp. 196-208. Here Friedman mentions O'Connor's fondness for *Miss Lonelyhearts* (p. 197).

116. Friedman, Melvin J. "Introduction." *The Added Dimension: The Art and Mind of Flannery O'Connor*, eds. Melvin J. Friedman and Lewis A. Lawson. New York: Fordham University Press, 1966, pp. 1-31. Friedman briefly summarizes West's influence on O'Connor's *Wise Blood*.

298. Greiner, Don. "Strange Laughter: The Comedy of John Hawkes." *Southwest Review*, 56, no. 4 (Autumn 1971), 318-327. Greiner sees West's *Miss Lonelyhearts* and Djuna Barnes' *Nightwood* as handing down a legacy to black humorists, particularly Hawkes.

131. Hassan, Ihab. *Contemporary American Literature 1945-1972: An Introduction*. New York: Frederick Ungar Publishing Company, 1973, pp. 52, 71, 81. Hassan lists West among those contributing to the "bizarre poetic sensibility of John Hawkes" (p. 52). He also lists West as a precursor of the modern Jewish urban novel, especially *Miss Lonelyhearts*, where "tragic fact and grotesque feeling, the aches of the ghetto and the anguish of dreams, are made available to the imagination" (p. 71). However, Hassan maintains that the line from West to Barth, Pynchon, and other black humorists "is not as straight as critics might wish" (p. 81).

307. Henkle, Roger B. "Pynchon's Tapestries on the Western Wall." *Modern Fiction Studies*, 17, no. 2 (Summer 1971), pp. 207-220. Henkle

briefly mentions that several critics have noted Thomas Pynchon's indebtedness to *A Cool Million* for the Benny Profane episode in *V*. However, he goes in to little detail here.

141. Hyman, Stanley Edgar. *Flannery O'Connor*. University of Minnesota Pamphlets on American Writers, No. 54. Minneapolis: University of Minnesota Press, 1966, pp. 43, 46. Hyman asserts that West is the greatest influence on O'Connor. In particular, "*Wise Blood* is clearly modeled on *Miss Lonelyhearts*" (p. 43). Too, like West, she had the writer's advantage "of multiple alienation from the dominant assumptions of our culture: he was an outsider as a Jew, and doubly an outsider as a Jew alienated from other Jews" (p. 46). At the same time, O'Connor was alienated as a woman, a Southerner, and a Catholic.

2. Hyman, Stanley Edgar. *Nathanael West*. Pamphlets on American Writers, No. 21. Minneapolis: University of Minnesota, 1962. Says Hyman, "The unique greatness of *Miss Lonelyhearts* seems to have come into the world with hardly a predecessor, but it has itself influenced a great many American novelists since" (p. 27), although Hyman does not specify who was so influenced.

144. Kazin, Alfred. *Bright Book of Life: American Novelists and Storytellers from Hemingway to Mailer*. Boston, Toronto: Little, Brown, and Company, 1973, pp. 17-18, 191. Kazin speaks of the "violently flashing images" of *Miss Lonelyhearts* and the "surrealistically overpainted Hollywood" of *The Day of the Locust* (p. 17) as signalling a new order in literature.

3. Light, James F. *Nathanael West: An Interpretative Study*. 2nd ed. Evanston: Northwestern University Press, 1971. Light speaks in more specific terms than most of West's influence on contemporary writers. Donald Barthelme's "Me and Miss Mandible" uses experimental techniques found in *The Dream Life of Balso Snell*. Terry Southern's *Candy* is influenced by the surrealistic distortion and "fleshly appetites" found in *The Dream Life of Balso Snell*. Joseph Heller's *Catch-22* probably was influenced by West, particularly in the theme of entrapped man. Malamud's *The Assistant*, Mailer's *The Deer Park*, and Vonnegut's *God Bless You, Mr. Rosewater* reflect West's suffering for the agonies of his fellow man. Flannery O'Connor's *Wise Blood* draws upon West's use of the grotesque. Most influenced perhaps, according to Light, is Edward Lewis Wallent-- *The Human Season, The Pawnbroker, The Tennants of Moonbloom,* and *The Children at the Gate*--in the use of characters morbid in their religious probings (see especially pp. 211-213).

64. Martin, Jay. *Nathanael West: The Art of His Life*. New York: Farrar, Straus, and Giroux, 1970. In citing West's influence on William Carlos Williams, Martin comments, "It is not too much to say that, though William's career began much earlier, the two writers had been working along similar lines, and William's understanding of West's imagination helped him to sharpen his own sensibility and define the direction he would pursue in literature after his time. To West's crucial influence are directly traceable the important developments which led Williams to *Paterson*". (p. 154).

174. May, John R. "Words and Deeds: Apocalyptic Judgment in Faulkner, West, and O'Connor." *Toward a New Earth: Apocalypse in the American Novel*. Notre Dame, London: University of Notre Dame Press, 1972, pp. 114-126. May mentions that O'Connor was much influenced by West, particularly in the use of condensed images.

179. Muller, Gilbert H. *Nightmares and Visions: Flannery O'Connor and the Catholic Grotesque*. Athens: University of Georgia Press, 1972, pp. 5, 20-21. Muller traces in some depth O'Connor's indebtedness to West for *Wise Blood* (pp. 20-21).

187. Orvell, Miles. *Invisible Parade: The Fiction of Flannery O'Connor*. Philadelphia: Temple University Press, 1972, pp. 21n, 51-52, 58, 73, 83n. Orvell finds that both West and O'Connor share an eye for the grotesque, but O'Connor is noted for "austere judgment" as opposed to West's "hazy compassion" (p. 52). However, West "confirmed in her what was there almost from the beginning--the odd comic look of her world" (p. 52). Also compared is both writers' use of a realistic style to handle fantastic subjects. Finally, Orvell notes in some detail *Wise Blood*'s indebtedness to West (p. 73).

364. Ratner, Marc L. "Rebellion of Wrath and Laughter: Styron's *Set This House on Fire*." *The Southern Review*, 7 (October 1971), 1007-1020. Ratner cites Styron's interest in West, particularly in the theme of the absurd catastrophe as described by R. W. B. Lewis (see [160]). Ratner finds that both writers present grotesques as an inevitable part of life. Says Ratner, "Like William Faulkner, John Hawkes, and Nathanael West, Styron gives us a comic-grotesque vision of the horror of the American nightmare" (p. 1020).

66. Reid, Randall. *The Fiction of Nathanael West: No Redeemer, No Promised Land*. Chicago and London: University of Chicago Press, 1967. In a change of tack, Reid finds West's influence on modern literature *less* than most would say. Concludes Reid, "The influence of grotesque art in general and of Faulkner in particular are probably more responsible for contemporary trends than West is" (p. 4). Neither does Reid find any connection between West's work and the surrealism found in drug culture literature. "In his work," maintains Reid, "most hallucination is involuntary and dreadful, not euphoric" (p. 5).

67. Scott, Nathan A., Jr. *Nathanael West: A Critical Essay*. Contemporary Writers in Christian Perspective. Grand Rapids, Michigan: William B. Eerdmans, 1971. Scott sees black humor as descending from West, although he thinks that West is important for more than merely his influence on that movement.

385. Skerrett, Joseph Taylor, Jr. "Dostoievsky, Nathanael West, and Some Contemporary American Fiction." *The University of Dayton Review*, 4, no. 1 (Winter 1967), 23-36. Skerrett sees Mark Twain and particularly West as forerunners of black humor. Black humorists such as Barth and Pynchon show West's "belief in the necessity of living life on a human scale, not in terms of impossible and absurd concepts and false importances" (p. 31).

207. Stephens, Martha. *The Question of Flannery O'Connor*. Baton Rouge: Louisiana State University Press, 1973, pp. 49, 96. Stephens notes West's influence on O'Connor's *Wise Blood*, which she compares to *Miss Lonelyhearts*. Stephens professes surprise that few early critics made the connection between the two novels. Concludes Stephens, "Even *Miss Lonelyhearts* is in one important respect a less forbidding book than *Wise Blood*, i.e., in that West's sense of life and of human suffering is not, finally, for all his weirdly contorted way of expressing it, nearly as peculiar as is O'Connor's" (p. 49).

167. Sturak, Thomas. "Horace McCoy's Objective Lyricism." *Tough Guy Writers of the Thirties*, ed. David Madden. Carbondale and Edwardsville: Southern Illinois University Press; London and Amsterdam: Feffer and Simons, Incorporated, 1968, pp. 137-162. Sturak mentions merely that West and McCoy are often placed in a context of writers of the thirties who greatly influenced contemporary writers.

30. Widmer, Kingsley. "The Last Masquerade." *Nathanael West: The Cheaters and the Cheated, A Collection of Critical Essays*. Deland, Florida: Everett/Edwards, Incorporated, 1973, pp. 179-193. Widmer finds West a forerunner of black humor, while not being a black humorist himself; West is more committed and less clever (using clever in a pejorative sense, I assume).

224. Widmer, Kingsley. "The Sweet, Savage Prophecies of Nathanael West." *The Thirties: Fiction, Poetry, Drama*, ed. Warren French. Deland, Florida: Everett/Edwards, Incorporated, 1967, pp. 97-106. Here Widmer calls West a precursor of black humor. "Especially concerned with the fatuous and machined dreams counterfeiting that reality [of the thirties], West foresaw apocalyptic violence of warped and cheated humanity" (p. 97).

VIII. Genre Studies

Almost all critics who deal with West (particularly those discussing
A Cool Million or *The Day of the Locust*) mention satire at least in passing,
but a few more obviously make satire (thus genre) one of the central
issues in their studies. An interesting dichotomy is evident in these
genre studies; for in one camp we find scholars who are much taken with
West's use of satire, while an equally vocal group finds West's failures
in handling the genre to be his greatest fault. Most--but not all--
of the genre studies cited below deal with West's use of satire.

81. Bier, Jesse. *The Rise and Fall of American Humor*. New York, Chicago,
San Francisco: Holt, Rinehart, and Winston, 1968, pp. 417-418. Bier
examines Evelyn Waugh and West as examples of British and American humor.
He finds that British satire has a "certain reformist belief" whereas
West's is a more general, "nameless" attack. Too, West's (thus America's)
humor is "grosser" than the witty British variety.

1. Comerchero, Victor. *Nathanael West: The Ironic Prophet*. Syracuse:
Syracuse University Press, 1964. Comerchero considers *Miss Lonelyhearts*
the best of West's novels, because there West best handles the delicate
balance between "agonizing pessimism" and "ironic amusement" (p. 72).
Comerchero compares the structure of the novel to a tragic drama, with
the hero journeying "from ignorance through experience to discovery"
(p. 73).

276. Cramer, Carter M. "The World of Nathanael West: A Critical Interpretation." *The Emporia State Research Studies*, 19, no. 4 (June 1971),
5-71. Cramer claims that *The Dream Life of Balso Snell* is more narrow
in focus than commonly imagined. It is not a dada novel--parodying
Dostoevsky, Joyce, *et al.*--but is an anatomy which buries the pseudo-
sophisticates of art in their own cliches. *A Cool Million* is also an
anatomy in Northrop Frye's sense, while *Miss Lonelyhearts* and *The Day of
the Locust* are more nearly novels in Frye's sense of the term. Concludes
Cramer, "West's extremely experimental attitude toward techniques of
style and structure was his attempt to find a vehicle to portray the
reality of the grotesque in a mass culture" (p. 8).

296. Gilmore, Thomas B., Jr. "The Dark Night of the Cave: A Rejoinder
to Kernan." *Satire Newsletter*, 2, no. 2 (Spring 1965), 95-100. A reply
to Kernan (see [146]). Gilmore claims that the assumption that *The Day
of the Locust* is a satire is false because 1) West's attitude is not that
of a satirist (West has pity and respect for his characters rather than
indignation or "amused contempt or scorn" [p. 95]); 2) West is more
interested in understanding his characters than in shaping attitudes;
3) the reader infers no alternate life style to the one shown in the novel.

146. Kernan, Alvin B. "The Mob Tendency: *The Day of the Locust*."
The Plot of Satire. New Haven and London: Yale University Press, 1965,
pp. 66-80. Included is an interesting discussion of the way that Tod
Hackett's changing taste in painters reflects the changing artistic

expression necessary to convey the world. More importantly, Kernan explains that the root meaning of "satire"--"filled with a variety of things" (p. 68)--is still functional in West's work. Says Kernan, "Whatever form dullness may take in a given satire, it moves always toward the creation of messes, discordancies, mobs, on all levels and in all areas of life" (p. 68). Kernan examines Tod Hackett's picture in *The Day of the Locust*-- "The Burning of Los Angeles"--as a manifestation of this type of satire. "West is not condemning all American life," concludes Kernan, "but isol- ating and expressing in grotesque forms a peculiar danger or brand of dullness within it. This is, specifically, the peculiar emptiness of many people and lives, and the search for compensation in vicarious excitement and glamour" (p. 72). Kernan sees the characters, scenes, and plot all moving toward disorder; thus, this particular kind of satire.

158. Levine, Paul. "Flannery O'Connor: The Soul of the Grotesque." *Minor American Novelists*, ed. Charles Alva Hoyt. Carbondale and Edwards- ville: Southern Illinois University Press; London and Amsterdam: Feffer and Simons, Incorporated, 1970, pp. 95-117. Levine discusses the evol- ution of the grotesque as a form and concludes that in West "grotesque satire comes into its own" (p. 97).

333. Linberg-Seyersted, Brita. "Three Variations of the American Success Story: The Careers of Luke Larkin, Lemuel Barker, and Lemuel Pitkin." *English Studies*, 53, no. 2 (April 1972), 125-141. Linberg-Seyersted traces the tradition of the success story as a genre (journeying from obscurity to renown, from ignorance to experience) and concludes that it is found world-wide, but especially in America. Horatio Alger (*Struggling Upward; or, Luke Larkin's Luck*) is a prime example. The author examines William Dean Howells' *The Minister's Charge; or, The Apprenticeship of Lemuel Barker* and West's *A Cool Million* as arising out of but reacting against that tradition. Howell's attitude toward the success ideal was ambivalent, but West rejected the myth completely. The author does not maintain that West was familiar with Howells' work but feels that it is possible, since Howells was on the Brown reading list. Perhaps the most obvious difference between the two was Howells' sqeamishness about sex; the same charge cannot be made, of course, about West.

64. Martin, Jay. *Nathanael West: The Art of His Life*. New York: Farrar, Straus and Giroux, 1970. Martin notes that "West was writing humorously and freely in well-defined traditions of satire" (p. 237). However, "West begins in comedy and ends by showing that beneath the comic froth lies the bitter, salt tragedy of betrayed ideals" (p. 239).

359. Pinsker, Sanford. "Charles Dickens and Nathanael West: Great Expectations Unfulfilled." *Topic*, 18 (1969), pp. 40-52. Pinsker maintains that little pure satire exists and that the most interesting forms are those blended with other literary genres, such as *Miss Lonelyhearts*. Both that novel and Dickens' *Great Expectations* lack the humor usually associated with satire. Both novels explore the difference between what one expects from life and what one receives.

392. Tibbetts, A. M. "The Strange Half-World of Nathanael West." *Prairie*

Schooner, 34, no. 1 (Spring 1960), 8-14. Like many other scholars, Tibbetts maintains that West was not a good satirist because he never indicates, either explicitly or implicitly, the standards actions are to be measured by (p. 14).

220. [White, William]. "The Complete Works of Nathanael West." *Best Masterplots, 1954-1964*, eds. Frank N. Magill and Dayton Kohler. New York: Salem Press, 1964, pp. 103-106. White says that West's novels do not succeed as satire because no possible alternative action is hinted at.

IX. Studies in the History of Ideas

This category is a curious one because nearly all of the criticism of West could be considered to a greater or lesser degree based on the history of ideas. Almost every article on *Miss Lonelyhearts*, for instance, discusses the importance of the Christ motif. Too, most of the works discussed in this chapter could be considered comparative criticism or possibly source studies. However, included in this section are only those studies which emphasize a particular philosophical or historical idea, archetype, or motif (other than the Christ motif, since it is universal to the criticism of *Miss Lonelyhearts*) in a historical context.

234. Andreach, Robert J. "Nathanael West's *Miss Lonelyhearts*: Between the Dead Pan and the Unborn Christ." *Modern Fiction Studies*, 12, no. 2 (Summer 1966), 251-261. Andreach finds that *Miss Lonelyhearts'* "unifying principle is the antagonism that pits the virile, sexual, natural paganism against the effeminate, ascetic, materialistic Christianity, a major theme in Western literature" (p. 251). The author briefly traces the myth that when Christ was born, Pan died. Pan personified nature and paganism and was denounced by Christianity. In particular, Andreach sees Shrike as representing Pan and Miss Lonelyhearts as trying to be Christ. Too, most of the misery of the letter writers comes from a conflict between natural desire and Christ-inspired guilt and absurd idealism. Miss Lonelyhearts is in the most hopeless position since he is so naturally a Pan follower but insists on seeking Christ instead. "What makes his predicament hopeless," explains Andreach, "is that belief in Christ is no solution since for West Christ was never born, and whenever Miss Lonelyhearts tries to make him a reality, he invariably brings back to life the dead Pan, the world of primitive sexuality" (pp. 254-255). Andreach traces part of the inspiration for the novel to Bulfinch's quotation of E. B. Browning's "The Dead Pan" (see p. 260).

260. Brown, Daniel R. "The War Within Nathanael West: Naturalism and Existentialism." *Modern Fiction Studies*, 20, no. 2 (Summer 1974), 181-202. After defining naturalism and existentialism, Brown explains that both have a positive and a negative side, with the negative side of naturalism similar to the positive side of existentialism. He also cites the influence of Marx, Darwin, Nietzche, and Freud on these ways of interpreting the world. West, Brown concludes, shares in both traditions. He finds the grotesque in West in keeping with naturalism, but the comedy not. Too, he claims that West is not so entirely pessimistic as some insist. "His war within his fiction is also between his desire to throw up his hands because of the absurdity of human behavior and all activity and his other desire to work to remedy social evils" (p. 187). Brown aligns West with the existentialists, also, but he sees little freedom in West's characters' choices.

301. Hassan, Ihab H. "Love in the Modern American Novel: Expense of Spirit and Waste of Shame." *Western Humanities Review*, 14, no. 2 (Spring 1960), 149-161. Hassan explores the relationship between love and sex in the modern American novel, particularly the theme of the sordidness of sex without love. Like Leslie Fiedler in *Love and Death in the*

American Novel (see [111]), Hassan finds a chronic inability or unwillingness in American fiction to deal with relations between the sexes in a natural fashion. West is a good example. In *"The Day of the Locust* or *Miss Lonelyhearts* sexual activity, brutalized and random, confessed to the radical failure of human relations in a society which offered no meaningful connectives between private and public relations. . . . The bitter fakeries of Miss Lonelyhearts, locked at the end in an embrace of death and Christian love with the cripple whom he has just cuckolded, parallel, in a sense, the profligacies of Fay Greener and her grotesque friends consumed in a holocaust of cheap illusions" (p. 156).

160. Lewis, R. W. B. "Days of Wrath and Laughter." *Trials of the Word: Essays in American Literature and the Humanistic Tradition.* New Haven and London: Yale University Press, 1965, pp. 184-236. Lewis describes world apocalypse as an old motif in literature, but recently this note of terror has seen the addition of the absurd. "It was West, following hard on Melville and Mark Twain, who established for contemporary American writing the vision of the ludicrous catastrophe" (p. 185). The ultimate example, finds Lewis, is *The Day of the Locust.*

327. Light, James F. *"Miss Lonelyhearts*: The Imagery of Nightmare." *American Quarterly*, 3, no. 4 (Winter 1956), 316-328. In discussing the chapter, "Miss Lonelyhearts and the Dead Pan," Light observes, "The dead pan refers to Shrike's lack of facial expression, but the word *pan* also suggests the dead nature god of flocks and pastures. Shrike is thus identified with the new mechanical world based on the emotionless physical sciences" (p. 320).

64. Martin, Jay. *Nathanael West: The Art of His Life.* New York: Farrar, Straus, and Giroux, 1970. For one of the better discussions of the Pan myth in *Miss Lonelyhearts*, see p. 198 *et passim.*

360. Pisk, George M. "The Graveyard of Dreams: A Study of Nathanael West's Last Novel, *The Day of the Locust." The South Central Bulletin*, 27, no. 4 (Winter 1967), 64-72. Pisk discusses the theme of horror in American literature played against the more common theme of American innocence. "Grotesqueries as they appear in Stephen Crane, Sherwood Anderson, Nathanael West, Carson McCullers, Truman Capote, Tennessee Williams (there is a school of the grotesque) have lent to them a quality of pathos and shock by their American *mise en scène*" (p. 206).

37. Wadlington, Warwick. "Nathanael West and the Confidence Game." *Nathanael West: The Cheaters and the Cheated, A Collection of Critical Essays.* Deland, Florida: Everett/Edwards, Incorporated, 1973, pp. 299-322. Wadlington explores West's connection to the tradition of American literature, particularly the theme of the confidence man as found in Melville and Mark Twain. America exists on confidence, claims Wadlington, and the failure of confidence in the twentieth century is failure for both the individual and American society in general. The confidence man of nineteenth century literature becomes the "conned man" of West's fiction. Melville's *The Confidence Man* is examined in particular. Too, in *The Dream Life of Balso Snell*, the protest against writing that so many see is the artist's protest against an audience which requires

him to be a confidence man. In *The Day of the Locust*, the novel is obviously about the cheated. Religious faith is attacked in *Miss Lonely-hearts*, the American dream in *A Cool Million*. Wadlington examines in detail how the development of character supports the non-confidence motif. Finally, Wadlington finds that West continually parodies himself as an artist, but achieves an objectivity in his better works.

X. Historical/Sociological Criticism

This category presents a special problem in that all the studies
herein are in a certain sense biography or biographical criticism.
However, included here are only those works which deal in some way with
the effect of the historical or social context on West's writing.

230. Aaron, Daniel. "Late Thoughts on Nathanael West." *Massachusetts
Review*, 6, no. 2 (Winter-Spring 1965), 307-317. States Aaron, "West be-
longed to that select company of socially committed writers in the
Depression decade who drew revolutionary conclusions in highly idio-
synchratic and undoctrinaire ways" (p. 308). Aaron claims that the
leftists had no quarrel with the content of West's writing but objected
to the style. "In misconstruing his humor and failing to explore his
baleful Wasteland, it [the Left] committed both a political and an aesthetic
blunder" (p. 110). Aaron concludes that West's humor was too universal
and did not serve the proper function or purpose for Communist taste.

74. Angoff, Allan, ed. *American Writing Today: Its Independence and
Its Vigor*. Washington Square: New York University Press, 1957, pp.
168, 206. Angoff claims that the writers who were well-regarded in the
thirties would not necessarily be the ones that we today (in the fifties)
would regard as the thirties best writers. Several unknowns (then)
would be added to the thirties list, including West (see p. 168). In
a later comment, Angoff observes that a "quality of pathos and shock"
is added to American grotesque writers (such as West) by the background
of the tradition of innocence in America (see p. 206).

276. Cramer, Carter M. "The World of Nathanael West: A Critical
Interpretation." *The Emporia State Research Studies*, 19, no. 4 (June
1971), 5-71. Cramer sees West as a product of and commentator on an age
of poverty, violence, and political and social insanity.

280. Edenbaum, Robert I. "A Surfeit of Shoddy: Nathanael West's
A Cool Million." *Southern Humanities Review*, 2, no. 4 (Fall 1968), 427-
439. Edenbaum's theme is that the world view of the novel is yellow press
journalism in general and the Hearst press in particular. Observes
Edenbaum, "In the Hearst ideology America is pure and innocent, the best
of all societies of the best of all possible people. But the destiny of
that society, story by story, page by page, is worked out in terms
of rapes, murders, sinister plots, sexual perversions, lynchings, fires,
revolutions, wars--the popular idiom of violence" (p. 429). Thus, the
lower middle class world of Hearst is the world that West is attacking
in his novel. Edenbaum examines West's prolific use of clichés to clinch
his point, particularly those clichés employing a racial stereotype.
Too, Edenbaum argues that W. H. Auden's complaint about West's inconsis-
tent focus--for instance, his sympathy for Wu Fong--is misguided. West
hated "shoddy" institutions, explains Edenbaum, not individuals: thus,
West's attack on Wu Fong's whore house.

109. Fiedler, Leslie A. "The Breakthrough: The American Jewish Novelist
and the Fictional Image of the Jew." *Recent American Fiction: Some*

Critical Views, ed. Joseph J. Waldmeir. Boston: Houghton Mifflin Company, 1963, pp. 84-109. Fiedler sees the thirties as beginning the influence of the Jewish writers, such as West. The favorite form for these Jewish writers was the proletarian novel; and even those who did not favor it tried to compensate, "like West feeding his more orthodox contemporaries at the family hotel and boasting of having walked the picket line with James T. Farrell and Leane Zugsmith" (p. 87).

284. Fiedler, Leslie A. "Master of Dreams." *Partisan Review*, 34, no. 3 (Summer 1967), 339-356. Fiedler sees the function of the Jewish writer in America as that of a dream/myth maker: "to read in the dreams of the present the past which never dies and the future which is always to come" (p. 346). Their stories waver between parable and essay, art and science. The purpose is therapeutic and prophetic. Fiedler says that the tone of Jewish literature--a wail of despair and a shout of discovery--is set once and for all by West. More specifically, he calls *The Dream Life of Balso Snell* "a fractured and dissolving parable of the very process by which the emancipated Jew enters into the world of Western culture" (p. 347). Too, he sees Mary in that same novel as the desirable *shiksah* that the Jew pants after, only to find her upon conquest less than desirable. Fiedler also examines Roth, Ginsberg, and Mailer in the same context (plus others, though in less depth).

113. Fiedler, Leslie A. *Waiting For the End*. New York: Dell Publishing Company, 1964, p. 37. Fiedler places West in a context of "pioneer exploiters of the ghetto [Jewish] milieu and the rhythms of Jewish American speech" (p. 37).

149. Goodman, Paul. "Underground Writing, 1960." *The American Novel Since World War II*, ed. Marcus Klein. Greenwich, Connecticutt: Fawcett Publications, Incorporated, 1969, pp. 186-195. Goodman claims that it is hard to understand why West is so admired by young writers, unless perhaps the world that he describes is the only one that the youth have experienced "and it seems that West teaches them a possible attitude to survive by" (p. 190).

311. Herbst, Josephine. "Nathanael West." *The Kenyon Review*, 23 (Autumn 1961), 611-630. Herbst discusses the intellectual context of the artistic ferment of the thirties as a background for a discussion of West.

5. Jackson, Thomas H. "Introduction." *Twentieth Century Interpretations of* Miss Lonelyhearts. Englewood Cliffs, New Jersey: Prentice-Hall, Incorporated, 1971, pp. 1-17. Jackson places West's major theme of dream/disillusionment in a context of the prosperity/bust decades of the twenties and thirties.

3. Light, James F. *Nathanael West: An Interpretative Study*. Evanston: Northwestern University Press, 1971. See pp. 120-128 for a thorough discussion of the historical background for *A Cool Million* and West's ideas on Communism. Other historical/sociological background information is found throughout Light's study.

333. Linberg-Seyersted, Brita. "Three Variations of the American Success Story: The Careers of Luke Larkin, Lemuel Barker, and Lemuel Pitkin." *English Studies*, 53, no. 2 (April 1972), 125-141. The author places West's attitude toward the American success ideal in a historical context. Before World War I, "Young intellectuals saw great promise in America and believed that a rich cultural and moral life would be realized in their country. After this optimism and enthusiasm, the disillusionment and cynicism of the postwar era turned the current against this variation in the American Dream" (pp. 135-136).

64. Martin, Jay. *Nathanael West: The Art of His Life*. New York: Farrar, Straus and Giroux, 1970. See Chapter Six in its entirety for the historical background to West's writing. Says Martin, "In the twenties, a decade of artistic experimentation had finally flowered in a stimulating literature. . . . The thirties, whether there had been a Depression or not, were to constitute a new beginning, an intellectual readjustment. . . . Perhaps only writers like Dos Passos, Hemingway, Faulkner, Fitzgerald, and West, whose consciousness extended from the twenties across into the thirties, could survive the oblivion which has overtaken many of the writers of the thirties and into which they fell, even then, daily" (pp. 98-99). See also pp. 256-260 on the pressure West and fellow writers felt from Marxist critics, and pp. 290-302 for a discussion of the anti-war climate which inspired West and Joseph Schrank to collaborate on *Good Hunting*.

174. May, John R. "Words and Deeds: Apocalyptic Judgment in Faulkner, West, and O'Connor." *Toward a New Earth: Apocalypse in the American Novel*. Notre Dame and London: University of Notre Dame Press, 1972, pp. 204-206. May claims that the Depression and social milieu of the thirties had a profound effect on West's writing.

92. Mottram, Eric. "The Hostile Environment and the Revival Artist: A Note on the Twenties." *The American Novel in the Nineteen Twenties*. Stratford-Upon-Avon Studies #13. eds. Malcolm Bradbury and David Palmer. London: Edward Arnold; New York: Crane, Russak, 1971, pp. 233- 262. Mottram says that West demonstrated that Hollywood was the incipient center of Fascism in the thirties (see p. 238).

360. Pisk, George M. "The Graveyard of Dreams: A Study of Nathanael West's Last Novel, *The Day of the Locust.*" *The South Central Bulletin*, 27, no. 4 (Winter 1967), 64-72. Observes Pisk, "Among the orange groves and motion picture studios [of Hollywood] West appears to have found in undiluted form certain social evils which are typical of the American scene" (p. 64). He feels that the change in titles of West's last novel--from *The Cheated* to *The Day of the Locust*--reflects West's ambivalence toward the American people: in the first version they are the plague's victims, in the second, the plague.

194. Ross Alan. "The Dead Center: An Introduction to Nathanael West." *The Complete Works of Nathanael West*. New York: Farrar, Straus, and Cudahy, 1957, pp. vii-xxii. Ross places West in the intellectual context of the twenties and thirties, along with Fitzgerald, Dos Passos, O'Hara,

etc. Concludes Ross, "It is this ruthless outline of collapse that Nathanael West created more savagely and poetically than any other contemporary writer in his two important novels, *Miss Lonelyhearts* and *The Day of the Locust*--blueprints of the faithless Christ-symbols that in the end stood for the American common man, like bitter flowers, as he lay on the ground at the stockyards of his own defeat" (p. ix). Ross claims that *Miss Lonelyhearts* is West's best novel, but *The Day of the Locust* represents his most mature effort "because in it his criticism of life is not intruding between the characters, nor his pity confronting them" (p. xi). Indeed, West was always a sociological writer anyway, according to Ross.

376. Schneider, Cyril M. "The Individuality of Nathanael West." *The Western Review*, 20, no. 1 (Autumn 1955), 7-28. Schneider places *A Cool Million* in a context of the thirties. He finds two reasons for the shift to political concerns in the novel: the unpopularity of *Miss Lonelyhearts* and West's association with radical writers at *Americana*. Says Schneider, "The magazine was characterized by a high degree of irreverence for most institutions dear to the American public" (p. 16). This cynicism is important, since *A Cool Million* is a reverse "Horatio Alger, mock *Candide* story" (p. 18).

67. Scott, Nathan A., Jr. *Nathanael West: A Critical Essay.* Contemporary Writers in Christian Perspective. Grand Rapids, Michigan: William B. Eerdmans, 1971. Scott begins by briefly describing the historical context for West's writing career: a decade when things seemed to be falling apart (see pp. 5-6).

386. Smith, Roger H. "Complete Works of Nathanael West." *The Saturday Review of Literature*, 40 (11 May 1957), 13-14. Smith briefly recounts the social and intellectual environment of the twenties and thirties out of which West developed. He finds that the twenties was a decade of exile and the thirties of envolvement, but, unlike his contemporaries, West managed to remain detached. Concludes Smith, "As a writer, his preoccupation was with the moral bankruptcy that underlay the surface ills" (p. 13).

387. Solberg, S. E. "The Novels of Nathanael West--A Sargasso of the Imagination." *The English Language and Literature*, 14 (October 1963), 125-146. Solberg finds that West uses the "norms of sexual behavior and attitude in a given situation to parallel the norms and attitudes of social or political behavior" (pp. 126-127). He concludes that West's attitude more closely resembles our day than his own. Too, although West is a "writer of conscience" and moral indignation is always close to the surface, he does not preach to the reader.

30. Widmer, Kingsley. "The Last Masquerade." *Nathanael West: The Cheaters and the Cheated, A Collection of Critical Essays*. **ed.** David Madden. Deland, Florida: Everett/Edwards, Incorporated, 1973, pp. 179-193. Widmer observes that the "masquerade" tendency in Hollywood (the people, the architecture, *etc.*) extends to the sensibilities of "all Southern California and beyond" (p. 179). Drawing from his own experiences in Hollywood, Widmer also concludes that West was not truly

a writer of the grotesque, as most critics believe, but was one who
fashioned a particular, but very real, reality.

XI. Comparative Criticism

Inspite of the fact (or perhaps *because* of the fact) that West's fiction is so distinctive, so seemingly out of the mainstream of American literature in the thirties, it has invited an abundance of comparisons to a striking number of his contemporaries in America and Europe, and also comparisons to earlier literature. The number of studies employing comparative criticism in some degree is so large that I have found it necessary to divide this chapter into five sections: one for comparative statements dealing with the entire canon of West's work and one section for each of the novels.

A) General Studies

71. Allen, Walter. *Tradition and Dream: A Critical Survey of British and American Fiction From the 1920's to the Present Day*. Middlesex, England: Penguin Books, 1965, p. 187. In West, Henry Roth, and Daniel Fuchs, states Allen, "We are lifted right above the purely economic, mechanical interpretation of life and are confronted with the human condition in its naked terror" (p. 187).

75. Asselineau, Roger. "Edgar Allan Poe." *American Writers: A Collection of Literary Biographies*, ed. Leonard Unger. New York: Charles Scribner's Sons, 1974. III: p. 425. Asselineau states that the theme of the grotesque as found in many Poe works was later taken up by West (although he does not claim Poe to be a source for West's inspiration).

79. Bertoff, Warner. *The Ferment of Realism: American Literature, 1884-1919*. New York: The Free Press; London: Collier-Macmillan, Limited, 1965, p. 37. In discussing Veblen's *Theory of the Leisure Class*, Bertoff observes that its "ironic tableau of business civilization and the moral types who flourish in it, broke much of the ground later occupied by social fabulists like Sinclair Lewis and John Dos Passos, Fitzgerald and Nathanael West" (p. 37).

81. Bier, Jesse. *The Rise and Fall of American Humor*. New York, Chicago, San Fransisco: Holt, Rinehart, and Winston, 1968, pp. 230-231. Bier compares West to the poet Don Marquis and finds West's work in contrast to Marquis' stoical tone. States Bier, "In *Lonelyhearts* [sic] and *Locust* [sic], West is mostly the strong comic realist, portraying malaise without indulging in extremity or sickness himself. That is what sets him apart from the post-World War II sickniks" (p. 231).

87. Bradbury, Malcolm. "Style of Life, Style of Art and the American Novel in the Nineteen Twenties." *The American Novel in the Nineteen Twenties*. Stratford-upon-Avon Studies #13. Eds. Malcolm Bradbury and David Palmer. London: Edward Arnold; New York: Crane, Russak, 1971, pp. 11-36. Bradbury places West in a context of experimental writers whose style is a comment on the "loss of language in American society" (p. 18).

266. Carlisle, Henry. "The Comic Tradition." *The American Scholar*, 28 (Winter 1958-1959), 96-108. In discussing the popular demand for "palliative" comedy, Carlisle observes, "Conversely, Nathanael West and H. L. Mencken, not being 'diverting' writers, are sometimes thought not to be comic."

268. Cheney, Brainard. "Miss O'Connor Creates Unusual Humor Out of Ordinary Sin." *The Sewanee Review*, 71, no. 4 (Autumn 1963), 644-652. In commenting upon John Hawkes' article on Flannery O'Connor (see [302]), Cheney admonishes, "In a *tour de force* remarkable only for its fool-hardiness, in which he brackets her with Nathanael West, Mr. Hawkes speaks of her 'inverted attraction for the reality of an absurd condition'" (p. 646). Cheney disagrees that O'Connor can be compared to West in the use of a "diabolic voice." Claiming that O'Connor was driven by religious revolution in a secular world, the author maintains that West's novels contain no genuine religion. However, Cheney does not support this last contention as well as one would wish.

109. Fiedler, Leslie A. "The Breakthrough: The American Jewish Novelist and the Fictional Image of the Jew." *Recent American Fiction: Some Critical Views*, ed. Joseph J. Waldmeir. Boston: Houghton Mifflin Company, 1963, pp. 84-109. States Fiedler, in the American Jewish novel of the thirties and before, "Wherever one turns, there is the sense of a revelation, mystic and secular and terrible as the only possible climax: . . . the baffled and destructive attempt of Nathanael West's *Miss Lonely-hearts* to become Christ in a Christless world . . ." (p. 89). More specifically, Fiedler compares West to Henry Roth. "In West, the comic butt is raised to the level of Everybody's victim, the sceptical and unbelieved-in Christ of a faithless world; in Roth, the *shlemiel* is moved back to childhood, portrayed as the victim of circumstances he can never understand, only transcend" (p. 91).

164. Fiedler, Leslie A. "The Two Memories: Reflections on Writers and Writing in the Thirties." *Proletarian Writers of the Thirties*, ed. David Madden. Carbondale and Edwardsville: Southern Illinois University Press; London and Amsterdam: Feffer and Simons, 1968, pp. 3-25. Fiedler claims that West successfully avoided the political clichés of the proletarian writers of the thirties, since "apocalypse was his special province" (p. 8). Still, West was deeply involved in the issues of the age and felt somewhat embarrassed that his work did not reflect proletarian ideals. Fiedler concludes that every revolution ultimately fails at everything except terror anyway, and just as the Marquis de Sade was the "laureate of terror" of 1789, so to was West in 1935 (p. 18).

113. Fiedler, Leslie A. *Waiting For the End*. New York: Dell Publishing Company, 1964, P. 83. Fiedler describes the "special Jewish" vulgarity which is capable of "metaphysical transcendance" at the hands of skillful writers such as West.

120. Friedrich, Otto. "Ring Lardner." *American Writers: A Collection of Literary Biographies*, ed. Leonard Unger. New York: Charles Scribners' Sons, 1974. II: 436. Friedrich sees the modern tendency to view

laughter as "the ally of evil" to be characteristic of both West and Lardner. He examines in particular the beginning of *Miss Lonelyhearts* (p. 436)..

122. Gehman, Richard. "Introduction." *The Day of the Locust*, by Nathanael West. New York: The New Classics, 1950, pp. ix-xxiii. Gehman compares West to his social protest contemporaries--Farrell, Caldwell, Herbst, and others. Finds Gehman, "He too deplored the emptiness of Twentieth Century life in the United States, but he chose to reflect that life in terms not of characters who were consciously involved in a struggle, but of those who were unconsciously trapped--characters who were, in the blindness of their lives, so tragic as to be true comic figures" (p. ix).

132. Hauck, Richard Boyd. *A Cheerful Nihilism: Confidence and "The Absurd" in American Humorous Fiction*. Bloomington, London: Indiana University Press, 1971. "One finds grim humor based on a sense of the absurd throughout other kinds of American fiction, too--a touch of it in Charles Brockden Brown or in John Neal; a lot of it in Ellen Glasgow or Nathanael West" (p. 243).

302. Hawkes, John. "Flannery O'Connor's Devil." *The Sewanee Review*, 70, no. 3 (Summer 1962), 395-407. Hawkes conducts an extended comparison of West and O'Connor. States Hawkes, "I would propose that West and Flannery O'Connor are very nearly alone today in their pure creation of 'aesthetic authority', and would also propose, of course, that they are very nearly alone in their employment of the devil's voice as vehicle for their satire or what we may call their true (or accurate) vision of our godless actuality" (p. 396). Hawkes defines satire as the establishing of a dominant ideal by analogy and irony. He claims that the implied dominant ideal in West is the "release from the pains of sexual struggle and of the dead-end of an impossible striving toward God" (p. 396). He claims that O'Connor's dominant ideal is the conflict between the need for religion and the disbelief in it. He then examines in depth the polarity of religious positions expressed by the two.

304. Hawkes, John. "Notes on the Wild Goose Chase" [in a symposium with D. J. Hughes and Ihab Hassan--"Fiction Today"]. *Massachusetts Review*, 3 (Summer 1962), 784-788. States Hawkes, "Djuna Barnes, Flannery O'Connor, Nathanael West--at least these three disparate American writers may be said to come together in that rare climate of pure and immoral creation--are very nearly alone in their use of wit, their comic treatments of violence and their extreme detachment" (p. 787). West was best able to maintain detachment from the violence he described, and he, therefore, generates "the deepest novelistic sympathy of all" (p. 787).

311. Herbst, Josephine. "Nathanael West." *The Kenyon Review*, 23 (Autumn 1961), 611-630. Observes Herbst, "What he shared with Dostoevsky was a horror of the emptiness of sterile intellect, a hatred of dogma."

313. Hollis, C. Carroll. "Nathanael West and Surrealist Violence." *Fresco*, 7, no. 5 (1957), 5-13. Hollis compares West to Celine. "*Journey to the End of Night* (1932) and *Death on the Installment Plan* (1936) may outdo West in their scatalogical detail, but there is the same savage

disgust with sexual violence, that sole remnant of the life force in the contemporary world" (p. 11).

318. Kanters, Robert. "Nathanael West perdu et retrouvé." *Figaro Littéraire*, 12 (August 1961), 2. Kanters begins by placing West in a context of American writers who came to Paris after World War I. In particular, he compares West to Hemingway. After a few sentences on each of the novels, a more general comparison to Hemingway follows. Kanters infers that each may be taken as emblematic of his generation, but West is more appropriate for the iconoclastic, disillusioned youth of today than is Hemingway.

158. Levine, Paul. "Flannery O'Connor: The Soul of the Grotesque." *Minor American Novelists*, ed, Charles Alva Hoyt. Carbondale and Edwardsville: Southern Illinois University Press; London and Amsterdam: Feffer and Simons, Incorporated, 1970, pp. 95-117. In a comparison of O'Connor and West, Levine comments, O'Connor's "characters are invariably blind Betty's or fanatical Miss Lonelyhearts" (p. 99). Too, both authors create a "wasteland of spiritually displaced persons" (p. 99).

160. Lewis, R. W. B. "Days of Wrath and Laughter." *Trials of the Word: Essays in American Literature and the Humanistic Tradition*. New Haven and London: Yale University Press, 1965, pp. 184-236. Lewis compares Terry Southern's *Dr. Strangelove* to West's novels. He finds West's vision more profound because he better understands the Judeo/Christian apocalyptic tradition (p. 194).

3. Light, James F. *Nathanael West: An Interpretative Study*. 2nd ed. Evanston: Northwestern University Press, 1971. Light sees West's need to find order as the same principle underlying much Jewish literature: J. D. Salinger's *The Catcher in the Rye*, Herman Wouk's *The Caine Mutiny* and *Marjorie Morningstar*, Saul Bellow's *Dangling Man* and *Henderson the Rain King*. See pp. 149-150.

338. Lund, Mary Graham. "Backwards-Forwards in Forbidden Lands." *Western World Review*, 3, no. 1 (Spring 1968), 21-27. The main thrust of Lund's essay is a comparison of West's novels and McLuhan's books, with the main difference being the latter's greater popularity. Both "probe" instead of explain; both were influenced by Joyce; both believe that life is not best understood as being linear, but that events are simultaneous (p. 21). Almost all of the insight on West comes from Randall Reid (see [66]).

163. Madden, David. "Introduction." *Proletarian Writers of the Thirties*, ed. David Madden. Carbondale and Edwardsville: Southern Illinois University Press; London and Amsterdam: Feffer and Simons, Incorporated, 1968, pp. xv-xlii. Madden mentions West in connection with several non-proletarian writers of the thirties who still employed themes and techniques often associated more strictly with the proletarians (p. xxv).

170. Magny, Claude-Edmonde. *The Age of the American Novel: The Film Aesthetic of Fiction Between the Two Wars*, trans. Eleanor Hochman. New York: Frederick Ungar Publishing Company, 1972, pp. 146, 225, 226, 229,

232. Magny cites West as the victim of a common American occurrence--novelists who die young. Too, Magny says that West, Fitzgerald, and O'Hara show two sides to America--the White Anglo-Saxon Protestant paradise on the one hand, but the insecurity and boredom at its basis on the other (p. 229). Magny claims that, like Faulkner, West and others tried to construct a church out of the world around them, but only Faulkner succeeded.

172. Martin, Jay. "Ambrose Bierce." *The Comic Imagination in American Literature*, ed. Louis D. Rubin, Jr. New Brunswick, New Jersey: Rutgers University Press, 1973, pp. 195-206. Martin compares Bierce's humor to several others', including West's "attacks upon convention" (p. 197).

344. McLaughlin, Richard. "West of Hollywood." *Theatre Arts*, 35 (August 1951), 46-47, 93. McLaughlin recognizes that West's protest was private compared to other proletarian writers of his day.

179. Muller, Gilbert H. *Nightmares and Visions: Flannery O'Connor and the Catholic Grotesque*. Athens: University of Georgia Press, 1972, p. 5. Muller cites West as one of those authors in the tradition of the grotesque, along with Faulkner, in the thirties.

348. Nichols, James W. "West, Lewis, Pope, and Satiric Contrasts." *Satire Newsletter*, 5, no. 2 (Spring 1968), 119-122. Nichols examines how the three authors use the same device of setting one idea against another "to insinuate that something is wrong, blameworthy, or ridiculous" (p. 119). *A Cool Million*, for instance, contrasts the naiveté of Alger's world to the raw truth of West's vision.

185. O'Connor, William Van. *The Grotesque: An American Genre and Other Essays*. Carbondale: Southern Illinois University Press, 1962, pp. 6, 8-9, 12, 18, 21, 55-56. O'Connor observes that the grotesque seems to flourish among southern writers, but West also described it in New York City, Vermont, and Hollywood.

188. Parkes, David L. "West, Nathanael." *Twentieth Century Writing: A Reader's Guide to Contemporary Literature*, eds. Kenneth Richardson and R. Clive Willis. London [*etc.*]: Newnes Books, 1969, p. 642. Parkes maintains that West reminds one "irresistibly of Voltaire." West's novels "juxtapose coolness and passion in a grotesque exposure of the political, economic, and social bankruptcy of his society" (p. 642).

62. Podhoretz, Norman. "Nathanael West: A Particular Kind of Joking." *Nathanael West: A Collection of Critical Essays*. Englewood Cliffs, New Jersey: Prentice-Hall, Incorporated, 1971, pp. 154-160. Podhoretz compares West to Fitzgerald--"who lacked West's capacity for intelligent self-criticism"--and Hemingway--"whose view of life seems to me rather more limited than West's" (p. 154).

368. Richmond, Lee J. "A Time to Mourn and a Time to Dance: Horace McCoy's *They Shoot Horses, Don't They.*" *Twentieth Century Literature*, 17, no. 2 (April 1971), 91-100. States Richmond, "With the exception of Nathanael West's *Miss Lonelyhearts* (1933) and *The Day of the Locust*

(1939), McCoy's novel is indisputably the best example of absurdist existentialism in American fiction" (p. 91). Richmond says that McCoy, like West, was unaccepted in America but found a small reading public among French existentialists.

376. Schneider, Cyril M. "The Individuality of Nathanael West." *The Western Review*, 20, no. 1 (Autumn 1965), 7-28. Schneider sees West as a distinctly regional author because he was so out of the mainstream of thirties literature, primarily because he was too bitter for proletarian writers. Concludes Schneider, "Where the protest novelists of the time, like Dos Passos, Steinbeck, and the Marxists, saw disorganization and chaos as a result of clashing social groups, West saw it as a natural outcome of the failure of Twentieth Century America to provide an outlet for creativity, expression, and the development of latent artistic talent" (p. 10).

202. Schulz, Max F. *Black Humor of the Sixties: A Pluralistic Definition of Man and His World*. Athens: Ohio University Press, 1973, pp. 12, 17, 113. Observes Schulz, "The protagonist of Black Humor does not despair with the savage bitterness of Nathanael West's *Miss Lonelyhearts*" (p. 12). Schulz also examines the difference between the satirist and the black humorist. He finds that the satirist sees a false/true ordering of reality. States Schulz, "The illogicality of action rampant in the Horatio Alger world of West's *A Cool Million* does not ultimately deny an underlying faith in the Puritan ethic of industry and perserverence" (p. 17).

204. Scott, Nathan A., Jr. *Modern Literature and the Religious Frontier*. New York: Harper and Brothers, 1958, p. 74. States Scott, "'The distance of God'--this might, indeed, be regarded as a major lesson of many of the most memorable books of our time, of Céline's *Journey to the End of Night*, of Djuna Barnes' *Nightwood*, of Nathanael West's *Miss Lonelyhearts*, of Robert Penn Warren's *World Enough and Time*, and of André Malraux's *The Walnut Trees of Attenburg*" (p. 74).

385. Skerrett, Joseph Taylor, Jr. "Dostoievsky, Nathanael West, and Some Contemporary American Fiction." *The University of Dayton Review*, 4, no 1 (Winter 1967), 23-36. Skerrett compares West's use of surrealistic techniques to James Purdy's in *Malcolm*. Both Miss Lonelyhearts and Malcolm are Christ figures. Clarity, documentary detachment, and deadpan satire are the major points of comparison between the two writers, feels Skerrett.

209. Swingewood, Alan. "Alienation, Reification, and the Novel: Sartre, Camus, and Nathanael West." *The Sociology of Literature*, by Diana T. Laurenson and Alan Swingewood. New York: Schocken Books, 1972, pp. 207-248. Swingewood explains that Sartre, Camus, and West "experienced alienation as nausea and the absurd, unlike earlier writers such as Fitzgerald, to whom life is meaningful despite failure" (p. 215). Too, "When Sartre and West tear away the apparently ordered nature of reality to disclose the unreason and chaos beneath, they do so within a specific socio-economic setting; they are novelists not of the human condition as such but of its specific contemporary form" (p. 216).

212. Walker, Franklin. *A Literary History of Southern Claifornia.*
Chronicles of California Series. Berkeley and Los Angeles: University
of California Press, 1950, p. 259. Walker lists West among those California writers who wrote on regional themes. He calls West a promising
writer who died young.

218. Wells, Walker. *Tycoons and Locusts: A Regional Look at Hollywood
Fiction of the 1930's.* Carbondale and Edwardsville: Southern Illinois
University Press; London and Amsterdam: Feffer and Simons, 1973,
pp. 49-70. Wells discusses West along with Schulberg, Fitzgerald, O'Hara,
and others as what he terms "Southland" writers.

225. Wiggins, Robert A. "Ambrose Bierce." *American Writers: A Collection
of Literary Biographies,* ed. Leonard Unger. New York: Charles Scribner's Sons, 1974. I: 190, 211. Wiggins claims that the techniques
developed by Bierce anticipated those of many major writers, including
West (p. 190). He also places West in a context of American writers
who had a markedly "dark side" in their art (p. 211).

228. Wilson, Edmund. *A Literary Chronicle: 1920-1950.* New York:
Doubleday and Company, Incorporated, 1956, p. 249. States Wilson,
"Both West and Fitzgerald were writers of a conscience and with natural
gifts rare enough in America or anywhere; and their failure to get the
best out of their best years may certainly be laid partly to Hollywood,
with its already appalling record of talent depraved and wasted" (p. 249).

B) *The Dream Life of Balso Snell*

21. Locklin, Gerald. "The Journey Into the Microcosm." *Nathanael West:
The Cheaters and The Cheated, A Collection of Critical Essays,* ed.
David Madden. Deland, Florida: Everett/Edwards, Incorporated, 1973,
pp. 23-56. Locklin claims that the epigraph to West's first novel
(from Anaxagoras) contains within it the multiple themes to be examined
in the book, just as the first two pages of Joyce's *Portrait of the
Artist as a Young Man* does. Locklin concludes that West--in techniques
used throughout the book--is both imitating and parodying Joyce.

335. Lorch, Thomas M. "The Inverted Structure of *Balso Snell.*" *Studies
in Short Fiction,* 4, no. 1 (Fall 1966), 33-41. Lorch claims that the
novel is West's *A Portrait of the Artist,* but less tender than Joyce's
or Fitzgerald's *This Side of Paradise.* (See p. 40).

66. Reid, Randall. *The Fiction of Nathanael West: No Redeemer, No
Promised Land.* Chicago and London: University of Chicago Press, 1967.
Reid compares *The Dream Life of Balso Snell* to Cabell's *Jurgen:* "the
school of affected paganism--genteel eroticism--playful irony--senti-
mental regret--Olympian resignation" (p. 15).

C) *Miss Lonelyhearts*

251. Balke, Betty Tevis. "Some Judeo-Christian Themes Seen Through the Eyes of J. D. Salinger and Nathanael West." *Cresset*, 31, no. 7 (1968), 14-18. Balke compares *Miss Lonelyhearts* and Salinger's *Franny and Zooie* and finds that, compared to Salinger, West was "loud and vehement in denying his heritage" (p. 14). Too, she finds that frequent references to Christ form a major theme in both authors' works.

85. Bluefarb, Sam. *The Escape Motif in the American Novel: Mark Twain to Richard Wright*. Columbus: Ohio State University Press, 1972, pp. 51, 139. Bluefarb compares George Willard in Sherwood Anderson's *Winesburg, Ohio* to Miss Lonelyhearts, but finds George incapable of making himself a Christ figure (p. 51).

264. Bush, C. W. "This Stupendous Fabric: The Metaphysics of Order in Melville's *Pierre* and Nathanael West's *Miss Lonelyhearts*." *Journal of American Studies*, 1, no. 2 (October 1967), 269-274. Bush begins by quoting the painter Washington Allston on the artist's need to create a visible incarnation that embodies the essence of the artist's scheme of society. He then examines West and Melville to show how this artistic principle operates. States Bush, "The nature of this 'stupendous fabric' where sense makes visible a non-sensuous object is a paradigm not only of the act of creation but of a plot structure which occurs again and again in American fiction" (p. 270). Pierre's created fabric suffers a jolt when he finds and falls in love with the illegitimate daughter of his dead father. His ordered, traditional, genteel life is suddenly insecure. So too, "Miss Lonelyhearts is also at a crisis: the old Christ myth he has constructed to keep himself sane and the readers of his newspaper column happy appears insufficient and hollow. The guilt experienced by both heroes leads them to reconstruct their roles in terms of a new order. In both cases the attempt leads to death" (p. 270).

1. Comerchero, Victor. *Nathanael West: The Ironic Prophet*. Syracuse: Syracuse University Press, 1964. Comerchero compares *Miss Lonelyhearts* and Sophocles' *Oedipus Rex* (pp. 84-85). He does not, however, claim Sophocles' play to be a source of West's novel.

121. Galloway, David D. *The Absurd Hero in American Fiction*. Revised edition. Austin and London: University of Texas Press, 1970, p. 93. Galloway compares Asa Lowenthal's "vision of suffering and responsibility" in Saul Bellow's *The Victim* to the same experience in *Miss Lonelyhearts*.

313. Hollis, C. Carroll. "Nathanael West and Surrealist Violence." *Fresco*, 7, no. 5 (1957), 5-13. Hollis compares West to Graham Greene. Finds that both author's pursue the Christian paradox of Christianity being a preparation for death, not life.

314. Hollis, C. Carroll. "Nathanael West and the 'Lonely Crowd'." *Thought*, 33 (Autumn 1958), 398-416. See [313] for a similar discussion by Hollis dealing with West's and Graham Greene's handling of the paradox of Christianity being a preparation for death, not life. Here, Hollis

also compares West to Céline. Céline's cynical conclusion "is almost true for West. The difference is that West has found that sufficient torture of the ex-Christian will force him back to a faith which the world may call insane but for which he can die" (p. 401).

159. Lewis, R. W. B. "The Aspiring Clown." *Learners and Discerners: A Newer Criticism*, ed. Robert Scholes. Charlottesville: The University Press of Virginia, 1964, pp. 61-108. In a discussion of the clown figure in Hart Crane's poetry, Lewis cites West as contributing "unforgettably to the modern image of the tortured clown in *Miss Lonelyhearts* of 1933, but in *The Day of the Locust* (1939), he suggested less appalling, more beguiling, and perhaps more mature aspects of the clown figure" (p. 103). Miss Lonelyhearts is hopelessly absurd, yet Harry Greener is a clown figure who represents in microcosm the post-World War II novelists' way of confronting the world--as a shuffling clown whose attempts at gaining affection are met with ridicule and a kick in the stomach, yet he achieves "an odd victory, oddly arrived at through a sort of comic humility and the instinct of love" (p. 104).

324. Lewis, R. W. B. "Hart Crane and the Clown Tradition." *The Massachusetts Review*, 4 (Summer 1963), 745-767. See [159] for a similar discussion. Lewis examines the artist as comedian as a tradition drawn upon by Hart Crane in his poem, "Chaplinesque." He sees West in that tradition, along with Wallace Stevens, E. E. Cummings, and Henry Miller. He finds Miss Lonelyhearts the perfect example of the tortured clown (such as Crane depicts in the earlier sections of "Chaplinesque"), while Harry Greener in *The Day of the Locust* represents a more mature vision: a clown/artist who is still tortured for his efforts but manages to take away an "odd Victory" (p. 765).

118. Malin, Irving. "Flannery O'Connor and the Grotesque." *The Added Dimension: The Art and Mind of Flannery O'Connor*, eds. Melvin J. Friedman and Lewis A. Lawson. New York" Fordham University Press, 1966, pp. 108-122. Malin briefly compares O'Connor's *Wise Blood* to West's *Miss Lonelyhearts*. He concludes that both employ black humor, but O'Connor abandons it and begins to "preach" to the reader (p. 112).

174. May, John R. "Words and Deeds: Apocalyptic Judgment in Faulkner, West, and O'Connor." *Toward a New Earth: Apocalypse in the American Novel*. Notre Dame, London: University of Notre Dame Press, 1972, p. 40. May says that Faulkner's *As I Lay Dying*, West's *Miss Lonelyhearts*, and O'Connor's *The Violent Bear It Away* do not have the cosmic scope of nineteenth century fiction, but "they employ an intensity and often subtlety of imagery" (p. 40) not seen before or since.

359. Pinsker, Sanford. "Charles Dickens and Nathanael West: Great Expectations Unfulfilled." *Topic*, 18 (1969), 40-52. Pinsker compares *Miss Lonelyhearts* to J. D. Salinger's *The Catcher in the Rye*, where the world is a mere straw man for Holden Caulfield to react against. However, in West's novel, the world does not allow Miss Lonelyhearts to live with his Christ vision. In comparing *Miss Lonelyhearts* to *Great Expectations*, Pinsker observes that both authors lack the humor usually associated with satire. Both novels explore the difference

in what one expects from the world and what one gets.

54. Ratner, Marc L. "Anywhere Out of This World: Baudelaire and Nathanael West." *Nathanael West: A Collection of Critical Essays*, ed. Jay Martin. Englewood Cliffs, New Jersey: Prentice-Hall, Incorporated, 1971, pp. 102-109. In what could as easily be taken as a source study as comparative criticism, Ratner links the economy and directness of *Miss Lonelyhearts* to the French symbolists, particularly Baudelaire. The primary thesis of the essay is that "the pivotal experience of *Miss Lonelyhearts*--the discussion in chapter seven of the alternatives of escape"--finds its inspiration in Baudelaire's poem, "Anywhere Out of This World" (p. 103). Ratner offers a close comparison of the structure and content of the two works. Of the possible optimistic interpretation of the final scene of *Miss Lonelyhearts*, Ratner says, "However, despite his plans for the future, he has become impossible for the world just as the world has become impossible for him" (p. 108). Thus, like Baudelaire, West sees all attempts to escape the world as fruitless.

66. Reid, Randall. *The Fiction of Nathanael West: No Redeemer, No Promised Land*. Chicago and London: University of Chicago Press, 1967. Reid compares the *menage a trois* grouping of Doyle, Mrs. Doyle, and Miss Lonelyhearts to a similar one of Wilson, Myrtle Wilson, and Gatsby in *The Great Gatsby*. "In both novels a crippled or devitalized cuckold is married to a vulgar but vital woman, and in both novels the cuckold mistakenly kills the 'spiritual' hero in revenge for his wife's betrayal" (p. 98). Another interesting comparison is to the wordless novels in woodcuts of Lynd Ward (especially *Madman's Drum*).

367. Richardson, Robert D. *"Miss Lonelyhearts." The University Review*, 32, no. 2 (December 1966), 151-157. Of the religious theme of the novel Richardson observes, "The shrill aetheism is much like Twain's violence over Christian Science; it is the protest of the more than half believer" (p. 155). Yet Richardson never tell us how this conclusion helps us to interpret the end of the novel.

384. Simonson, Harold P. "California, Nathanael West, and the Journey's End." *The Closed Frontier: Studies in American Literary Tragedy*. New York [*etc.*]: Holt, Rinehart, and Winston, Incorporated, 1970, pp. 99-124. Simonson's essay includes a fine comparison between Melville's *Pierre* and *Miss Lonelyhearts*. Miss Lonelyhearts, like Pierre, dedicates himself to the chronometrical standard (ideal) rather than the sublunary standard. Shrike represents the latter (p. 113).

385. Skerrett, Joseph Taylor, Jr. "Dostoievsky, Nathanael West, and Some Contemporary American Fiction." *The University of Dayton Review*, 4, no. 1 (Winter 1967), 23-36. Included is a comparison of Miss Lonely-hearts to several of Dostoevsky's heroes.

390. Thale, Mary. "The Moviegoer of the 1950's." *Twentieth Century Literature*, 14, no. 2 (July 1968), 84-89. Thale compares West's *Miss Lonelyhearts* to Walker Percy's *The Moviegoer*. Both novels were ignored by large segments of the reading public, though both were critically praised. Too, both novels concern urban men in search of something to

make life significant. Each examines and rejects "art, enlightened hedonism, non-urban simplicity" (p. 84). Each ends his search in insanity. Included incidentally (though at some length) is a comparison of West's novel and Samuel Johnson's *Rasselas*. Thale concludes that Shrike and Miss Lonelyhearts, like Imlac and Rasselas "are the same characters at different stages of development" (p. 84). In the same way, Percy's two protagonists merge into one in the person of Binx Bolling.

12. Volpe, Edmund L. "The Waste Land of Nathanael West." *Twentieth Century Interpretations of* Miss Lonelyhearts, ed. Thomas H. Jackson. Englewood Cliffs, New Jersey: Prentice-Hall, Incorporated, 1971, pp. 81-92. Volpe believes that *Miss Lonelyhearts* "is the answer of the 1930's to the great poem of the 1920's--T. S. Eliot's *The Waste Land*" (p. 81). Volpe finds the aridity of the poem due to the aridity of man's soul. Therefore, it is within man's power to regenerate the spiritless world. The world itself has an order, founded in the traditions of the past. The same is not the case in West. There nature is naturally orderless and man "appears as a misfit in an undirected universe" (p. 82). Thus, "The heroic ages Eliot recalls in his poem are for West simply periods in which man's illusions and dreams were more powerful, and therefore more effective in disguising the realities" (pp. 82-83).

228. Wilson, Edmund. *A Literary Chronicle: 1920-1950*. New York: Doubleday and Company, 1956, p. 358. Wilson says that Evelyn Waugh's *The Loved One* recalls both *Miss Lonelyhearts* and *The Day of the Locust*.

D) *A Cool Million*

84. Blotner, Joseph. *The Modern American Political Novel, 1900-1960*. Austin and London: University of Texas Press, 1966, pp. 40, 145. Blotner compares the diction in Samuel G. Blythe's *The Fakers* to West's in *A Cool Million* (p. 40). Also compared is the anonymous author's use of clichés in *Philip Dru, Administrator* and West's clichés in *A Cool Million* (p. 145).

279. Edenbaum, Robert I. "Dada and Surrealism in the United States: A Literary Instance." *Arts in Society*, 5, no. 1 (1968), 114-125. Edenbaum compares Lemuel Pitkin to the poet in Apollinaire's *Le Poete Assassine*, in that they have similar deformities. Connected with this is the dadaist techniques of imagery: scatology, obscenity, and sacrilege.

280. Edenbaum, Robert I. "A Surfeit of Shoddy: Nathanael West's *A Cool Million*." *Southern Humanities Review*, 2, no. 4 (Fall 1968), pp. 427-439. Edenbaum begins with a comparison of West's novel and Voltaire's *Candide*--fairly detailed.

121. Galloway, David D. *The Absurd Hero in American Fiction*. Revised edition. Austin and London: University of Texas Press, 1970, p. 95. Galloway briefly compares Saul Bellow's Augie March to Lemuel Pitkin in *A Cool Million*.

297. Graham, John. "Struggling Upward: *The Minister's Charge* and
A Cool Million." Canadian Review of American Studies, 4 (1974), 184-196.
Graham compares West's *A Cool Million* not only to Horatio Alger's novels
but also to William Dean Howells' *The Minister's Charge; or, The Apprenticeship of Lemuel Barker* (1887). States Graham, "Unlike Alger, both Howells
and West emphasize the human costs implicit in the illusion that ambition, hard work, and thrift will automatically bring success" (p. 184).
He concludes that West's style is deliberately antithetical to Howell's.

117. Hoffman, Frederick J. "The Search for Redemption: Flannery
O'Connor's Fiction." *The Added Dimension: The Art and Mind of Flannery
O'Connor*, eds. Melvin J. Friedman and Lewis A Lawson. New York: Fordham
University Press, 1966, pp. 32-48. Hoffman compares Hazel Motes of
O'Connor's *Wise Blood* to both Miss Lonelyhearts and Lemuel Pitkin (p. 38,
continued on p. 47n).

158. Levine, Paul. "Flannery O'Connor: The Soul of the Grotesque."
Minor American Novelists, ed. Charles Alva Hoyt. Carbondale and Edwardsville: Southern Illinois University Press; London and Amsterdam: Feffer
and Simons, Incorporated, 1970, pp. 95-117. Levine compares O'Connor's
"A Late Encounter With the Enemy" to *A Cool Million* and finds that both
combine social and moral insights with grotesque distortion of the real
world (pp. 101-102).

160. Lewis, R. W. B. "Days of Wrath and Laughter." *Trials of the
Word: Essays in American Literature and the Humanistic Tradition*. New
Haven and London: Yale University Press, 1965, pp. 184-236. Lewis
compares the dismantling of Benny Profane in Pynchon's *V* to the similar
dismantling of Lemuel Pitkin in *A Cool Million*.

341. Matthews, T. S. "A Gallery of New Novels." *The New Republic*,
79 (18 July 1934), 271-272. In a one paragraph review of *A Cool Million*,
Matthews compares West's novel to Voltaire's *Candide*. Concludes Matthews,
"It is true that 'Candide' is an etching whose lines are more subtle
and more biting than the broad strokes of 'A Cool Million', but Mr.
Nathanael West has the heart of the matter in him" (p. 271).

348. Nichols, James W. "Nathanael West, Sinclair Lewis, Alexander Pope
and Satiric Contrasts." *Satire Newsletter*, 5 (Spring 1968), 119-122.
States Nichols, "The satiric device that *A Cool Million, Babbitt*, and
The Rape of the Lock use is the basic and very common device of playing
one set of ideas or values against another to insinuate that something
is wrong, blameworthy, or ridiculous" (p. 119). Nichols draws on Douglas
Shepard's "Nathanael West Rewrites Horatio Alger, Jr." (see [383]) for
much of his comment on West.

357. Petrullo, Helen B. "Clichés and Three Political Satires of the
Thirties." *Satire Newsletter*, 8, no. 2 (Spring 1971), 109-117. Petrullo examines West's *A Cool Million*, Sinclair Lewis' *It Can't Happen
Here*, and James Thurber's *The Last Flower*, noting the theme in each
of "uncritical masses who make possible the rise of dictatorships by
responding uncritically to meaningless clichés" (p. 109). Each author
examines through satiric fantasy an impossible world. The type of satire
employed in West's novel reflects its creation during Hitler's rise to

power and the Great Depression. Petrullo claims that the novel was not as popular as similar ones because it lacked focus: through cliché, all was reduced--both the trivial and the important--to the same level of abstraction.

359. Pinsker, Sanford. "Charles Dickens and Nathanael West: Great Expectations Unfulfilled." *Topic*, 18 (1969), pp. 40-52. Pinsker sees a parallel between *A Cool Million* and the "America" chapters of *Martin Chuzzlewit*: an attack on the Eden image of America.

202. Schulz, Max F. *Black Humor of the Sixties: A Pluralistic Definition of Man and His World*. Athens: Ohio University Press, 1973, p. 113. Schulz sees Richard Wright in *The Wig* reaching the same conclusion about patterning oneself after a national ideal that West does in *A Cool Million*. Observes Schulz about Lester in *The Wig*, "To pattern himself thus is to dehumanize himself. This is an insight Nathanael West dramatized in his satire on the Horatio Alger ideal in *A Cool Million*" (p. 113).

383. Shepard, Douglas. "Nathanael West Rewrites Horatio Alger." *Satire Newsletter*, 3, no. 1 (Fall 1965), 13-28. In what could as easily be considered a source study (this essay is also discussed in that chapter), Shepard offers an in depth examination of West using Horatio Alger as a brunt of satire. States Shepard, "Clearly the satirical thrust of the plot line depends on its inverting the usual Alger rags-to-riches-through-honest-effort pattern" (p. 13). West also parodies Alger's style. Most of the essay is taken up with a two column juxtaposition of passages from the two authors.

384. Simonson, Harold P. "California, Nathanael West, and the Journey's End." *The Closed Frontier: Studies in American Literary Tragedy*. New York [*etc.*]: Holt, Rinehart, and Winston, Incorporated, 1970, pp. 99-124. Simonson compares Lemuel Pitkin to Twain's Huck Finn at some length and concludes that Lemuel never has a means of escape, as does Huck.

E) *The Day of the Locust*

232. Aaron, Daniel. "Writing For Apocalypse." *Hudson Review*, 3 (Winter 1951), 634-636. Aaron finds that *The Day of the Locust* is somewhat similar to the proletarian novels of the thirties, but in contrast, West was "saved from being naive and doctrinaire by his compulsive irony, by his delight in the incongruous, and perhaps most of all by his profound disgust with life itself" (p. 634). Aaron compares West's last novel to Waugh's *The Loved One* and Fitzgerald's *The Last Tycoon*. All are arraignments of Hollywood, but West, rather than being witty or romantic, is despairing. Aaron feels that West lacked the comic detachment of the true satirist, and the novel is a failure because the images of the cock fight and the "dream dump" of Hollywood are never related. "No conscious idea or metaphor holds this book together" (p. 636), claims Aaron. Too, Homer Simpson "is nothing more than a botched

reworking of Sherwood Anderson's grotesque in his story, 'Hands'" (p. 636).

71. Allen, Walter. *Traditions and Dreams:A Critical Survey of British and American Fiction From 1920 to the Present Day*. Middlesex, England: Penguin Books, 1965, p. 192. Allen compares *The Day of the Locust* to John Steinbeck's *The Grapes of Wrath*. Steinbeck's "Okies" were in search of the Good Earth, but West's characters "crawled from Iowa to die in an exaccerbated boredom in a Never-Never land that has deceived them" (p. 192).

72. Allen, Walter. *The Urgent West: The American Dream and Modern Man*. New York: E. P. Dutton and Company, Incorporated, 1969, pp. 217-219. See [71] for a similar discussion by Allen. Here Allen again compares *The Day of the Locust* to Steinbeck's *The Grapes of Wrath*. States Allen, "Whereas Steinbeck's 'Okies' flood into California in search of the good earth, West's anonymous crowds are retired people . . . who have migrated from the Middle West, driven, as the title of the novel suggests, by an instinctive urging to California, to wait for death there in a sort of indignant boredom in what has proven to be a Never-Never land, a phony paradise" (p. 218). Allen claims that West belongs in a school of writers-- like Ralph Ellison (*Invisible Man*) and Joseph Heller (*Catch-22*)--motivated by "the vision of a ludicrous catastrophe" (p. 218).

233. Alter, Robert. "The Apocalyptic Temper." *Commentary*, 41, no. 6 (June 1966), 61-66. Alter describes in pejorative terms the literature of apocalypse, which offers "nothing but revelations of what already is known" (p. 62). He compares *The Day of the Locust* to E. M. Forster's *Howard's End* to illustrate his contention. We are not as interested in Homer Simpson as in Leonard Bast, claims Alter, because the details of Homer's life are not as important, because "they are so simple and so known--Homer is merely the perfect product and paradigm of American society's insidious sterility" (p. 63). Alter concludes, "*The Day of the Locust* is a brilliant book, but its achievement is of a lesser order-- finally, I think because of the schematic imagination which its apocalyptic assumptions impose" (p. 63). Also included are briefer comparisons to Ellison, Barth, Heller, and Pynchon. Some fine insights offered here, but unfortunately not on West.

34. Apple, Max. "History and Case History in Babel's *Red Cavalry* and West's *The Day of the Locust*." *Nathanael West: The Cheaters and the Cheated, A Collection of Critical Essays*, ed. David Madden. Deland, Florida: Everett/Edwards, Incorporated, 1973, pp. 235-248. In a comparison of the two works, Apple finds that the most striking similarity is between the "precision of their syntax and the imagistic speed of their sentences" (pp. 235-236). Both authors' styles come from the contrast between the "physical awesomeness of events and the paltry resources of language" (p. 236). Apple claims that a certain playfulness is evident in West's syntax. Too, West does not fall back on literary tradition, like Babel, nor does he attempt to justify violence.

36. Bowden, James H. "No Redactor, No Reward." *Nathanael West: The Cheaters and the Cheated, A Collection of Critical Essays*, ed. David Madden. Deland, Florida: Everett/Edwards, Incorporated, 1973, pp.

283-298. Bowden compares *Miss Lonelyhearts* to Ecclesiastes (without the "Summing Up of the Duty of Man") and *The Day of the Locust* to Revelations (with no hint of heavenly reward for the faithful).

274. Collins, Carvel. "Nathanael West's *The Day of the Locust* and *Sanctuary.*" *Faulkner Studies*, 2, no. 2 (Summer 1953), 23-24. Collins sees parallel themes in the two novels--the "authors' disgust with a machine-made society" (p. 23). There is also a close parallel between Faulkner's Popeye and Earl Shoop of West's novel. Collins cites other parallels, but admits that they are tenuous. He concludes that, overall, *The Day of the Locust* is more depressing and shocking than Faulkner's novel. But in West is no character so admirable as the "dignified, stoical, realistic Ruby Lamar, who gives to *Sanctuary* a tragic air above the shock and corncob scandal" (p. 24).

112. Fiedler, Leslie. *The Return of the Vanishing American.* New York: Stein and Day, 1968, pp. 144, 147-149, 150. Fiedler maintains that Hemingway's *The Torrents of Spring* and West's *The Day of the Locust* are ways of redeeming the Western for American literature (pp. 143-144).

121. Galloway, David D. *The Absurd Hero in American Fiction.* Revised edition. Austin and London: University of Texas Press, 1970, p. 135. Galloway sees Faye Greener in *The Day of the Locust* as an ancestor of Saul Bellow's Madeline in *Herzog.*

290. Galloway, David, D. "Nathanael West's Dream Dump." *Critique: Studies in Modern Fiction*, 6, no. 3 (Winter 1963-64), 46-64. Galloway first compares *The Day of the Locust* to Fitzgerald's *The Great Gatsby.* "West has gone farther than Fitzgerald in dehumanizing the contemporary female, but the fey heroine dominates the macabre development of both *The Great Gatsby* and *The Day of the Locust*" (p. 60). Galloway next compares the lives and attitudes of the two authors (pp. 60-61), followed by a comparison of *The Day of the Locust* and Fitzgerald's *The Last Tycoon* (pp. 61-63). Galloway claims that West influenced Fitzgerald on the writing of this last novel. Galloway concludes that Fitzgerald "and West created sympathetic monographs of a world which, by distorting and negating man's needs and desires, leaves him a senseless shell, unable to fulfill his dreams" (p. 63).

126. Greenberg, Alvin. "Choice: Ironic Alternatives in the World of the Contemporary American Novel." *American Dreams, American Nightmares*, ed. David Madden. Carbondale and Edwardsville: Southern Illinois University Press; London and Amsterdam: Feffer and Simons, Incorporated, 1970, pp. 175-187. Greenberg discusses *The Day of the Locust* in a context of works--such as *The Sound and the Fury, The Sun Also Rises, The Man With the Golden Arm*--which explore "a world running down, in the midst of which stands the often solitary individual" in a process of predeter- mined disintegration (p. 176). In only *The Day of the Locust*, however, does the dream of demonic apocalypse occur (pp. 183-184).

139. Hoffman, Frederick J. *The Modern Novel in America 1900-1950.* Chicago: Henry Regnery Company, 1951, pp. 115n, 129. Hoffman compares West's use of architectural descriptions in *The Day of the Locust* to

Sinclair Lewis' description of the Zenith Athletic Club (p. 115n).
Too, Hoffman claims that *The Day of the Locust* is a more successful picture
of Hollywood than Fitzgerald's *The Last Tycoon* (p. 129).

154. Korges, James. "Erskine Caldwell." *American Writers: A Collection
of Literary Biographies*, ed. Leonard Unger. New York: Charles Scribner's
Sons, 1974. I: 298. In comparing Caldwell's *God's Little Acre* to
The Day of the Locust Korges observes, "It is a novel of rich sexuality,
sexuality being, in this symbolic landscape, as grim and spectral as the
Hollywood landscape of Nathanael West's *The Day of the Locust*" (p. 298).

159. Lewis, R. W. B. "The Aspiring Clown." *Learners and Discerners:
A Newer Criticism*, ed. Robert Scholes. Charlottesville: The University
Press of Virginia, 1964, pp. 61-108. In comparing Hart Crane's and
West's use of the clown figure, Lewis observes that Harry Greener is a
clown figure who represents in microcosm the post-World War II novelists'
way of confronting the world, as a shuffling clown whose attempts at
gaining affection are met with a kick in the stomach, yet who achieves
"an odd victory, oddly arrived at through a sort of comic humility and
the instinct of love" (p. 104).

176. Millgate, Michael. *American Social Fiction: James to Cozzens*.
Edinburgh and London: Oliver and Boyd, 1964, pp. 154-156, 163-164.
Millgate compares *The Day of the Locust* to Evelyn Waugh's *The Loved One*,
but finds the latter more narrow in scope.

33. Mueller, Lavonne. "Malamud and Nathanael West: Tyranny of the
Dream Dump." *Nathanael West: The Cheaters and the Cheated, A Collection
of Critical Essays*. Deland, Florida: Everett/Edwards, Incorporated,
1973, pp. 221-234. Mueller compares Malamud's *The Natural* to *The Day of
the Locust* and finds, "Both writers describe mindless fans who are conditioned into automated spectators and the hoodwinked by illusions,
drugged by yellow journalism, the tabloids, the cinema, and headed almost
willingly and happily to certain disaster" (p. 221). In both novels
the crowd's created heroes must perform to a certain American code of
success. Too, both worlds are filled with grotesques, and Mueller feels
that Malamud's Ray is in his own way an artist, like Tod Hackett.
Memo Paris may also parallel West's Faye Greener in that both are sexually
alluring but frightening. Finally, both novels have dwarves as their
most grotesque characters.

189. Parry, Idris. "Kafka, Gogol, and Nathanael West." *Kafka: A
Collection of Critical Essays*, ed. Ronald Gray. Englewood Cliffs, New
Jersey: Prentice-Hall, Incorporated, 1962, pp. 85-90. Parry compares
Homer Simpson of *The Day of the Locust* to Gregor Samsa of Kafka's *The
Metamorphosis* and to Kovalyov of Gogol's "The Nose." He finds Homer's
hands, like Kovalyov's nose, a symbol of repression. West receives less
attention then the other two writers in this essay.

352. Pearce, Richard. "'Pylon', 'Awake and Sing!' and the Apocalyptic
Imagination of the 30's." *Criticism*, 13, no. 2 (Spring 1971), 131-142.
Pearce claims that the fear of apocalypse expressed by such thirties
writers as Henry Roth, West, Faulkner, Dos Passos, and Odets parallels

our current fear; thus, this generation is most capable of interpreting the thirties. Pearce compares *The Day of the Locust* to *The Great Gatsby* to show the change in attitude between the twenties and the thirties. In Fitzgerald's novel, a romantic view of the new world is the goal, and the romantic protagonist is finally destroyed. Therefore, the novel demonstrates a recognition of lost values. In *The Day of the Locust*, the goal itself is Hollywood, but the motive power is never clear. The novel ends in apocalypse: the destruction of the characters and their world. Pearce concludes that West accurately evokes the irrational violence of the apocalypse, but not the forces underlying it.

358. Phillips, Robert S. "F [*sic*] and The Day of the Locust." *Fitzgerald Newsletter*, 15 (Fall 1961), 68-69. Phillips briefly explores the similarity between *The Day of the Locust* and Fitzgerald's *Tender is the Night*. In particular, he notes both authors' use of the "masquerade" theme, or the distance between reality and illusion. Too, both plumb the "falsity of our present values" (p. 68). Phillips does not assume that one novel was a source for the other.

89. Piper, Henry Dan. "Social Criticism in the American Novel of the Nineteen Thirties." *The American Novel in the Nineteen Thirties*, eds. Malcolm Bradbury and David Palmer. London: Edward Arnold; New York: Crane, Russak, 1971, pp. 59-84. Piper says that the measure of success of Fitzgerald's *The Last Tycoon* is best guaged by comparing it to *The Day of the Locust*, but he fails to give us the result of such a comparison.

190. Powell, Lawrence Clark. "*The Day of the Locust*: Nathanael West." *California Classics: The Creative Literature of the Golden State*. Los Angeles: The Ward Ritchie Press, 1971, pp. 344-356. Powell compares West's novel to an earlier "sugar-coated" Hollywood novel--*Merton of the Movies*, by Harry Leon Wilson. Both concern a Hollywood that lures people, only to destroy their dreams. However, Wilson's characters are not destroyed by their new knowledge as West's are. Concludes Powell, West "perceived Hollywood and its product as the pure epitome of all that is wrong with life in the United States" (p. 345).

66. Reid, Randall. *The Fiction of Nathanael West: No Redeemer, No Promised Land*. Chicago and London: University of Chicago Press, 1967. Reid finds a correspondence to Greek theatre in general in West's novels and to Euripides in particular in *The Day of the Locust*. Concludes Reid, "The Euripidean sense of disproportion is everywhere in West" (p. 124). Reid examines in depth West's use of song and dance in the novel. He also traces the "immortal whore" quality of Faye Greener to Baudelaire and Huysmans (p. 130 *et passim*). A final comparison is the choreographed pattern of West's novel to a similar effect in Sherwood Anderson's *Winesburg, Ohio*. In both novels the characters "are like figures who briefly detach themselves from a crowd and dance to the center of the stage, then retreat back into the anonymous mass which fills the wings and overbalances the central action" (p. 139). Too, West intensifies Anderson's use of the thwarted climax.

421. Widmer, Kingsley. "The Hollywood Image." *Coastlines*, 5, no. 1 (1961), 17-27. Widmer examines the distance between fact and fantasy as a prevailing theme in Hollywood novels. After commenting on West's use

of the mock-heroic in *The Day of the Locust* and West's use of "fantastic disproportion" (p. 18), the author claims that West and other Hollywood novelists--such as Mailer and Wright Morris--adore the Hollywood "bitch" in their own way as much as the adolescent does.

30. Widmer, Kingsley. "The Last Masquerade." *Nathanael West: The Cheaters and the Cheated, A Collection of Critical Essays*, ed. David Madden. Deland, Florida: Everett/Edwards, Incorporated, 1973, pp. 179-193. Widmer places *The Day of the Locust* in a context of Hollywood novels. "The Hollywood novelists force us to see symbols and morals as merely props to other props." He concludes that these novels are not so much satire as exposé.

228. Wilson, Edmund. *A Literary Chronicle: 1920-1950*. New York: Doubleday and Company, Incorporated, 1956, p. 241. Wilson discusses *The Day of the Locust* in a context of Hollywood novels--"a novel on a higher level of writing than any other I have mentioned" (p. 241).

XII. General Criticism

        This chapter is admittedly a catch-all, containing just about any
critical view of West's work not dealt with in the previous eleven. The
reader may expect to find here books, material in books, articles in
periodicals, and reviews. Annotations will center on "pure" criticisms,
if such truly exist: that is, critical views which do not make overt
use of biographical criticism, historical criticism, source studies,
etc. Once again, the large amount of works annotated here has forced me
to divide this chapter into five sections: one for West's canon in general, and a section for each of the novels.

                A) General Criticisms of West's Canon

231. Aaron, Daniel. "'The Truly Monstrous': A Note on Nathanael West."
Partisan Review, 14, no. 1 (1947), 98-106. Aaron says that *The Dream Life
of Balso Snell* demonstrates West's "predilection for the grotesque"
(p. 100). Describing the wasteland atmosphere of *A Cool Million*, he
concludes, "West's unpleasantly genial parody is only a weak tour de force
which is hardly saved by its serious undertones and occasional insights"
(p. 102). He finds that the Hollywood inhabitants in *The Day of the
Locust* "suffer from a cosmic ennui which only lynchings and love-nests
can mitigate" (p. 103). Too, though West does not rate with Farrell or
Dos Passos, according to Aaron, he "tells us more about the fascist men-
tality and the coming cataclysm than most class-conscious novels of the
thirties" (p. 104). He concludes that *Miss Lonelyhearts* will probably
remain a "minor classic" and "West may come to rate a footnote in the
histories of academicians. But he will always appeal to readers with
a taste for the grotesque" (p. 106).

71. Allen, Walter. *Tradition and Dream: A Critical Survey of British
and American Literature From the 1920's to the Present Day*. Middlesex,
England: Penguin Books, 1965, pp. 187, 188-190, 190-192. Allen cites
West for his "extraordinarily economic and nervous prose; and he was the
most economical novelist who ever wrote."

235. Angell, Richard C. [Review of two new editions of West's novels].
New Mexico Quarterly, 33, no. 2 (Summer 1963), 237-238. In a review of
the New Directions edition (1962) of *Miss Lonelyhearts* and *The Day of
The Locust* and the Noonday Press edition (1963) of *The Dream Life of Balso
Snell* and *A Cool Million*, Angell comments, "These editions are . . .
belated and richly deserved recognition of an artist of decided talent
if not genius" (p. 237). Angell relies in Stanley Hyman for much of his
comment on West (see [2]).

238. Anon. "The Great Despiser." *Time*, 69 (17 June 1957), 102-106.
This review of the *Complete Works* contains a summary and comment (mostly
laudatory) on each of the novels, but primarily on *Miss Lonelyhearts*.
Of West, "He was one of those men in whom pity must take the form of anger,
but his anger was not anything as simple as anti-American or anti-Babbitt;
it was anti-human nature" (p. 104).

244. Anon. "Nathanael West." *Times Literary Supplement*, 57, (24 January 1958), 44. "The motive power of West's work, from beginning to end, was a fascinated disgust with the processes of the body and accompanying obsession with physical violence" (p. 44). The author concludes that West's limited range is compensated for by his intensity.

247. Anon. "Rubbing Off the Sheen." *Newsweek*, 49 (May 13, 1957), 126-127. In a review of the *Complete Works*, the author mentions only *Miss Lonelyhearts* and *The Day of the Locust*--calls them "among the most mordantly incisive works in modern American letters" (p. 126).

76. Auden, W. H. "Interlude: West's Disease." *"The Dyer's Hand" and Other Essays*. New York: Random House, 1962, pp. 238-245. Auden begins by enumerating West's possible faults: his dreams are not realistic as dreams, nor his books realistic as "real" life. Too, the sameness of theme from book to book is a failing. Says Auden, "A writer may concern himself with a very limited area of life and still convince us that he is describing the real world, but one becomes suspicious when, as in West's case, whatever world he claims to be describing . . . no married couples have children, no child has more than one parent, a high percentage of the inhabitants are cripples, and the only kind of personal relations is the sado-masochistic" (p. 239). Auden concludes, "His books should, I think, be classified as Cautionary Tales, parables about a Kingdom of Hell whose ruler is not so much the Father of Lies as the Father of Wishes. . . . West's descriptions of the Inferno have the authenticity of first-hand experience: he has certainly been there, and the reader has the uncomfortable feeling that his was not a short visit" (p. 241).

252. Bellamy, W. J. "Nathanael West." *The Cambridge Quarterly*, 4, no. 1 (Winter 1968-69), 95-106. Bellamy contends that West's current high reputation is merely "trendy," particularly since he appeals to the "atmosphere of disillusion" (p. 95) in America, where "the social process is still felt to be destructive" (p. 95). West is "in his finest work, as effectively brief as the American novelists today tend to be wordy." In this review of the *Complete Works*, Bellamy contends that two of the novels are worth re-reading; two not worth reading at all. Says Bellamy, "The problem is that there is much to admire in West's work--but not that much" (p. 97). Contained in the essay is a long diatribe against Ross's introduction to the *Complete Works*. Too, of Stanley Hyman's claim that *Miss Lonelyhearts* is one of the three finest American novels of the century (see [2]), Bellamy scoffs, "This is not an especially exalted rank" (p. 101).

253. Berolzheimer, Hobart H. [Review of the *Complete Works*]. *Library Journal*, 82 (1 June 1957), 1539. A sentence or so on each of the novels. He recommends the volume to "mature and sophistocated readers who are not easily shocked."

254. Bittner, William. "A la recherche d'un écrivain perdu." *Les Langues Modernes*, 54 (July-August 1960), 274-282. Bittner examines the themes of love and religion in *The Dream Life of Balso Snell* and *Miss Lonelyhearts*.

255. Bittner, William. "Catching Up With Nathanael West." *The Nation*, 184, no. 18 (4 May 1957), 394-396. In a review of the *Complete Works*,

Bittner says that the symbols and satire appear more grotesque and striking, oddly, because they more resemble the real.

271. Coates, Robert M. "The Four Novels of Nathanael West, That Fierce, Humane Moralist." *The New York Herald Tribune Book Review*, 33 (9 May 1957), 4. A brief, laudatory review of the *Complete Works*.

1. Comerchero, Victor. *Nathanael West: The Ironic Prophet*. Syracuse: Syracuse University Press, 1964. Comerchero cites West for exploiting psychoanalysis but not probing deeply. "He is not interested in analysing character;" explains Comerchero, "he is interested in crystallizing it by using Freudian images as symbols or objective correlatives of a psychological state" (p. 3). He describes West as a strident Jeremiah, but with an underlying compassion. Comerchero's entire book applies here, of course, but chapter three--"A Study in Tension"--is a particularly fine discussion. Observes Comerchero, "It is in this delicate balance between intense feeling and humorous expression that West achieves some of his greatest effects" (pp. 24-25). And in connection with this, "By carefully maintaining a fine line between comedy and tragedy, West uses the comic both as relief and as preparation" (p. 27). This heightens the reader's sensitivity to pathos and makes him receptive to slight shifts in tone. The remainder of the chapter is a fine discussion of West's manipulation of tone in his novels. Of the four novels, Comerchero observes, "Thus, despite certain prevalent motifs in all four novels, the first two are personal, psychological, and philosophical; the latter two, more social-psychological and political. Moreover, the second novel in each pair treats the problem in a darker, less comic fashion" (p. 73).

275. Cowley, Malcolm. "It's the Telling That Counts." *The New York Times Book Review* (May 12, 1957), pp. 4-5. In a review of the *Complete Works* (including a portrait of West), Cowley claims that the spirit of the novels is the twenties, not the thirties. He comments that *The Dream Life of Balso Snell* and *A Cool Million* are "barely worth reprinting" (p. 4), but he praises the other two novels. Some biographical information is included with the critical comments; Cowley concludes that West's chief skill is not his grotesque imagination; but simply his power with words.

107. [The Editors of *Time*]. "Editor's Preface." *The Dream Life of Balso Snell*, by Nathanael West. Time Reading Program Special Edition. New York: Time Incorporated, 1965, pp. vii-xii. The editors conclude, "His satire, his haunting bitterness--which after all were negative manifestations that reflected the search for the beauty of humanity that he must have sensed--were rarely equalled in our time" (p. xii).

281. Engle, Paul. "The Exciting Prose of Nathanael West." *The Chicago Sunday Tribune* (12 May 1957), Section 4, p. 3. In a review of the *Complete Works*, Engle cites West as a fine satirist with an "imaginative precision of phrase" (p. 3). Most of the review concerns *Miss Lonelyhearts* and *The Day of the Locust*.

109. Fiedler, Leslie A. "The Breakthrough: The American Jewish Novelist and the Fictional Image of the Jew." *Recent American Fiction: Some*

Critical Views, ed. Joseph J. Waldmeir. Boston: Houghton Mifflin Company, 1963, pp. 84-109. Fiedler claims that West's former obscurity is now being overbalanced by enthusiastic rediscoverers. "There is no use in being carried away, however; no use in concealing from ourselves the fact that what has been restored to us is only another tragically incomplete figure, whose slow approach to maturity ends in death" (pp. 85-86). Fiedler sees West as a humorist of the grotesque who uses violence as a theme, tone and method, much as the surrealists do. "West does not seem to me finally a really achieved writer," concludes Fiedler; "his greatness lies like a promise just beyond his last novel and is frustrated by his early death; but he is the inventor for America of a peculiarly modern kind of book whose claims to credence are perfectly ambiguous. One does not know whether he is being presented the outlines of a nightmare endowed with a sense of reality or the picture of a reality become indistinguishable from nightmare" (p. 93).

110. Fiedler, Leslie A. "The Dream of the New." *American Dreams, American Nightmares*, ed. David Madden. Carbondale and Edwardsville: Southern Illinois University Press; London and Amsterdam: Feffer and Simons, Incorporated, 1970, pp. 19-27. Here Fiedler comments on the thirties writers who think of the novel as an embryonic form of film, and he uses West as an example. He also cites West as an example of the American tendency to mock the *avante-garde*, particularly in *The Dream Life of Balso Snell*.

111. Fiedler, Leslie A. *Love and Death in the American Novel*. New York: Stein and Day, 1966, pp. 326-328, 485-491. Fiedler finds Faye Greener in *The Day of the Locust* "the most memorable and terrible woman in an American novel of the 30's . . . a kind of *ersatz* Jean Harlow" (p. 326). Fiedler concludes that the same worry of the usurpation of male roles by the female which bothered Faulkner also troubled West, particularly in *The Dream Life of Balso Snell*, where Miss McGeeney turns into a mannish figure when Balso kisses her. Faye is the epitome of the lust for love (i. e., in Fiedler's terms, for death). West's attitude (and his male characters') toward the female is one of mixed sado-masochism. He concludes that West was the "chief neglected talent of the age" (p. 485). West refused to follow the program of proletarian writers and instinctively realized that literary truth was not synonymous with fact. The chief effect in his works is a kind of horror/comedy inspired by surrealism. Finally, Fiedler places West in a context of Jewish writers (like Kafka) who are bent on universalizing their experience to make it emblematic of Western man as a whole.

113. Fiedler, Leslie A. *Waiting For the End*. New York: Dell Publishing Company, 1964, pp. 37, 45, 46, 48, 49, 50, 51, 52, 63, 64, 83, 108, 143, 226. Fiedler finds that West is a "tragically incomplete figure" (p. 46), who exploited violence; and to West even sex is a horror. He claims that West must finally be considered a comic writer and his characters comic characters in the *shlemiel* tradition.

285. Flavin, Robert J. "Animal Imagery in the Works of Nathanael West." *Thoth*, 6, no. 2 (Spring 1965), 25-30. Flavin finds that West's frequent use of animal imagery underscores the theme of man's degeneracy. He examines all the novels, save *A Cool Million*, because there West

"sacrificed the stylistic hallmark that makes a writer's work compact
and homogenous" (p. 25). He concludes that *The Dream Life of Balso
Snell*'s theme is bestial, *Miss Lonelyhearts*' is that bestiality is
predatory, and *The Day of the Locust*'s is that the predatory beast
"delights most in incessant violence" (p. 30).

127. Grigson, Geoffrey, ed. *The Concise Encyclopedia of World Literature*. New York: Hawthorne Books, Incorporated, 1963, p. 483 (portrait
on p. 473). "He was a brilliant comedian; yet he saw the world as a
desert of panic and emptiness, and his books mercilessly analyse the
human condition. . . . His outspokenness, his refusal to sugar the pill,
may well be the reason why his reputation is only gradually matching
his achievement" (p. 483).

303. Hawkes, John. "John Hawkes on His Novels [an interview with John
Graham]." *The Massachusetts Review*, 7 (Summer 1966), 449-461. In
commenting on West, Hawkes observes, "Nathanael West, I think, did make
use of a kind of sick joke, but I think he uses the sick joke always
so that you feel behind it the idealism, the need for innocence and
purity, truth, strength and so on" (p. 461).

305. Hayes, E. Nelson. "Recent Fiction." *The Progressive*, 21 (June
1957), 35-39 (see especially p. 38). A one paragraph review of the
Complete Works, with a mere mention of the novels.

137. Herzberg, Max J. *et. al.*, eds. *The Reader's Encyclopedia of
American Literature*. New York: Thomas Y. Crowell Company, 1962, p.
1211. West is cited for being "a major figure in American fiction,"
and *Miss Lonelyhearts* and *The Day of the Locust* are cited for effectively
rendering the horror of contemporary life.

312. Hogan, William. "Nathanael West, Symbol of the Literary 1930's."
San Fransisco Chronicle (22 May 1957), p. 23. A laudatory review of the
Complete Works, containing a few lines on each of the novels. West's
is "a talent that even at this late date still burns with an icy blue
flame."

315. Hollis, C. Carroll. "Nathanael West: Diagnostician of the Lonely
Crowd." *Fresco*, 8, no. 1 (1957), 5-21. Mostly on *The Day of the Locust*,
but some general comments on West's canon throughout.

316. Hough, Graham. "New Novels." *Encounter*, 53 (February 1958),
84-87 (see especially p. 86). Hough reviews the *Complete Works*, which
he believes is hardly more than a "period piece." *The Dream Life of
Balso Snell* was "better left buried." *A Cool Million* is told in a
"parody best-seller style inapt for sustained irony," and *The Day of the
Locust*'s comment is a "hopeless theme for any but the most narrow kind
of success" (p. 86). In *Miss Lonelyhearts*, however, West "succeeds in
capturing a mood of megalopolitan despair with great success" (p. 86).

145. Kearns, G. A. "West, Nathanael." *Cassell's Encyclopedia of World
Literature*, ed. J. Buchanon-Brown. Revised and Enlarged. New York:
William Morrow and Company, Incorporated, 1973. III: 736. A brief
paragraph defining the common theme in West's work: it "projects a

113

manic vision of the pressures of modern urban mass society on characters
who are physical and emotional cripples" (p. 736). The four novels are
listed, plus five studies on West.

3. Light, James F. *Nathanael West: An Interpretative Study*. 2nd ed.
Evanston: Northwestern University Press, 1971. Says Light of what I
consider the primary theme in West's work, man's dreams and their conse-
quences, "In this world of decay and violence man is able to exist only
through dreams. The search for a dream to believe in is right--and in
this connection *Miss Lonelyhearts* and *Balso* agree--for it is only through
dreams that men can fight their misery. However, the commercialization
and stereotyping of man's dreams have led to a weakening of their power,
a puerility in their content. This is the worst betrayal of modern man"
(p. 85). Thus, Light does not see the act of dreaming itself as being
the culprit in West's fiction. The entirety of Light's study, of course,
concerns criticism, so no summary is possible; but it might be well to
direct the reader to critical discussions that would be difficult to
find in other works. For instance, see pp. 113-114 for a discussion of
"Business Deal," which Light claims is important as a forerunner of *The
Day of the Locust*. Other short stories are discussed on pp. 114-115.
See pp. 154-160 for a discussion of West's movie scripts produced while
he was working for Republic studios. Included here are lengthier examinations of *The President's Mystery*, *Five Came Back*, and *The Spirit of
Culver*. West's one produced play--*Good Hunting*--is discussed on pp.
162-163.

39. Malin, Irving. *Nathanael West's Novels*. Carbondale and Edwardsville: Southern Illinois University Press; London and Amsterdam: Feffer
and Simons, Incorporated, 1972. Malin's approach is New Critical:
close readings of the texts, a lack of which he feels is the major failure
of earlier criticisms. He observes, "The novels are formal designs
which create their powerful effects by the accumulation of significant
recurring details" (p. 7). He feels that ambivalence is West's chief
effect, and it is caused by his refusal to make black/white decisions.
Malin largely discounts the importance of the psychological interpretation
favored by many critics. He sees the sources of the characters' sexual
reactions in narcissism, not homosexuality, *etc*. "Their bodies become
totemic, holding secret and mysterious power. Their narcissism is
strikingly ambiguous. They are in love-and-hate with their physical
being; they would like to surrender it . . . but they cannot let go. Thus
they are caught in a vicious circle. They hate what they need to live
with. This psychological phenomena is the novelistic axiom" (p. 57).
Another interesting observation is that all the novels end in a flight
into the "womb of self" (p. 5). The novels are "childish" but for a
reason. They deal with fears that any child would feel in the adult
world. All the novels are patterned after the child's dream. The final
chapter examines West's prose on the paragraph level to show what a
skilled craftsman West was: interesting, but the kind of exercise
where the reader can find just about what he wants to find.

40. Martin, Jay. "Introduction." *Nathanael West: A Collection of
Critical Essays*, ed. Jay Martin. Englewood Cliffs, New Jersey: Prentice-
Hall, Incorporated, 1971, pp. 1-10. Martin includes a brief critical

statement on each of the novels. He concludes, "West's world, however distorted its people may sometimes be, is perfectly clear and complete. If it seems to lack the largeness of Tolstoy's . . . still it is precisely drawn to scale, richly complete in its own terms, and boldly directed in its concentrated vision" (p. 9).

64. Martin, Jay. *Nathanael West: The Art of His Life*. New York: Farrar, Straus, and Giroux, 1970. A great deal of critical information is included in Martin's biography, so much that it is impossible to succinctly summarize it, but it might be useful to direct the reader to a few discussions that are rarely found in other sources. See pp. 164 and following, for instance, for a discussion of West's unpublished stories. States Martin, "He set out in them to define form and character anew" (p. 165). For a discussion of West's movie scripts, see pp. 401 and following.

185. O'Connor, William Van. *The Grotesque: An American Genre and Other Essays*. Carbondale: Southern Illinois University Press, 1962, pp. 6, 8-9, 12, 18, 21, 55, 56. Comments on West as a writer of the grotesque.

186. Olsen, Bruce. "Nathanael West: The Use of Cynicism." *Minor American Novelists*, ed. Charles Alva Hoyt. Carbondale and Edwardsville: Southern Illinois University Press; London and Amsterdam: Feffer and Simons, Incorporated, 1970, pp. 81-94. Olsen comments on West's hatred of the dream life, "West would have us implacably undeceived against the storymakers. Life, as he seemed to proclaim it, did blindly run with unconscious desires, uncharted social forces, and the indifferent blows of accident" (p. 81).

353. Peden, William. "Nathanael West." *The Virginia Quarterly Review*, 33, no. 3 (Summer 1957), 468-472. In a review of the *Complete Works*, Peden comments on West's "savage indictments of what has been aptly termed the 'horrible emptiness of mass lives'" (p. 469).

62. Podhoretz, Norman. "Nathanael West: A Particular Kind of Joking." *Nathanael West: A Collection of Critical Essays*, ed. Jay Martin. Englewood Cliffs, New Jersey: Prentice-Hall, Incorporated, 1971, pp. 154-160. Observes Podhoretz, "His 'particular kind of joking' has profoundly unpolitical implications; it is a way of saying that the universe is always rigged against us and that our efforts to contend with it invariably lead to absurdity" (p. 155). He concludes that this type of laughter is distinctly unAmerican in its unrelieved pessimism. Of West's two greatest works, *Miss Lonelyhearts* and *The Day of the Locust*, he observes that they "are comic novels, not simply because they contain funny passages but because they are about the inability of human beings to be more than human, the absurdity of the human pretense to greatness and nobility" (p. 160). He concludes that at the bottom lies West's compassion yet resolve not to be "taken in" by human pretense.

191. Pritchett, V. S. *"Miss Lonelyhearts." The Living Novel and Later Appreciations*. New York: Random House, 1968, pp. 276-282. Pritchett claims that West "was preoccupied with hysteria as the price paid for accepting the sentimentalities of the national dream" (p. 276). Life, however, was not tragic for West because tragedy was not possible in

modern life, only banality.

91. Raban, Jonathan. "A Surfeit of Commodities: The Novels of Nathanael West." *The American Novel in the Nineteen Twenties*, eds. Malcolm Bradbury and David Palmer. Stratford-upon-Avon Studies #13. London: Edward Arnold; New York: Crane, Russak, 1971, pp. 215-232. Raban bemoans the "slavish" adoration of West by critics such as Leslie Fiedler (curious that Fiedler should be pointed out since he consistently tempers his praise of West by noting his present "overbalanced" reputation; see [113]). Concludes Raban, "West's work is pathetically incomplete: re-reading his novels one watches again and again as the shrill personality of the author extrudes from behind the papery mask of his assumed style" (p. 216).

365. Raven, Simon. "Sub-Men and Super Women." *Spectator*, 199 (6 December 1957), 810. In a review of the Complete Works, Raven comments that the books have two things on common: "laconic and viciously hard writing, and an implacable vision of a pagan world from which all the traditional pagan consolations [such as sex and liquor] have been removed" (p. 810).

66. Reid, Randall. *The Fiction of Nathanael West: No Redeemer, No Promised Land*. Chicago and London: University of Chicago Press, 1967. Reid finds the main characteristic of West's style to be its simplicity and pictorial quality. "At times his pictorial technique closely resembles collage--but only at times. It also resembles cartoon strips, movies, and several different schools of painting, as well as such nongraphic visual arts as the tableau and the dance" (p. 9). He claims that West is neither a realist or a fantasist because his works imitate art, not life. Concludes Reid, "Perhaps no one has understood so well, or revealed so accurately, the nature of our favorite lies" (p. 11).

369. Rosenfield, Isaac. "Faulkner and Contemporaries." *Partisan Review*, 18, no. 1 (January-February 1951), 106-114. Of those who wrote about the pop culture, Rosenfield asserts, "The only man who, in my opinion, really knew what he was doing was Nathanael West, and this is because of his theme--it runs through both *Miss Lonelyhearts* and *The Day of the Locust*, and it makes him unique among American novelists-- the secret inner life of the masses" (p. 110). Concludes Rosenfield, "He saw, as everybody has seen, the starvation latent in the popular media. . . . The starvation is not only for good books and fine music, it is a starvation for all of life, for sexual fulfillment, for decent work, for pleasure and happiness and relief from the desolation that drives people insane" (p. 111).

197. [Ross, Alan]. "West, Nathanael." *The Concise Encyclopedia of Modern World Literature*, ed. Geoffrey Grigson. New York: Hawthorne Books, Incorporated, 1963, p. 483. Contains a one page summary and critical comment on the novels. Concludes Ross, West was "a brilliant comedian; yet he saw the world as a desert of panic and emptiness, and his books mercilessly analyse the human condition" (p. 483). He says that West's style--"rare in fiction now--is economical, concrete, undiluted, and highly charged with poetry" (p. 483).

370. Russell, Ralph. "He Might Have Been a Major Novelist." *The Reporter*, 16 (30 May 1957), 45-46. A review of the *Complete Works* containing a few sentences on each of the novels, plus a one page discussion of West's style and common themes. Russell concludes, "But West's talent seemed to be growing, and one may surmise that had he lived he might have gone far beyond the merely grotesque, the merely disgusting, the merely hopeless" (p. 46).

373. Sanders, David. [Review of the *Complete Works*.] *Books Abroad*, 31 (1957), 376-377. Sanders praises *Miss Lonelyhearts* although he virtually dismisses *The Dream Life of Balso Snell* and *A Cool Million*. He claims that *The Day of the Locust* is not the best of the hollywood novels, as many critics assert; rather, it shows the limitations of surrealism. Sanders concludes, "West was surely the most dedicated Surrealist among twentieth century American writers, and, in his application of this technique to an examination of the Great Depression, he was virtually unique" (p. 376).

376. Schneider, Cyril M. "The Individuality of Nathanael West." *The Western Review*, 20, no. 1 (Autumn 1955), 7-28. Schneider finds that West's novels typically center around the plight of a frustrated hero. He concludes, "His work will always appeal to readers with a taste for the bizarre and to those who can find a meaning in his fantastic realism" (p. 28).

378. Schoenewald, Richard L. "No Second Act." *Commonweal*, 66 (10 May 1957), 162-163. A review of the *Complete Works*. Schoenewald praises West, often comparing him to Fitzgerald. He concludes, "Like an expressionistic artist, he saw the breaking up of life's surface, and in his prose he drew the fragments" (p. 163).

382. Seymour-Smith, Martin. "Prophet of Black Humor." *Spectator*, 221 (19 July 1968), 94-95. Seymour-Smith believes that none of the novels is perfect, but each in its own way is a masterpiece.

384. Simonson, Harold P. "California, Nathanael West, and the Journey's End." *The Closed Frontier: Studies in American Literary Tragedy*. New York [*etc.*]: Holt, Rinehart, and Winston, Incorporated, 1970, pp. 99-124. Claims the author, "The work of Nathanael West must be read as a profound interpretation of how the great myth of the West came to end" (p. 104). The intertwining of life and death in the novels is reflected in the West as a place to live and a place to die. Simonson sees the journey in one form or another as a key motif in West's works and he finds that motif tragic in nature. He explores the motif in each of the novels, but it reaches its culmination in *The Day of the Locust*.

385. Skerrett, Joseph Taylor, Jr. "Dostoievsky, Nathanael West, and Some Contemporary American Fiction." *The University of Dayton Review*, 4, no. 1 (Winter 1967), 23-36. Skerrett sees West as being bleakly pessimistic, disapproving to a degree of all his characters. "In the Westian view, the essence of the American dream lies in its impossibility, in the failure of ourselves as a nation to concretize in reality" (p. 26). Too, West "was probably the first major American writer to recover from

Freud, and as a result West's characterization is free from the heavy-handed determinism that ruined so many novels of the 20's and 30's" (p. 26).

386. Smith, Roger H. "Complete Works of Nathanael West." *The Saturday Review of Literature*, 40 (11 May 1957), 13-14. Smith finds that each novel is based on a polarized concept--man's dreams on the one hand, and the violence of the man-made world on the other. He concludes that *A Cool Million* is West's worst novel and *The Day of the Locust* his most mature. West wrote of an age where dreams were perverted, where noble actions could no longer be conceived: thus, his dark pessimism.

208. Straumann, Heinrich. *American Literature in the Twentieth Century*. 3rd revised edition. New York: Harper and Row, 1965, pp. 78-79. Straumann's comment is specifically intended for *Miss Lonelyhearts*, but I think that it applies equally well to the entire canon of West's works. "The borderline between reality and nightmare is intentionally defaced and the devastating force at work in the dissolution of all values at all levels, is only equalled by the power and precision with which symbols and imagery are handled" (p. 78).

209. Swingewood, Alan. "Alienation, Reification, and the Novel: Sartre, Camus, Nathanael West." *The Sociology of Literature*, by Diana T. Laurenson and Alan Swingewood. New York: Shocken Books, 1972, pp. 207-248. Swingewood's discussion of the relationships of West's male characters to the female characters is especially good. He concludes that West's heroes are either passive or are raped. "Sexual failure is used to emphasize the failure of modern industrial society to provide man with genuine creative and human activity" (p. 243).

210. Symons, Julian. *Critical Occasions*. London: Hamish Hamilton, 1966, pp. 99-105. Symons finds that the motive power for West's work is his "fascinated disgust with the processes of the body and an accompanying obsession with physical violence" (p. 100).

392. Tibbetts, A. M. "The Strange Half-World of Nathanael West." *Prairie Schooner*, 34, no. 1 (Spring 1960), 8-14. In trying to stem the recent flood of critical adulation of West, Tibbetts warns, "West was simply not that good a writer; indeed in some ways he was a very bad writer" (p. 8). He complains that West deals with only half of the world and, indeed, the half left out is the more important: "real people doing real things" (p. 8). Too, "West did not understand the nature of satire" (p. 8). Tibbetts goes to some length to show that West's characters and situations simply are not realistic. Particularly unrealistic is the characters' complete inability to love.

35. Torchianna, Donald T. "The Painter's Eye." *Nathanael West: The Cheaters and the Cheated, A Collection of Critical Essays*, ed. David Madden. Deland, Florida: Everett/Edwards, Incorporated, 1973, pp. 249-282. Torchianna remarks on the variety of narrative perspectives used by West in dealing with the same basic themes and materials. The themes which he finds continually repeated are broken dreams, the innate destructiveness of man, and the "bankruptcy of the middle class" (p. 250).

224. Widmer, Kingsley. "The Sweet Savage Prophecies of Nathanael West."
The Thirties: Fiction, Poetry, Drama, ed. Warren French. Deland,
Florida: Everett/Edwards, Incorporated, 1967, pp. 97-106. Observes
Widmer, "West's work curiously fuses poetic style and naturalistic subjects,
clinical undercutting and poetic over-reaching, empathetic immediacy
and disinterested mockery" (p. 98).

422. Williams, David. "A Lancashire Boyhood." *The Manchester Guardian*
(3 December 1957), p. 4. In a review of the *Complete Works*, Williams
states that West's common theme is the "brittle falsities of life in the
boom towns of the American Pacific coast." He calls *Miss Lonelyhearts*
a "sad, savage, freakish, exceptional book."

45. Williams, William Carlos. "A New American Writer." *Nathanael West:
A Collection of Critical Essays*, ed. Jay Martin. Englewood Cliffs,
New Jersey: Prentice-Hall, Incorporated, 1971, pp. 48-49. Williams
notes that West's strength "is that he has taken seriously a theme of
great importance so trite that all of us thought there would be no life
in it: I mean that terrible moral impoverishment of our youth in the
cities" (p. 48).

424. Williams, William Carlos. "Sordid? Good God!" *Contempo*, 3
no. 11 (25 July 1933), pp. 5, 8. Williams applauds West's insistence
on the truth. Much of the essay is a diatribe against contemporary
criticism and a call for the great American novelist. He concludes,
"Anyone using American must have taste in order to be able to select
from among the teeming vulgarisms of our speech the personal and telling
vocabulary which he needs to put over his effects. West possesses
this taste" (p. 8).

425. Wilson, Edmund. [Ad for *Miss Lonelyhearts*]. *Contempo*, 3 (25
July 1933), 7. Wilson finds West more "philosophic-poetic" than most
American humorists. Too, West goes deeper than dada although he was
obviously influenced by them. "West is in short, an original, comic
poet."

429. Zimmer, Dieter E. "Nathanael West, oder Warnungen vorm Tag der
Heuschrechen." *Neue Rundschau*, 83 (1972), 287-302 [in German]. The
essay explores Auden's contention that West's works concern mainly the
distance between illusion and reality and the violence that often results
from destroyed dreams.

B) *The Dream Life of Balso Snell*

244. Anon. "Nathanael West." *Times Literary Supplement*, 57 (24 January
1958), 44. "The motive power of West's work, from beginning to end,
was a fascinated disgust with the processes of the body and an accompanying
obsession with physical violence." The author maintains that *The Dream
Life of Balso Snell*--"a work of some originality which contains images,
and even scenes, of remarkable power"--is too often underestimated.

255. Bittner, William. "Catching Up With Nathanael West." *The Nation*, 184, no. 18 (4 May 1957), 394-396. Bittner maintains that the true subject of *The Dream Life of Balso Snell* is love, and West "apparently considers organized religion a sublimation of more natural emotion" (p. 395).

99. Coates, Robert M. "Introduction." *Miss Lonelyhearts*, by Nathanael West. New York: The New Classics, 1950, pp. ix-xiv. Coates calls *The Dream Life of Balso Snell* "a little too determined in its evident desire to shock and scandalize the reader. But it also contained passages of extraordinarily vivid and sensitive writing" (p. x).

1. Comerchero, Victor. *Nathanael West: The Ironic Prophet*. Syracuse: Syracuse University Press, 1964. Of *The Dream Life of Balso Snell* Comerchero notes, "West's protest against writing books is as much a protest against reading literature--the artificiality and sense of unreality, the self-consciousness and poisonous awareness that result from wide reading" (p. 52). Like many other critics, Comerchero sees the novel as important for prefiguring themes and techniques employed more successfully in later novels. He concludes that the novel fails because West took on too much, but it contains flashes of brilliance. He claims that the images are less functional than those in *Miss Lonelyhearts* and *The Day of the Locust*, and the theme is a more personal one than in the later novels. Comerchero concludes that in the novel West is writing from a matrix of his own "psychic experience" but he still directs his satire at the world in general.

276. Cramer, Carter M. "The World of Nathanael West: A Critical Interpretation." *The Emporia State Research Studies*, 19, no. 4 (June 1971), 5-71. Cramer claims that *The Dream Life of Balso Snell* is more narrow in focus than commonly imagined. It is not a dada novel, parodying Dostoevsky, Joyce, and others, but it is an anatomy (in Northrop Frye's sense of the term) which buries the pseudo-sophisticates in their own clichés. Concludes Cramer, "To criticize *A Cool Million* or *The Dream Life of Balso Snell* as inferior novels in comparison to West's other works is to state a preference for the novel form over the anatomy--little more" (p. 38).

289. G., V. N. *"The Dream Life of Balso Snell."* Contempo, 1 (21 August 1931), 3. A one paragraph review of the novel. Though the author finds little significant in the book, "There is a suavity of phrase and execution in *The Dream Life of Balso Snell* that makes for excellent reading" (p. 3).

291. Galloway, David D. "A Picaresque Apprenticeship: Nathanael West's *The Dream Life of Balso Snell* and *A Cool Million*." *Wisconsin Studies in Contemporary Literature*, no. 2 (Summer 1964), 110-126. Galloway comments on the lack of attention paid these two novels and believes that it was caused by West's being at "a nearly neurotic point of artistic isolation, and their polemical tone recalls the worst products of the cult of violence of the 1930's" (p. 110). However, Galloway finds the novels valuable for their very lack of constraint because here we find West's themes and techniques in purest form. "In *Balso Snell*, West introduced his readers to the eccentric, the mystic, the pervert, the crippled,

and the disillusioned who were to be credibly presented as major players
in his later novels" (p. 111).

122. Gehman, Richard. "Introduction." *The Day of the Locust*, by Nathanael West. New York: The New Clasics, 1950, pp. ix-xxiii. States
Gehman, "*The Dream Life of Balso Snell* was an inverted book, a young
man's intellectual parlor trick performed chiefly for his own amusement"
(p. xix).

295. Gehman, Richard. "Nathanael West" A Novelist Apart." *The Atlantic
Monthly*, 186, no. 3 (September 1950), 69-72. Condensed from his introduction to *The Day of the Locust*. See [122].

127. Grigson, Geoffrey, ed. *The Concise Encyclopedia of World Literature*.
New York: Hawthorne Books, Incorporated, 1963, p. 483. Of *The Dream
Life of Balso Snell*, the author comments, "Whatever its solemnly rational
detractors may declare, this book is funny down to its words."

313. Hollis. C. Carroll. "Nathanael West and Surrealist Violence."
Fresco, 7, no. 5 (1957), 5-13. Of *The Dream Life of Balso Snell*, Hollis
observes, "Unlike the other three novels in which he diagnoses the inward-
eating cancer of secular society, this first work is blatantly an account
of the dissolution of self" (p. 7).

314. Hollis, C. Carroll. "Nathanael West and the 'Lonely Crowd'."
Thought, 33 (Autmun 1958), 398-416. Hollis claims that *The Dream Life
of Balso Snell* is more of a protest against the self than a protest
against society, like the other novels. See also [313].

2. Hyman, Stanley Edgar. *Nathanael West*. Pamphlets on American Writers,
no. 21. Minneapolis: University of Minnesota, 1962. Hyman finds the
strength of *The Dream Life of Balso Snell* to be its "garish comic imagination" (p. 13); its weakness is its immaturity--"obsessive scatology"
(p. 15), for instance. "The book has no form, and consists merely of
a series of encounters and complications, terminated rather than resolved
by orgasm" (p. 15).

165. Klein, Marcus. "The Roots of Radicals: Experience in the Thirties."
Proletarian Writers of the Thirties, ed. David Madden. Carbondale and
Edwardsville: Southern Illinois University Press; London and Amsterdam:
Feffer and Simons, Incorporated, 1968, pp. 134-157. Klein finds that the
irony in *The Dream Life of Balso Snell* is so pervasive, so self-conscious,
and builds upon itself so constantly that the narrative is lost; the
intensity of the irony is so great that West is unable to make any sort
of statement about anything. Klein finds that West, like Balso, is trying
to strip himself of all poses in the novel. The novel "declares an
aesthetic requirement: literature must rid itself of a literary in-
heritance" (p. 144).

328. Light, James F. "Nathanael West." *Prairie Schooner*, 31, no. 3
(Fall 1957), 279-283. Light observes that all of the artistic endeavors
in *The Dream Life of Balso Snell* "are attempts by the physically inferior
to compensate for being a dull, ugly bird rather than the brilliantly

plumed Bird of Paradise" (p. 279). Thus, all art is a lie. Flesh is
the only truth. The basic theme of the novel, that from dreams comes misery,
is examined in detail in the following three novels.

3. Light, James F. *Nathanael West: An Interpretative Study*. 2nd ed.
Evanston: Northwestern University Press, 1971. Says Light, "*Balso*
[*sic*] is a rejection of the artistic, the rational, and the spiritual
pretensions of man. In revealing man's ultimate phoniness, *Balso* emphasizes the illogic and confusion of man's dream life. At the same
time, *Balso* asserts that the dream life reaffirms common everyday truths"
(p. 44). Observes Light, "From the beginning one notes a conflict
within Balso between the philosophies of monism (idealism) and pluralism
(or materialism). . . . Balso's song, concerned with the eternal roundness
of things, dramatizes the monistic yearnings of Balso for some Emersonian
Over Soul or a Nietzchean Primordial Unity" (p. 46). At the end of the
novel, the body [balls of Snell] achieves complete victory over the
spirit. Also included here is a fine discussion of the novel's
influence on West's later works (pp. 56-57).

21. Locklin, Gerald. "The Journey Into the Microcosm." *Nathanael West:
The Cheaters and the Cheated, A Collection of Critical Essays*. Deland,
Florida: Everett/Edwards, Incorporated, 1973, pp. 23-56. Locklin claims
that the negative criticism of *The Dream Life of Balso Snell* is unjust.
"It is one of the most complex books this side of James Joyce, and its
complexity is coherent, not chaotic" (p. 24). He feels that the novel,
like *Finnegans Wake*, is a microcosm of humanity, resulting in an "original
generalization about man's total condition" (p. 24).

335. Lorch, Thomas M. "The Inverted Structure of *Balso Snell* [*sic*]."
Studies in Short Fiction, 4, no. 1 (Fall 1966), 33-41. Lorch finds that
the two prevailing motifs of inversion in the novel are sex and excrement.
The circle motif (monism) and the dream structure (from erection and
entrance to climax) are also unifying effects. Lorch concludes that the
novel is not an attack on literature itself, but on its "misuses, abuses,
and perversions" (p. 37). Too, he argues that *The Dream Life of Balso
Snell* is worthwhile in its own right, not merely as a precursor of later
works. He claims that the failure of the book is not in its conception,
but in its execution. He also argues that the novel is not necessarily
"a dismissal of man's spiritual pretensions in general and of his [West's]
literary aspirations in particular" (p. 33). He describes the novel as
inverted in structure and theme--"an *advocatus diaboli*, as strong an
argument as West can generate against the very things he wants most to
believe in" (p. 34). For example, Balso as a poet should be idealistic,
yet he is cynical and materialistic.

39. Malin, Irving. *Nathanael West's Novels*. Carbondale and Edwardsville:
Southern Illinois University Press; London and Amsterdam: Feffer and
Simons, Incorporated, 1972. Malin concludes that *The Dream Life of
Balso Snell* is unsuccessful because it surrenders to its controlling
metaphors: circularity, excrement, and so forth (see p. 29).

64. Martin, Jay. *Nathanael West: The Art of His Life*. New York:
Farrar, Straus and Giroux, 1970. Observes Martin, "In *The Dream Life
of Balso Snell*, West conducts a moral experiment in the nature and

principles of values by plunging into the underworld of the mind, where ordinary values are transformed, strangely twisted--in effect, trans-valued--and alternating moralities are given painful birth" (p. 126). Martin sees the novel as prefiguring themes, character types, and stylistic techniques polished in later works.

344. McLaughlin, Richard. "West of Hollywood." *Theatre Arts*, 35 (August 1951), 46-47, 93. McLaughlin calls *The Dream Life of Balso Snell* a work of promise, but with youthful faults.

186. Olsen, Bruce. "Nathanael West: The Use of Cynicism." *Minor American Novelists*, ed. Charles Alva Hoyt. Carbondale and Edwardsville: Southern Illinois University Press; London and Amsterdam: Feffer and Simons, Incorporated, 1970, pp. 81-94. Olsen finds that *The Dream Life of Balso Snell* comes closest to *Miss Lonelyhearts* as a true work of art. He maintains, "It is not, after all, a Dadaist performance, but an intense execution of the art of anti-art" (p. 93).

353. Peden, William. "Nathanael West." *The Virginia Quarterly Review*, 33, no. 3 (Summer 1957), 468-472. Peden finds the chapters of *The Dream Life of Balso Snell* "objectifications of man's most submerged passions, dreams, and desires. For all its flashes of brilliance, however, *The Dream Life of Balso Snell* is little more than a one-dimensional tour de force, with ciphers for characters" (p. 469).

62. Podhoretz, Norman. "Nathanael West: A Particular Kind of Joking." *Nathanael West: A Collection of Critical Essays*. Englewood Cliffs, New Jersey: Prentice-Hall, Incorporated, 1971, pp. 154-160. Podhoretz finds that *The Dream Life of Balso Snell* "is a battleground on which West the sentimentalist is pitted against West the cynic" (p. 156). The battle ends in a draw.

190. Powell, Lawrence Clark. "*The Day of the Locust:* Nathanael West." *California Classics: The Creative Literature of the Golden State*. Los Angeles: The Ward Ritchie Press, 1971, pp. 344-356. Of *The Dream Life of Balso Snell* Powell states, "Readable only as a literary tour de force, it is interesting as a stage in West's development" (p. 348).

66. Reid, Randall. *The Fiction of Nathanael West: No Redeemer, No Promised Land*. Chicago and London: University of Chicago Press, 1967. Reid observes that the three main targets of West's satire are the dream, sex, and art. He also finds that the frequent failure of low comedy (as in *The Dream Life of Balso Snell*) comes in part from West's instinctive pessimism. I personally feel that Reid's contention that Balso Snell is a "thinly disguised variant of 'asshole smell'--with perhaps an overtone of 'Branch Cabell'" (p. 16) is a little far-fetched.

367. Richardson, Robert D. "*Miss Lonelyhearts.*" *The University Review*, 33, no. 2 (December 1966), 151-157. Richardson comments that *The Dream Life of Balso Snell* is written in "furious waste" (p. 151).

194. Ross, Alan. "The Dead Center: An Introduction to Nathanael West." *The Complete Works of Nathanael West*. New York: Farrar, Straus, and

Cudahy, 1957, pp. vii-xxii. Ross observes that West's last three novels chart the disintegration of society while *The Dream Life of Balso Snell* charts the disintegration of self. Too, "*Balso Snell* [*sic*] is a sneer in the bathroom mirror at art" (p. xii).

376. Schneider, Cyril M. "The Individuality of Nathanael West." *The Western Review*, 20, no. 1 (Autumn 1955), 7-28. Schneider says that the chief worth of *The Dream Life of Balso Snell* is as a measure of growth of the later novels.

203. Schulz, Max F. *Radical Sophistication: Studies in Contemporary Jewish American Novelists*. Athens: Ohio University Press, 1969, pp. 36-55, 179, 185. Schulz observes that each one of West's novels confronts and denounces a false dream. He then examines in detail the contrast in *The Dream Life of Balso Snell* between romantic love and the procreative instinct (pp. 38-41). He finds that this is also a dominant theme in the later novels.

381. Schwartz, Edward Greenfield. "The Novels of Nathanael West." *Accent*, 17 (Autumn 1957), 251-262. Schwartz is effusive in his praise of *The Dream Life of Balso Snell*--"One of the most profane, bawdy, and humorous novels in American literature" (p. 252). He claims that the novel shows the ultimate desire of the artist to be sexual satisfaction. Concludes Schwartz, Balso's "most important discovery during his dream journey is that man's pretensions, his romantic conception of himself, lead to the abnegation of basic human needs and to tragic frustrations" (p. 252).

67. Scott, Nathan A. Jr. *Nathanael West: A Critical Essay*. Contemporary Writers in Christian Perspective. Grand Rapids, Michigan: William B. Eerdmans, 1971. Scott argues that James Light's contention (see [3]) that *The Dream Life of Balso Snell* is essentially an attack on all art misses the point. "West's primary purpose in *The Dream Life of Balso Snell* is that of hinting at how much, in a fallen world bereft of any great hope, human existence does indeed inevitably become itself a matter of art" (p. 16). He describes the novel as a "metafiction" in that the life portrayed is a life acted upon a stage: life as a work of art. He concludes that when life has no moral center, men make only a pretense of living.

210. Symons, Julian. *Critical Occasions*. London: Hamish Hamilton, 1966, pp. 99-105. Symons believes that *The Dream Life of Balso Snell*'s primary purpose is to shock, but it does contain some scenes of power. "The blasphemy, the obscenity, the deep sense of personal anguish about his own life and the condition of the world, they are all in this early phantasy" (p. 101), along with the regrettable propensity for turning the tragedy into a joke.

391. Tibbetts, A. M. "Nathanael West's *The Dream Life of Balso Snell*." *Studies in Short Fiction*, 2, no. 2 (Winter 1965), 105-112. Tibbetts rejects James Light's interpretation (see [3]) of the novel as a quest by the protagonist for some principle of unity, resulting ultimately in an attack on artistic endeavor. Rather, Tibbetts feels that the novel

is about "*fractured personality*, a person who is cut off from humanity and whose world is without sanity or meaning" (p. 105). He finds three fractured personalities at work: John Gilson, Saniette's lover, and Beagle Darwin. All three are pulled by opposing forces. All want order, but "lust for disorder" (p. 110). Tibbetts concludes that the novel cannot be satire because the fractured personalities disallow a discernible point of view--always necessary for satire.

414. White, William. "A Novelist Ahead of His Time: Nathanael West." *Orient/West*, 6 (January 1961), 55-64. White maintains that neither *The Dream Life of Balso Snell* nor *A Cool Million* is very good. The former is valuable mainly as a statement on nihilism. "What West seems to say in these disjointed episodes is that neither art nor culture nor religion can save man from his own animal self, and all pretensions to more than animality are essentially phony" (p. 62).

224. Widmer, Kingsley. "The Sweet Savage Prophecies of Nathanael West." *The Thirties: Fiction, Poetry, Drama*, ed. Warren French. Deland, Florida: Everett/Edwards, Incorporated, 1967, pp. 97-106. Widmer says that *The Dream Life of Balso Snell* "satirizes art as a pseudo-sublimation of sex by the incompetent" (p. 98).

228. Wilson, Edmund. *A Literary Chronicle: 1920-1950*. New York: Doubleday and Company, Incorporated, 1956, p. 245. Wilson calls *The Dream Life of Balso Snell* "a not very successful exercise in this vein of phantasmagoria" (p. 245).

C) *Miss Lonelyhearts*

236. Anon. "Books and Reviews." *New Outlook*, 162 (July 1933), 55, 58-59. A one paragraph laudatory review of *Miss Lonelyhearts*. The author calls the novel a "modernized, faithless, 'Pilgrim's Progress'" (p. 58).

241. Anon. "'Miss Lonelyhearts' and Some Other Recent Works of Fiction." *The New York Times Book Review* (23 April 1933), p. 6. A brief review of the novel. The author praises its wit and humor and finds its satire more profound than the common run.

244. Anon. "Nathanael West." *Times Literary Supplement*, 57 (24 January 1958), 44. The author comments that "structurally *Miss Lonelyhearts* splits off into a number of brilliant fragments which could be put together again in another order without any very noticeable effect on the style's impact." Too, the novel is flawed by the lack of any moral viewpoint.

69. Abrahams, Roger D. "Androgynes Bound: Nathanael West's *Miss Lonelyhearts*." *Seven Contemporary American Authors: Essays on Cozzens, Miller, West, Golding, Heller, Albee, and Powers*, ed. Thomas B. Whitbread. Austin and London: University of Texas Press, 1966, pp. 49-72. Abrahams notes that *Miss Lonelyhearts* "is a work of utter despair, yet its ironic approach causes despair itself to be branded ridiculous" (p. 51). To fully experience life is a painful process for West's characters. Miss

Lonelyhearts is on a quest, but he arrives nowhere. His problem is that he cannot harmonize head and heart. He is offered two major alternatives in the novel: cynicism (Shrike) and sentimental optimism (Betty), which results in male/female, paternal/maternal, sadism/masochism, city/country dichotomies. Miss Lonelyhearts tries to see love as a unifying force (an androgynous force), but "The response to an act of love is the same as that to any other stimulus, absurd destruction and death" (p. 72).

234. Andreach, Robert J. "Nathanael West's *Miss Lonelyhearts*: Between the Dead Pan and the Unborn Christ." *Modern Fiction Studies*, 12, no. 2 (Summer 1966), 251-261. Says Andreach, "For West all that Christianity does for a man is give him a consciousness of a higher reality, which prevents him from enjoying his sexual nature without feeling guilty. The paradox which destroys Miss Lonelyhearts is that it takes violence to bring Christ to life but violence is just what Christianity banished" (p. 259).

80. Bertoff, Warner. *Fictions and Events: Essays in Criticism and Literary History.* New York: E. P. Dutton and Company, Incorporated, 1971, p. 173. Bertoff briefly mentions *Miss Lonelyhearts* under the heading of "lonely men on the edges of madness" (p. 173).

255. Bittner, William. "Catching Up With Nathanael West." *The Nation*, 184, no. 8 (4 May 1957), 394-396. Bittner maintains that West's sympathies are with Miss Lonelyhearts, but he agrees with Shrike.

256. Britten, Florence Haxton. "Grotesquely Beautiful Novel." *The New York Herald Tribune Books* (30 April 1933), p. 6. In a laudatory review of *Miss Lonelyhearts*, Britten says that the novel is a "lineal descendant of the New England Puritan tradition" (p. 6). She finds that the technique of the love scenes resembles that of Ben Hecht and the dadaists.

264. Bush, C. W. "This Stupendous Fabric: The Metaphysics of Order in Melville's *Pierre* and Nathanael West's *Miss Lonelyhearts.*" *Journal of American Studies*, 1, no. 2 (October 1967), 269-274. Bush claims that Miss Lonelyhearts' attempt to order existence by the Christ myth runs afoul of the needs of the body; great sexual tension is a result. "Love prompted by some metaphysical paradigm of order is achieved only at the expense of the human. Miss Lonelyhearts rejects Betty for God" (p. 272).

265. Caldwell, Erskine. [Ad for *Miss Lonelyhearts*]. *Contempo*, 3 (25 July 1933), 7. "I haven't read such good satire on life and living in this era of the twentieth century in a long time" (p. 7).

270. Coates, Robert M. [Ad for *Miss Lonelyhearts*]. *Contempo* 3, (25 July 1933), 7. Coates cites West's gift for verbal agility and fantastic metaphor.

99. Coates, Robert M. "Introduction." *Miss Lonelyhearts*, by Nathanael West. New York: The New Classics, 1950, pp. ix-xiv. Coates observes that in the novel West insists on the "unpleasantness of all primary human relations" (p. xii). The book is written with "passionate sustained intensity that gives it rare dignity and importance" (p. xiii).

272. Coates, Robert M. "Messiah of the Lonely Heart." *The New Yorker*, 9 (15 April 1933), 59. Coates describes the writing in *Miss Lonelyhearts* as crisp, clever and impishly ironical, but "it has no particular message and it's all about practically nothing at all" (p. 59). He observes that the fourteen chapters of the book (plus one as prologue) might be a parallel to the fourteen stations of the cross.

1. Comerchero, Victor. *Nathanael West: The Ironic Prophet*. Syracuse: Syracuse University Press, 1964. Comerchero argues that James Light's contention (see [3]) that Miss Lonelyhearts found the true answer in the end, even if those around him consider him insane, is wrong. West offers us no solution. "As a result of his Spenglerian vision [materialistic nature of progress] and religious skepticism, West is placed in the paradoxical position of debunking religion while using the decline of Christianity to symbolize the decline of the West" (p. 83). Comerchero finds a logical contradiction here, but not an artistic one, particularly with West's skillful handling of the paradoxes. Too, Comerchero examines Miss Lonelyhearts as an archetypal hero in the Joseph Campbell (*The Hero With a Thousand Faces*) sense. Finally, Comerchero traces Miss Lonelyhearts' oedipal homosexuality, finding a proliferation of phallic images. See pp. 72-102 for the bulk of the discussion on West's *Miss Lonelyhearts*.

100. Connolly, Cyril. *The Modern Movement: One Hundred Key Books From England, France, and America, 1880-1950*. New York: Atheneum, 1966, pp. 73-74. A one paragraph synopsis of *Miss Lonelyhearts*, which concerns "the exploitation of emotion by modern methods of publicity" (p. 73).

103. Cowley, Malcolm. *Exile's Return: A Literary Odyssey of the 1920's*. New York: The Viking Press, 1951, p. 237. Included is a brief discussion of *Miss Lonelyhearts*--"a tender and recklessly imaginative novel" (p. 237).

104. Cowley, Malcolm. *Exile's Return: A Narrative of Ideas*. New York: W. W. Norton and Company, Incorporated, 1934, p. 231. Cowley describes *Miss Lonelyhearts* as "a brilliant novel that had few readers" (p. 231).

276. Cramer, Carter M. "The World of Nathanael West: A Critical Interpretation." *The Emporia State Research Studies*, 19, no. 4 (June 1971), 5-71. States Cramer, "Sexual impotence is directly related with spiritual death in West's works, as it is in the novels of D. H. Lawrence and the poems of T. S. Eliot. Randall Reid (see [66]) errs in asserting that any homosexual interpretation of the novel requires us to ignore many of 'the novels' details', for West uses sexual impotence and perversion as metaphors for man's total psychic misery" (p. 48). Concludes Cramer, "There is not even narrow existential hope in West's world" (p. 52).

277. D[avies], H[ugh] S[ykes]. "American Periodicals." *The Criterion*, 11 (July 1932), 772-775. In a review of *Contact*, Davies decries the emphasis on violence in the publication, and cites the lamb slaughter episode (later included in *Miss Lonelyhearts*) as an example. Davies asserts that it is impossible to render such a scene without high emotion, yet West insists upon impersonal, scientific observation. Davies sniffs,

"If it really happened, then it must be regretted that Mr. West feels like that about it" (p. 772).

24. Distasi, Lawrence W. "Nowhere to Throw the Stone." *Nathanael West: The Cheaters and the Cheated, A Collection of Critical Essays*. Deland, Florida: Everett/Edwards, Incorporated, 1973, pp. 83-102. Distasi examines violence in *Miss Lonelyhearts* as a part of man's fundamental nature and West's "desperation that the dreams and rituals founded on containment of that agression were dissipating, leaving only naked violence in their place" (p. 83). Also examined is the parallel between West's pessimism and Freud's, as expressed in *Civilization and Its Discontents*. The advance of civilization requires repression of natural agressive tendencies, resulting in guilt; either man succumbs to his guilt or violence errupts. Miss Lonelyhearts is the "prototypical guilty man of the twentieth century" (p. 84), because of his added dimension of the connection to the mass media. Miss Lonelyhearts' guilt manifests itself in two ways: his Christ complex and the "protective deadening of the senses" (p. 85). Finally, Distasi claims that Reid's rejection of Stanley Hyman's interpretation of the novel (that homosexuality is Miss Lonelyhearts' chief problem)--see [2] and [66]--is correct for the most part, yet he feels that it is incorrect to say that homosexuality has nothing to do with the story. Homosexuality characterizes a demand for self-liberation (see pp. 94, 101).

10. Edenbaum, Robert I. "To Kill God and Build a Church: Nathanael West's *Miss Lonelyhearts.*" *Twentieth Century Interpretations of* Miss Lonelyhearts, ed. Thomas H. Jackson. Englewood Cliffs: New Jersey: Prentice-Hall, Incorporated, 1971, pp. 61-69. States Edenbaum about the theme of the novel, "In a mechanized world, the energy that once went into old, lost symbols goes into the manufacture and worship of objects themselves instead of into the ordering of them into some sort of meaningful whole; the objects usurp the function of some ordering principle beyond them. Instead of working toward reality, America fragments it and substitutes the fantasies offered by the movies, newspapers and radio" (p. 66). Miss Lonelyhearts offers an ineffectual platitude (Christ) to combat this spiritlessness, but fails. The only reality that remains is his ego. Thus, Edenbaum disputes the claim that Miss Lonelyhearts found the true answer at the end, even though he was misunderstood by others. "Certainly West is searching for a religion, but to suggest that his dementia is a usable solution is ludicrous" (p. 68). Although no solution is found, Miss Lonelyhearts' confronting the truth is closer to a solution than anyone else in the novel comes.

111. Fiedler, Leslie A. *Love and Death in the American Novel*. New York: Stein and Day, 1966, pp. 326-328, 485-491. Fiedler sees Miss Lonelyhearts' function as the absurd Christ the same as the writer's function.

113. Fiedler, Leslie A. *Waiting For the End*. New York: Dell Publishing Company, 1964, p. 50. Fiedler observes that, in *Miss Lonelyhearts*, apocalypse means defeat for everybody.

287. Frank, Mike. "The Passion of *Miss Lonelyhearts* According to Nathanael West." *Studies in Short Fiction*, 10, no. 1 (Winter 1973),

67-73. Frank finds two dominant themes in the criticism of *Miss Lonely-hearts*: Either Miss Lonelyhearts is warped or the world is warped. He sees Stanley Hyman (see [2]) as combining the views by saying that Betty represents good but is overwhelmed by Miss Lonelyhearts, who represents the world of man as opposed to the world of nature. Frank claims that the inference that goodness and innocence are appropriate responses to West's world is erroneous. The only valid response belongs to Miss Lonelyhearts. Too, the old cliché about insanity being the only sane response to a mad world holds here, but for a different reason than in, say, *Catch-22*, where a sane norm is inferred. In *Miss Lonelyhearts* cynicism is the only response, and the ultimate cynicism is toward Christ, who came to save the world but failed so miserably.

293. Geha, Richard, Jr. *"Miss Lonelyhearts*: A Dual Mission of Mercy." *Hartford Studies in Literature*, 3 (1971), 116-131. Geha claims that West constantly rehashed "the psychological issues that obsessed him" (p. 116) in all four of the novels. The essay is an attempt to deal psychoanalytically with *Miss Lonelyhearts*, but Geha does not extend his conclusions to West himself (although the inference is that this would be valuable if enough were known about West). The novel deals with its hero's progressively depressive tendencies until "in the terminal stages of psychotic regression, a delusion evolves of his own salvation and messianic powers" (p. 117). Geha is Freudian with a vengeance. Miss Lonelyhearts "unconsciously attempts to undo the inadequately repressed childhood memory of mutilation to the woman's body, her castration" (p. 118). The hero suffers from the shock of recognition of the sex difference, and his struggle is to "ensure the safety of his threatened penis" (p. 118), and so on.

127. Grigson, Geoffrey, ed. *The Concise Encyclopedia of World Literature*. New York: Hawthorne Books, Incorporated, 1963, p. 483. Of *Miss Lonely-hearts*--"West's masterpiece is one of the notables of modern fiction."

299. Hammett, Dashiell. [Ad for *Miss Lonelyhearts*]. *Contempo*, 3 (25 July 1933), 7. "A new motif in American writing; in his work there are no echoes of other men's books."

300. Hand, Nancy Walker. "A Novel in the Form of a Comic Strip: Nath-anael West's *Miss Lonelyhearts*." *The Serif*, 5, no. 2 (June 1968), 14-21. Hand contends that the novel "deals with much more than a class struggle; it deals, instead, with man's struggle for belief in something larger and more constant than himself. West's ultimate statement in *Miss Lonelyhearts* is that such a struggle is self-deluding and doomed to frustration, that order and meaning in life do not exist" (p. 14). Hand finds that the characters, except for Miss Lonelyhearts, are stereotypes (Shrike is the comic strip villain) and grotesques. She concludes that, in a world where all dreams and ambitions are reduced to such a level of absurdity, the only viable reaction is laughter, but Miss Lonely-hearts takes it all too seriously.

308. Herbst, Josephine. [Ad for *Miss Lonelyhearts*]. *Contempo*, 3 (25 July 1933), 7. "This story, apart from its extreme readability, is a sort of morality play. . . . The miserable contradictions of our

times make webs for their [the characters'] feet, and the whole drama of man's wish for escape and solution runs through" the novel.

310. Herbst, Josephine. *"Miss Lonelyhearts*: An Allegory." *Contempo*, 3 (25 July 1933), 4. Herbst sees Miss Lonelyhearts as the archetypal sufferer, emblematic of a diseased society. She also notes the dream quality of the novel.

26. Hickey, James W. "Freudian Criticism." *Nathanael West: The Cheaters and the Cheated, A Collection of Critical Essays*, ed. David Madden. Deland, Florida: Everett/Edwards, Incorporated, 1973, pp. 111-150. Hickey observes that Freudian criticism is irrelevant if merely an application of psychology which does not help in understanding the work, but it can be useful if the theory occupies a significant place in the work itself. Hickey summarizes the psychological positions taken by other critics of *Miss Lonelyhearts*, particularly Hyman and Reid (see [2] and [66]), and he decides that both were wrong. West was not using Freudian psychology in the way suggested by Hyman, but he was using it in a certain way, contrary to Reid's contention. Hickey offers his own interpretation. He says that it is necessary to see the themes in more than just a literary light, but rather as "symptoms of ML's [*sic*] disturbance" (p. 117). Such a reading of course assumes that the problem is in Miss Lonelyhearts, not the world. Hickey says the reality of Miss Lonelyhearts' world is utter chaos, and the two "sub-realities"are the Christ vision and order. He claims that the Christ complex is a result of Miss Lonelyhearts' "phrenetically ambiguous relationship to his father" (p. 122).

313. Hollis, C. Carroll. "Nathanael West and Surrealist Violence." *Fresco*, 7, no. 5 (1957), 5-13. Hollis argues that the ending to *Miss Lonelyhearts* is not so bleak as many suppose but is "essentially true to Christian psychology. Paradoxical as West may have thought it, he was basically realistic in presenting Christianity as a preparation not for life but for death" (p. 10). Hollis claims that Shrike is the final victor in the novel, however, since his view triumphs.

314. Hollis, C. Carroll. "Nathanael West and the'Lonely Crowd'." *Thought*, 33 (Autumn 1958), 398-416. See [313] for the same basic discussion.

2. Hyman, Stanley Edgar. *Nathanael West*. Pamphlets on American Writers, No. 21. Minneapolis: University of Minnesota, 1962. Hyman cites Betty in *Miss Lonelyhearts* as "the principle of order" and he seems to see her as the saving grace or the solution to the anguish. "She is an innocent Eve to his [Miss Lonelyhearts'] fallen Adam, and he alone is driven out of Eden" (p. 17). Of the last scene in the novel Hyman writes, "It is of course a homosexual tableau--the men locked in an embrace while the women stand helplessly by--and behind his other miseries Miss Lonelyhearts has a powerful latent homosexuality. It is this that is ultimately the joke of his name" (p. 22). Hyman sees Miss Lonelyhearts' case as "a classic Oedipus complex" (p. 23). He concludes that *Miss Lonelyhearts*--along with *The Sun Also Rises* and *The Great Gatsby*--is one of the three great American novels of the twentieth century.

11. Hyman, Stanley Edgar. "Nathanael West." *Twentieth Century Interpretations of* Miss Lonelyhearts, ed. Thomas H. Jackson. Englewood Cliffs: New Jersey: Prentice-Hall, Incorporated, 1971, pp. 70-80. An abbreviated version of [2], this section dealing with *Miss Lonelyhearts* exclusively.

5. Jackson, Thomas H. "Introduction." *Twentieth Century Interpretations of* Miss Lonelyhearts, ed. Thomas H. Jackson. Englewood Cliffs, New Jersey: Prentice-Hall, Incorporated, 1971, pp. 1-17. Jackson traces the order/disorder theme throughout *Miss Lonelyhearts* to show how everything else has some relationship to it. He concludes, "It is a measure of the bitterness in his view of modern life that his version of the heroic plot is expressed through a set of almost purely symbolic characters whose essential claims as persons are undercut and denied by their reductive symbolic values. . . . His technique becomes an embodiment of his theme in the sense that his people have no being, only symbolic value" (p. 7).

317. Jacobs, Robert G. "Nathanael West: The Christology of Unbelief." *Iowa English Yearbook*, 9 (Fall 1964), 68-74. Jacobs sees Miss Lonelyhearts as the archetypal Puritan, assuming the Christ function of "sin-eating" in a world in the process of self-destruction. He first attempts to save the people around him, but fails. He then draws into his rock-like state, oblivious to the outside, and has a religious experience. He sees Doyle as the outward sign of grace, but gets killed. At the end he is suspended between the bottom and top of the stairs, creating an aura of ambiguity. Even if Christ is the answer, there is too much suffering in the world for one man to help much.

160. Lewis, R. W. B. "Days of Wrath and Laughter." *Trials of the Word: Essays in American Literature and the Humanistic Tradition.* New Haven and London: Yale University Press. 1965, pp. 184-236. Lewis claims that *Miss Lonelyhearts* is West's vision of the world under the dominion of Antichrist.

6. Light, James F. "The Christ Dream." *Twentieth Century Interpretations of* Miss Lonelyhearts, ed. Thomas H. Jackson. Englewood Cliffs, New Jersey: Prentice-Hall, Incorporated, 1971, pp. 19-38. Taken completely from [3].

327. Light, James F. "*Miss Lonelyhearts*: The Imagery of Nightmare." *American Quarterly*, 3, no. 4 (Winter 1956), 316-328. Light sees Miss Lonelyhearts trying to come to grips with a world of decay, violence, and pain. The hero sets out on a quest of mystical salvation, but he is murdered, ironically, by one of the "desperate of the universe" (p. 316) who inspired him to his quest. Light's analysis of Shrike is particularly good. Light concludes that the characters, save Miss Lonelyhearts, "become merely simplified states of mind" (p. 326). The entire essay is included in revised form in [3].

3. Light, James F. *Nathanael West: An Interpretative Study.* 2nd ed. Evanston: Northwestern University Press, 1971. Light finds *Miss Lonelyhearts* the best of West's novels because there form and content are best combined. Too, it is West's most compassionate work. See [327] for a synopsis of a similar discussion of the novel by Light.

336. Lorch, Thomas M. "Religion and Art in *Miss Lonelyhearts*." *Renascence*, 20, no. 1 (Autumn 1967), 11-17. Lorch claims that the traditional view of the novel's end--a negative conclusion about the possiblity of religious hope in the modern world--is wrong because it fails to take into account Miss Lonelyhearts' "very real Christian development and improvement, and, second, the inseparability of his positive growth and the equally real negative forces which question and undercut it" (p. 11). Lorch contends that the Christ pictured in the novel is the most humane and loving of men and is in direct contrast to Shrike, the devil figure. Lorch admits that as Miss Lonelyhearts grows closer to Christ, he grows more ineffectual, ridiculous, and withdrawn from the world. He concludes that West intends for the reader to see both the positive and negative side of religious committment. The real problem in the novel is not with religious experience itself but with the problem of expressing religion in modern society. Miss Lonelyhearts fails to function because of inherent weaknesses and because of the grotesque and "debased communications media" (p. 16) which surrounds him. Miss Lonelyhearts is also an artist, and religious experience is as much imaginative as mystical. Therefore, his failure is also a failure of artistic expression.

39. Malin, Irving. *Nathanael West's Novels*. Carbondale and Edwardsville: Southern Illinois University Press; London and Amsterdam: Feffer and Simons, Incorporated, 1972. Malin sees the characters in *Miss Lonelyhearts* as merely projections of its hero. All of West's major characters act compulsively and fail because their visions do not acknowledge the demands of others. Malin's study is particularly helpful in describing the patterns of opposition and juxtaposition of character and image in the novel.

342. Matthews, T. S. "Novels--A Fortnight's Grist." *The New Republic*, 74 (26 April 1933), 314-315. A three sentence review of *Miss Lonelyhearts*--"a centrifugal extravaganza" (p. 314).

174. May, John R. "Words and Deeds: Apocalyptic Judgment in Faulkner, West, and O'Connor." *Toward a New Earth: Apocalypse in the American Novel*. Notre Dame, London: University of Notre Dame Press, 1972, pp. 114-126. May contends that Miss Lonelyhearts' primary concern is to find an order amidst the chaos around him. All of nature is chaos, symbolically and otherwise; the only instance of order in the novel is the rock which the hero eventually becomes. May supports the image of Shrike as the demon by maintaining that his temptations of Miss Lonelyhearts are a parody of Satan's three temptations of Christ (with "Luke" as the basis). The final temptation is to become Christ, which Miss Lonelyhearts falls for and, of course, fails at. Thus, the rock becomes a parody of the symbol of fidelity to God. May sees Miss Lonelyhearts' death as the final judgment on his efforts. May concludes that West asserts man's needs for illusions, yet paradoxically illusions lead only to death.

345. Milburn, George. "The Hollywood Nobody Knows." *The Saturday Review of Literature*, 20, no. 4 (20 May 1939), 14-15. Predicts that *The Day of the Locust* will not be received as enthusiastically as *Miss Lonelyhearts*.

347. Mott, Frank Luther. [*Miss Lonelyhearts*]. *Journalism Quarterly*, 10 (June 1933), 170-171. In an unfavorable review, Mott says, "The book is maudlin, hysterical, bawdy. Mercifully, it is brief . . . " (p. 171).

182. Nelson, Gerald B. "Lonelyhearts." *Ten Versions of America*. New York: Alfred A. Knopf, 1972, pp. 77-90. Nelson finds that Miss Lonely-hearts mixes a Puritan conscience with mother love, with conflicting results. He wants to love his readers but cannot because they are "naughty children" (p. 80). Miss Lonelyhearts wishes to sacrifice himself for the principle of love, which translates to a desire for death because of his hatred of others, says Nelson. His messianic impulse "is the urge of self-destruction of the mother who feels herself unnatural because she can't bring herself to love her deformed child" (p. 80). Nelson examines in rather sweeping terms Puritanism from its initial impulse to its final destructive bent. Too, he claims that Shrike speaks for West. Miss Lonelyhearts is a "pathetic fool" (p. 83), but Shrike represents rationality. However, that offers no more hope than Miss Lonelyhearts' Puritan vision. Miss Lonelyhearts fails, ultimately, because he can offer only suffering instead of a release from pain and an increase in pleasure, which is what America really wants.

185. O'Connor, William Van. *The Grotesque: An American Genre and Other Essays*. Carbondale: Southern Illinois University Press, 1962, pp. 8-9. O'Connor describes the one-dimensional characters and the influence of the comic strip on *Miss Lonelyhearts*. They add to the "frightening sense of emptiness that pervades" the novel (p. 8).

186. Olsen, Bruce. "Nathanael West: The Use of Cynicism." *Minor American Novelists*, ed. Charles Alva Hoyt. Carbondale and Edwardsville: Southern Illinois University Press; London and Amsterdam: Feffer and Simons, Incorporated, 1970, pp. 81-94. Olsen claims that *Miss Lonely-hearts* is all that saves West from oblivion, and the reason it is worth-while has nothing to do with its philosophy, but for "old fashioned formal reasons" (p. 82). There, instead of telling us his views, West shows us. He compares the novel to *A Cool Million* on these grounds. *A Cool Million* is "univocal" while *Miss Lonelyhearts* "is a marvelous example of emotions deferred in internal structure" (p. 84). The only point of view in the lesser works is the narrator's because the characters are in service of an idea only.

351. Orvell, Miles D. "The Messianic Sexuality of Miss Lonelyhearts." *Studies in Short Fiction*, 10, no. 2 (Spring 1973), 159-167. Orvell agrees with Reid's view (see [66]) that the homosexual interpretation of *Miss Lonelyhearts* is fallacious, yet he disagrees that the hero's problem is a conflict between Agape and Eros. He claims that Miss Lonelyhearts' response is not abnormal but is the only one possible in West's world-view. Orvell claims that Miss Lonelyhearts fears the power of Christ, associating the messianic energy with the sexual; he both desires potency and fears failure. Too, Orvell sees West as sharing Whitman's view of America heading toward an "impoverishing materialism" (p. 167), but for West, no optimism, no hope of regeneration is possible.

353. Peden, William. "Nathanael West." *The Virginia Quarterly Review*,

33, no. 3 (Summer 1957), 468-472. Peden observes that the deterioration of the individual (*The Dream Life of Balso Snell*) becomes the destruction of a whole social group in *Miss Lonelyhearts*.

65. Perry, Robert M. *Nathanael West's* Miss Lonelyhearts: *Introduction and Commentary*. New York: Seabury Press, 1969. Perry concludes that the novel represents a new emphasis on religion. "*Miss Lonelyhearts* is an honest cry, based on the faith that human society can be and will be responsible to human agony, once its collective heart has been touched by its literary prophets" (p. 32).

62. Podhoretz, Norman. "Nathanael West: A Particular Kind of Joking." *Nathanael West: A Collection of Critical Essays*, ed. Jay Martin. Englewood Cliffs, New Jersey: Prentice-Hall, Incorporated, 1971, pp. 154-160. Podhoretz observes that the sparseness of style and coherence of conception show *Miss Lonelyhearts* to be vastly more mature than West's first novel. "The letters make the fact of evil a concrete presence in the novel" (p. 157), and since the letters are the most objective reality present, evil is the greatest reality in West's world. To combat the evil, West offers three views of salvation in the novel: Miss Lonely-hearts' "sentimental spiritualism," Shrike's cynicism, and Betty's "naive unconcern." All three are obviously failures.

191. Pritchett, V. S. *"Miss Lonelyhearts." The Living Novel and Later Appreciations*. New York: Random House, 1968, pp. 276-282. *Miss Lonely-hearts* is a "selection of hard, diamond-fine miniatures, a true American fable" (p. 279).

66. Reid, Randall. *The Fiction of Nathanael West: No Redeemer, No Promised Land*. Chicago and London: University of Chicago Press, 1967. Reid finds that the parody of literary technique in *The Dream Life of Balso Snell* becomes a human problem in *Miss Lonelyhearts*. "When West's people try to be serious, they are ridiculous. When they try to be funny, they are frightening. Thus the dual vision of the novel yields a precise statement about its characters: despite their pretensions, their pain is real" (p. 42). Reid goes to some length to refute Hyman's and Comerchero's Freudian readings of the novel (see [2] and [1]).

367. Richardson, Robert D. *"Miss Lonelyhearts." The University Review*, 33, no. 2 (December 1966), 151-157. Richardson states that the theme of the novel is order versus disorder, yet "while the story plunges into chaos, West's carefully controlled telling of the story asserts the other side, the orderly side of the conflict" (p. 151). Richardson examines the stone motif of the novel, which eventually replaces flesh and blood entirely. The novel has a furious pace, yet it holds together, unlike West's other novels whose very intensity makes them fall apart. He concludes that the novel is about language: 1) the apparently illiterate but superb letters; 2) Miss Lonelyhearts' inability to communicate; 3) Shrike the superb rhetorician (compared here to Cassius and Antony, while Miss Lonelyhearts is the good but inarticulate Brutus [p. 153]); and 4) West himself, who orders all.

194. Ross, Alan. "The Dead Center: An Introduction to Nathanael West."

The Complete Works of Nathanael West. New York: Farrar, Straus, and Cudahy, 1957, pp. vii-xxiii. Ross says that *Miss Lonelyhearts* "is the formalizing and objectifying of the rebellious vision of *Balso Snell* [*sic*]" (p. xiii). Too, Miss Lonelyhearts' final Christ vision is but a delusion. Ross claims that the characters in *Miss Lonelyhearts*, as in the other novels, are not types, but they "let in light on a central character . . . to show, but not to offer him, escape" (p. xvi). The minor characters function in much the same way as a Greek chorus.

197. [Ross, Alan]. "West, Nathanael." *The Concise Encyclopedia of Modern World Literature*, ed. Geoffrey Grigson. New York: Hawthorne Books, Incorporated, 1963, p. 483. West makes us feel Miss Lonelyhearts' death "as an ironic parody of Christian martyrdom and as the final victory of the gospel of Shrike" (p. 483).

203. Schulz, Max F. *Radical Sophistication: Studies in Contemporary Jewish-American Novelists*. Athens: Ohio University Press, 1969, pp. 36-55, 179, 185. The clash between romantic love and the procreative instinct is more complex in *Miss Lonelyhearts* than in West's other novels, for there love is translated into a quest for religious faith, which is constantly undercut by the "underlying metaphoric insinuation of oedipal obscenities" (p. 44).

381. Schwartz, Edward Greenfield. "The Novels of Nathanael West." *Accent*, 17 (Autumn 1957), 251-262. Scwartz draws a brief parallel between *Miss Lonelyhearts* and *Pilgrim's Progress*, the obvious difference being in philosophy. "For West, the old gods are dead" (p. 256).

67. Scott, Nathan A., Jr. *Nathanael West: A Critical Essay*. Contemporary Writers in Christian Perspective. Grand Rapids, Michigan: William B. Eerdmans, 1971. Scott says of *Miss Lonelyhearts*, "For his Christ dream-- in its lack of any anchorage in a coherent structure of belief, and in its bootless sentimentality--does finally appear to be itself nothing more than an example of the peurility to which the religious vision has been reduced in the world" (p. 25). Too, Scott finds, "Though the comedy is macabre, it is, like all true comedy, quite without any cynicism at all: it only wants to say 'beware'--of all the false ecstacy" (p. 26).

382. Seymour-Smith, Martin. "Prophet of Black Humor." *Spectator*, 221 (19 July 1968), 94-95. Seymour-Smith claims that the irony in *Miss Lonelyhearts* was beyond anything in American fiction and "possibly no novelist anywhere had exhibited West's capacity for sardonic economy" (p. 94).

25. Smith, Marcus. "The Crucial Departure: Irony and Point of View." *Nathanael West: The Cheaters and The Cheated, A Collection of Critical Essays*, ed. David Madden. Deland, Florida: Everett/Edwards, Incorporated, 1973, pp. 103-110. Smith cites the critical polarity over *Miss Lonely-hearts*--either he is a viable modern saint or a fool--and claims that the ambiguous effect is intentional, examining technical features of the novel which contribute to the effect. He finds that we see Miss Lonelyhearts as admirable at one time, but then West deliberately undercuts this with a pejorative view the next.

389. Swan, Michael. "New Novels." *The New Statesman and Nation*, 38 (6 August 1949), 153-154. A favorable review of the Grey Walls Press edition of *Miss Lonelyhearts*, Swan cites West for conciseness of thought and phrase. He concludes that the novel "is a savage Christian parable, the product of that interesting type of mind which seems to be controlled by a Christian background and yet is repelled by it" (p. 153).

209. Swingewood, Alan. "Alienation, Reification, and the Novel: Sartre, Camus, and Nathanael West." *The Sociology of Literature*, by Diana T. Laurenson and Alan Swingewood. New York: Schocken Books, 1972, pp. 207-248. Swingewood sees the problem of Miss Lonelyhearts in part as being the clichéd life of the thirties; he finally turns to Christ, but finds himself outside of Christian love.

210. Symons, Julian. *Critical Occasions*. London: Hamish Hamilton, 1966, pp. 99-105. Symons claims that *Miss Lonelyhearts* (along with the other novels) is not really a work of art but is a "reflection of reality in a mirror of pain" (p. 102). Symons feels that the novel could be rearranged in another order with little effect on the novel's impact. The book is also hurt by its style of "bright impersonal smartness" (p. 102) and West's hesitancy to commit himself to any positive view.

392. Tibbetts, A. M. "The Strange Half-World of Nathanael West." *Prairie Schooner*, 34, no. 1 (Spring 1960), 8-14. Tibbetts claims that West's only really good novel is *Miss Lonelyhearts*--"The power of this extremely short novelette comes not from its satire, but from its beautifully ordered, tight structure; its clear, brilliant imagery; and the traces of high comedy played out in its fine, sharp scenes" (p. 11).

393. Troy, William. "Four Newer Novelists." *The Nation*, 136 (14 June 1933), 672-673. In a review of *Miss Lonelyhearts*, Troy states, "If it were not for Mr. West's prose, which leans too much to the baroque, and for a certain ambiguity of genre ('the actual and the fanciful' are here too often confounded), 'Miss Lonelyhearts' would be a better book. As it stands, however, it is one of the most readable and one of the most exceptional books of the season" (p. 673).

12. Volpe, Edmund L. "The Waste Land of Nathanael West." *Twentieth Century Interpretations of* Miss Lonelyhearts, ed. Thomas H. Jackson. Englewood Cliffs, New Jersey: Prentice-Hall, Incorporated, 1971, pp. 81-92. Volpe claims that the reader has sympathy for Miss Lonelyhearts throughout, until the last few chapters, when he becomes a madman. Volpe feels that West loses control here, and this is the chief failure of the novel. He concludes that given the world as it is for West, the Christ dream itself is a form of madness.

219. Whitbread, Thomas B. "Introduction." *Seven Contemporary Authors: Essays on Cozzens, Miller, West, Golding, Heller, Albee, and Powers*, ed. Thomas B. Whitbread. Austin and London: University of Texas Press, 1966. "*Miss Lonelyhearts* may be the most convincingly bleak book herein discussed" (p. vii).

221. [White, William]. "*Miss Lonelyhearts.*" *Masterpieces of World Literature in Digest Form*, ed. Frank N. Magill. 3rd series. New York:

Harper and Brothers, 1960, pp. 664-667. White lists the setting, characters, *etc.*, and the type of plot ("social satire"). In the "Critique" he calls *Miss Lonelyhearts* a tale of the "often disgusting life man has made for himself in his despair" (p. 665). A two-an-one-half page précis of the novel follows.

414. White, William. "A Novelist Ahead of His Time: Nathanael West." *Orient/West*, 6 (January 1961), 55-64. *Miss Lonelyhearts* is "a grotesque picture of the miserable, monstrous, often disgusting life man has made for himself in his despair" (p. 63).

224. Widmer, Kingsley. "The Sweet Savage Prophecies of Nathanael West." *The Thirties: Fiction, Poetry, Drama*, ed. Warren French. Deland, Florida: Everett/Edwards, Incorporated, 1967, pp. 97-106. Widmer finds that West "sympathetically annihilates Christianity" (p. 100) in *Miss Lonelyhearts*. "West sardonically makes his ordinary-American-Christ equally sick and saintly" (p. 101). The only possible hope is through complete social and cultural apocalypse.

425. Wilson, Edmund. [Ad for *Miss Lonelyhearts*]. *Contempo*, 3 (25 July 1933), 7. Wilson is effusive in his praise of the novel.

228. Wilson, Edmund. *A Literary Chronicle: 1920-1950*. New York: Doubleday and Company, Incorporated, 1956, pp. 245-248. Wilson comments that *Miss Lonelyhearts*' philosophic-poetic point of view and "a sense of phrase as well as of chapter" made it seem more European than American (p. 245).

427. Wilson, T. C. "American Humor." *The Saturday Review of Literature*, 9 (13 May 1933), 589. In a review of *Miss Lonelyhearts*, Wilson foresees that the novel will "enrich the tradition of American humor," but he feels that the humor has "tragic implications." The novel is a book about "men whose warped lives do not offer any theme considerable enough for tragedy" (p. 589).

D) *A Cool Million*

237. Anon. Under "Brief Review." *New Masses*, 12 (August 21, 1934), 25. A one paragraph review of *A Cool Million*, mostly summarizing the plot. The author claims that West was "impressed by the posthumous fame of Horst Wessel."

239. Anon. "In the Jungle." *Review of Reviews*, 90 (August 1934), 6-7. In a one paragraph review of *A Cool Million*, the author comments on the inverted parallel to Horatio Alger and concludes, "'A Cool Million' is a delightful parody, with satire which hits uncomfortably near the truth" (p. 7).

244. Anon. "Nathanael West." *Times Literary Supplement*, 57 (24 January 1958), 44. The author says that *A Cool Million* is, in a way, West's most interesting work, but it fails because of its pastiche style.

249. Anon. "Shorter Notices." *The Nation*, 139 (25 July 1934), 112.
In a one paragraph review of *A Cool Million*, the author concludes,
"Mr. West is heavy-handed but his book is stimulating and at times
bitterly hilarious."

76. Auden, W. H. "Interlude: West's Disease." *"The Dyer's Hand"*
and Other Essays. New York: Random House, 1962, pp. 238-245. Auden
compares *A Cool Million* to de Sade's *Justine* and finds that both are
founded upon the principle that the "creation is essentially evil and
that goodness is contrary to its laws" (p. 244). But West would not
carry this to its logical conclusion: that it is man's duty to be evil.

254. Bittner, William. "A la recherche d'un écrivain perdu." *Les*
Langues Modernes, 54 (July-August 1960), 274-282. Bittner compares
West's comic technique in *A Cool Million* to S J. Perelman's. "There
can be little doubt that each contributed to the technique of ridicule
through over-literalness and comic surprise through style and vocabulary
either too formal or abruptly informal" (p. 280), but West went further
with this technique that Perelman.

255. Bittner, William. "Catching Up With Nathanael West." *The Nation*,
184, no. 18 (4 May 1957), 394-396. Remarks Bittner on *A Cool Million*,
"For West to have seen as early as 1934 that fascism grows on making the
patsy the hero seems sheer genius" (p. 394).

84. Blotner, Joseph. *The Modern American Political Novel, 1900-1960*.
Austin and London: University of Texas Press, 1966, p. 247. Blotner
claims that *A Cool Million* "showed how, even with the self-imposed handicap
of a confining style, he could use this talent [for parody and comic
absurdity] to satirize contemporary concerns just as he had attempted
to analyze more personal ones in the bizarre but penetrating novels by
which he is better known" (p. 247).

36. Bowden, James H. "No Redactor, No Reward." *Nathanael West: The*
Cheaters and the Cheated, A Collection of Critical Essays, ed. David
Madden. Deland, Florida: Everett/Edwards, Incorporated, 1973, pp.
283-298. Bowden claims that *A Cool Million* fails because Alger's works
are already satires on themselves, and "it is simply not possible to
satirize a satire" (p. 288).

258. Britten, Florence Haxton. "Youth Against Age in Recent Leading
Fiction." *The New York Herald Tribune Books*, 10 (1 July 1934), 8-9.
In a review of *A Cool Million*, Britten finds the book intelligent and
witty, but a step down from *Miss Lonelyhearts*. The novel is fun, but
exploiting the American myth is passé, and the satire is not incisive
enough to be a proper attack on fascism.

267. Chamberlain, John. "Books of the Times." *The New York Times*,
(19 June 1934), p. 17. In a largely favorable review of *A Cool Million*,
Chamberlain observes, "One must either laugh at this sort of thing or
go mad because of the insane reality that lies behind it. . . . Mr.
West has shown, in violently comic form, just what may be expected if
and when the time comes for a last-ditch defense of the American myth"
(p. 17).

99. Coates, Robert M. "Introduction." *Miss Lonelyhearts*, by Nathanael West. New York: The New Classics, 1950, pp. ix-xiv. Coates calls *A Cool Million* "a mistake. . . . There is none of the savage poetry and sharpness of phrase which illuminated every other piece of writing he ever turned out" (p. x). However, it is important for showing us how America could fall to fascism.

1. Comerchero, Victor. *Nathanael West: The Ironic Prophet*. Syracuse: Syracuse University Press, 1964. Of *A Cool Million* Comerchero comments, "As a work of art it is hardly worthy of sustained comment. It is a bag of tricks, some of which are brilliantly effective, and it fails to achieve anything beyond a few laughs" (p. 103). He says that West's theme is success and failure in American society, and the conclusion is that the success finally betrays the society while the society betrays the failure. Comerchero finds that the primary purpose of the novel is to destroy clichés and illusions, "the blind, uncritical idealism, the simple, uncomplicated world view of society at large" (p. 111).

276. Cramer, Carter M. "The World of Nathanael West: A Critical Interpretation." *The Emporia State Research Studies*, 19, no. 4 (June 1971), 5-71. Comments Cramer, "To criticize *A Cool Million* or *The Dream Life of Balso Snell* as inferior novels in comparison to West's other works is to state a preference for the novel form over the anatomy-- little more" (p. 38).

291. Galloway, David D. "A Picaresque Apprenticeship: Nathanael West's *A Cool Million* and *The Dream Life of Balso Snell*." *Wisconsin Studies in Contemporary Literature*, 5, no. 2 (Summer 1964), 110-126. Galloway sees *A Cool Million* mainly as a work of apprenticeship in preparation for the writing of *The Day of the Locust*. He also traces the influence of S. J. Perelman's humor, particularly the use of American commonplaces as targets of satire, on the novel. Concludes Galloway, West "suffers less with Lemuel than with his other misguided 'fools'. It is the content of their dreams, however, which makes the suffering of Balso Snell, Miss Lonelyhearts, and Tod Hackett ennobling. Even though *A Cool Million* makes a violent critique of the milieu in which Lemuel's dream is culti- vated, West is so out of sympathy with the character of that dream that he has little sympathy for Lemuel" (p. 124).

292. Gannett, Lewis. "Books and Things." *The New York Herald Tribune*, (21 June 1934), 19. In an unfavorable review of *A Cool Million*, Gannett comments, "I don't think good writing is laid on with a trowel" (p. 19).

315. Hollis, C. Carroll. "Nathanael West: Diagnostician of the Lonely Crowd." *Fresco*, 8, no. 1 (1957), 5-21. "The real flaw of *A Cool Million* is that West's passionate castigation of American society is too strong to be contained successfully in the fanciful framework" (p. 6). He compares Lemuel to Gulliver, except that West's hero never learns from his experiences. Hollis observes that the trauma of the savage ending "is most forcefully comprehended by imagining the spiritual state of the American Jew who has lost his faith" (p. 10). However, Hollis does not claim to make his reading biographical. He finds that in the last two novels, the "lonely crowd becomes increasingly made up of apostates;" yet "there is no apostacy in an age without faith" (p. 11).

2. Hyman, Stanley Edgar. *Nathanael West*. Pamphlets on American Writers, No. 21. Minneapolis: University of Minnesota, 1962. Of *A Cool Million* Hyman states, "What form the book has comes from these ritual stages of dismemberment, but in a truer sense *A Cool Million* is formless, an inorganic stringing together of comic set-pieces, with the preposterous incidents serving merely to raise the various topics West chooses to satirize" (p. 29). He concludes, "The book is strongest as a political warning" (p. 30).

160. Lewis, R. W. B. "Days of Laugh and Laughter." *Trials of the Word: Essays in American Literature and the Humanistic Tradition*. New Haven and London: Yale University Press, 1965, pp. 184-236. Lewis claims that *A Cool Million* is "this country's most vigorous narrative vision of the political apocalypse" (p. 214). Art is West's weapon against evil (hate).

328. Light, James F. "Nathanael West." *Prairie Schooner*, 31, no. 3 (Fall 1957), 279-283. Light claims that *A Cool Million* is West's weakest novel. Although the use of clichés had a purpose there, it destroyed his distinctive prose style--his strongest asset.

3. Light, James F. *Nathanael West: An Interpretative Study*. 2nd ed. Evanston: Northwestern University Press, 1971. Light suggests that *A Cool Million* was written largely to make money (p. 138). However, "Like the previous novels, *A Cool Million* offers no real solutions. It mocks the American way, derides the 'conspiracies' of the Bolsheviki and the International Jewish Bankers, and attacks bitterly the American fascist movement. If the novel suggests anything affirmatively, it is that life was better in earlier times" (p. 137).

333. Linberg-Seyersted, Brita. "Three Variations of the American Success Story: The Careers of Luke Larkin, Lemuel Barker, and Lemuel Pitkin." *English Studies*, 53, no. 2 (April 1972), 125-141. Linberg-Seyersted claims that *A Cool Million* is a powerful novel, and the numbed effect most readers feel is the only proper response.

39. Malin, Irving. *Nathanael West's Novels*. Carbondale and Edwardsville: Southern Illinois University Press; London and Amsterdam: Feffer and Simons, Incorporated, 1972. Malin says that the last thirty pages almost saves *A Cool Million*, but, "We should see the novel clearly as a misguided, faulty effort--an attempt to write a lighthearted piece of propaganda. Propaganda, black comedy, and allegory do not usually mix" (p. 83).

340. Marsh, Fred T. "*A Cool Million* and Other Recent works of Fiction." *The New York Times Book Review* (1 July 1934), p. 6. In a favorable review of *A Cool Million*, Marsh notes that it is almost perfect parody, but it hits too close to home to be completely enjoyable. The style is self-limiting, however, and it is not as good as *Miss Lonelyhearts*.

56. Martin, Jay. "The Black Hole of Calcoolidge." *Nathanael West: A Collection of Critical Essays*, ed. Jay Martin. Englewood Cliffs, New Jersey: Prentice-Hall, Incorporated, 1971, pp. 114-131. Slightly revised version of the discussion of *A Cool Million* in [64].

344. McLaughlin, Richard. "West of Hollywood." *Theatre Arts*, 35 (August 1951), 46-47. McLaughlin calls *A Cool Million* "a grave mistake" (p. 47).

185. O'Connor, William Van. *The Grotesque: An American Genre and Other Essays*. Carbondale: Southern Illinois University Press, 1962, pp. 6, 8-9, 12, 18, 21, 55-56. O'Connor feels that *A Cool Million* is too exaggerated to be taken seriously.

99. Peden, William. "Nathanael West." *The Virginia Quarterly Review*, 33, no. 3 (Summer 1957), 468-472. Peden calls *A Cool Million* West's weakest novel.

66. Reid, Randall. *The Fiction of Nathanael West: No Redeemer, No Promised Land*. Chicago and London: University of Chicago Press, 1967. Reid finds that the problem with *A Cool Million* is that, "In a world so dominated by moronic gullibility, a reader can neither identify with the characters nor feel much complicity in the folly and evil they represent" (p. 106). He claims that part of the reason for the novel's failure is the fact that it was hurriedly written as West was trying to escape the hotel business. Like many other critics, Reid observes that in the novel West imposes the pattern of *Candide* upon the Horatio Alger myth.

194. Ross, Alan. "The Dead Center: An Introduction to Nathanael West." *The Complete Works of Nathanael West*. New York: Farrar, Straus, and Cudahy, 1957, pp. vii-xxii. Ross says that the mock heroic style of *A Cool Million* is "brilliantly successful" (p. xvii), but it also forces him to sacrifice the terse, compact style that is his strongest feature. The novel attacks "the way in which the sheeplike dependence of the mob, their malleableness, is made use of for ulterior political ends" (p. xviii).

197. [Ross, Alan]. "West, Nathanael." *The Concise Encyclopedia of Modern World Literature*, ed. Geoffrey Grigson. New York: Hawthorne Books, Incorporated, 1963, p. 483. *A Cool Million* is "written in a style which too much parodies the magazine best seller."

371. S., G. "The New Books." *The Saturday Review of Literature*, 10 (30 June 1934), 785. In an unfavorable one paragraph review of *A Cool Million*, the author concludes, "The present reviewer finds only a straining for effect and an impenetrable tedium."

203. Schulz, Max F. *Radical Sophistication: Studies in Contemporary Jewish-American Novelists*. Athens: Ohio University Press, 1969, pp. 36-55. Schulz suggests that probably few readers miss the point of *A Cool Million*, as Comerchero (see [1]) claims; but he does think that the book seems to laugh at itself, has a curious aura of reserve stemming from its excess. He feels that the problems with the American dream as exposed in the novel are obvious, but their solutions are not.

381. Schwartz, Edward Greenfield. "The Novels of Nathanael West." *Accent*, 17 (Autumn 1957), 251-262. Schwartz concludes that *A Cool Million* is a good outline for an American *Candide*, but little more (p. 257).

141

67. Scott, Nathan A., Jr. *Nathanael West: A Critical Essay.* Contemporary
Writers in Christian Perspective. Grand Rapids, Michigan: William B.
Eerdmans, 1971. Scott asserts that *A Cool Million* "does now appear to
be the shrewdest essay in political discrimination to be found anywhere
in the American fiction of its period" (p. 27). West's "characters are
drawn with the kind of extravagantly parodistic flatness that precludes
psychological analysis; his chain of incident, in its travesty of the
Alger myth, mounts horror upon horror, without any slight concession to
plausibility; and the whole burlesque moves with the rapidity and deliberate
crudeness of an animated cartoon" (p. 28).

382. Seymour-Smith, Martin. "Prophet of Black Humor." *Spectator*, 221
(19 July 1968), 94-95. The author claims that *A Cool Million* is entirely
successful as satire, the best of its kind in American fiction.

388. Steiner, T. R. "West's Lemuel and the American Dream." *The Southern
Review*, 7, no. 4 (October 1971), 994-1006. Steiner says that *A Cool
Million* has been unappreciated because it is not read properly. Like
the Horatio Alger novels and *Gulliver's Travels*, "*A Cool Million* frequently
purports to be a children's book. As such, although its literary mode
may be parody or mock-heroic, West's novel is also fantasy myth, dream-
wish identification, imaginative 'redemption', and pure play" (p. 994).
Steiner claims that West was not so much interested in fascism as in the
type of psyche that would allow such a state to thrive. Too, he rejects
the idea that the frequent unfavorable portraits of Jews in West's fiction
represents anti-Jewishness. Rather, all ethnic groups who fall victim
to sterile dreams are attacked. He concludes that the novel is West's
spiritual biography--evoking the Jew's confrontation with the American
myth.

210. Symons, Julian. *Critical Occasions.* London: Hamish Hamilton,
1966, pp. 99-105. Symons claims that *A Cool Million* has a magnificent
theme for satire, but West's mind was not broad enough to handle it.

414. White, William. "A Novelist Ahead of His Time: Nathanael West."
Orient/West, 6 (January 1961), 55-64. White maintains that *A Cool Million*
is a failure because the slapstick manner is so pervasive that the satire
is not effective.

224. Widmer, Kingsley. "The Sweet Savage Prophecies of Nathanael
West." *The Thirties: Fiction, Poetry, Drama*, ed. Warren French. Deland,
Florida: Everett/Edwards, Incorporated, 1967, pp. 97-106. Widmer terms
A Cool Million a "trite treatment of the trite" (p. 103).

E) *The Day of the Locust*

71. Allen, Walter. *Tradition and Dream: A Critical Survey of British
and American Fiction From the 1920's to the Present Day.* Middlesex,
England: Penguin Books, 1965, pp. 187, 188-190, 190-192. Allen feels
that *The Day of the Locust* is more ambitious than *Miss Lonelyhearts* but
less intense since Tod Hackett is merely an observer of the action.

244. Anon. "Nathanael West." *Times Literary Supplement*, 57 (24 January 1958), 44. The author comments that *The Day of the Locust* "has a fine, brittle brilliance, the book marks an advance on his previous work: but he paid the price for it . . . in a slackening of energy and concentration" (p. 44).

245. Anon. "Neglected Novelist." *Newsweek*, 36 (4 September 1950), 77-78. In a brief review of *The Day of the Locust* the author concludes, "West's humor was harried, and the mood of his novels jumpy and nervous, like that of a respectable citizen caught in a gangster hideout, and never sure of what anyone around is going to do" (p. 78).

250. Anon. "Truly Monstrous." *Time*, 33 (19 June 1939), 84. In a brief review of *The Day of the Locust* the author says that West started well, but long before the end "his intended tragedy turns into screwball grotesque, and groggy author West can barely distinguish fantastic shadow from fantastic substance."

254. Bittner, William. "A la recherche d'un écrivain perdu." *Les Langues Modernes*, 54 (July-August 1960), 274-282. Bittner briefly compares Fitzgerald's treatment of Hollywood in *The Last Tycoon* to West's in *The Day of the Locust*. He finds Fitzgerald's treatment more romantic; West "mocks it furiously" (p. 282).

257. Britten, Florence Haxton. "New Novels From Far and Near." *The New York Herald Tribune Books* (21 May 1939), p. 7. Britten mostly retells the plot in this review of *The Day of the Locust*. She finds it more disciplined, less surreal than *Miss Lonelyhearts*, but "by comparison with the other, 'The Day of the Locust' is emotionally inert" (p. 7), perhaps because West is aware of the "futility of his materials--for certainly the locusts *have* feasted here."

98. Coan, Otis W. and Richard G. Lillard. *America in Fiction: An Annotated List of the Novels That Interpret Aspects of Life in the United States, Canada, and Mexico*. Palo Alto: Pacific Books, Publishers, 1967, p. 113. Under "Traditional America--City Life" the authors list *The Day of the Locust*: "a sensational picture of the lunatic fringe in Hollywood."

1. Comerchero, Victor. *Nathanael West: The Ironic Prophet*. Syracuse: Syracuse University Press, 1964. Comerchero says that *The Day of the Locust* "differs from the other novels by failing to focus indignation upon any single aspect of existence. . . . In many respects, the reader's inability to do so [focus on any one central point] comprises the chief failing of the novel" (p. 120). Like many other critics, Comerchero feels that the novel lacks the intensity of *Miss Lonelyhearts* because Tod Hackett does not take part in, but merely observes, the action. Too, the novel is too long and does not use the incremental effect that West is so good at. Comerchero finds that the novel is best read as a prose *Waste Land*, not as a normal narrative; the importance lies in its symbolic impressions, not plot. Tod's comments should not be taken as merely clarification of his character but as analysis of American society. He is the unifying priciple in the novel. The reader finds nearly all of West's themes here, but most important are the twin themes of apathy and lechery. Hollywood

143

itself is a false land of escape; even Tod's chaining to Faye is a form of escape. Homer (West's symbol for the crowd) is the only one who cannot adopt a pose. And of Faye, Comerchero concludes, "Sexual sanity is impossible in the 'Unreal City', but compared to the other characters, she is neither apathetic nor lecherous; and in a world of half-men, promiscuity is paradoxically a pardonable quest" (p. 141).

103. Cowley, Malcolm. *Exile's Return: A Literary Odyssey of the 1920's.* New York: The Viking Press, 1951, pp. 237-240. Cowley calls *The Day of the Locust* "still the best of the Hollywood novels" (p. 237n).

276. Cramer, Carter M. "The World of Nathanael West: A Critical Interpretation." *The Emporia State Research Studies,* 19, no. 4 (June 1971), 5-71. Cramer sees *The Day of the Locust* as a natural extension of *Miss Lonelyhearts,* with the scope broadened to include all society in its despair. Cramer comments on the common complaint about the shift in focus in the novel: "The validity of such critical arguments is reduced, however, when the reader considers the prophetic nature of the work-- a work that, unlike the conventional dramatic or psychological novel or the realistic or naturalistic novel, operates on a plane of pure symbol, in an effort not to dramatize a single character or problem but, instead, to dramatize the death rattle of a civilization" (p. 54). Concludes Cramer, "The profound, disquieting despair captured by West has at its very vortex West's insistence that the boundaries between reality and nightmare may be irredeemably lost" (p. 57).

32. Edenbaum, Robert I. "From American Dream to American Nightmare." *Nathanael West: The Cheaters and the Cheated, A Collection of Critical Essays,* ed. David Madden. Deland, Florida: Everett/Edwards, Incorporated, 1973, pp. 201-216. Edenbaum finds the basic structure of *The Day of the Locust* follows the two-level world pictured by Tod Hackett in his paintings: 1) the world of the grotesques, such as Abe, Harry and Faye and 2) the world of midwesterners who flock to California, such as Homer. The midwesterners "provide, by allusion and appearance, a constant background against which the grotesques perform" (p. 202). Hollywood itself is a masquerade world, but West is careful to try to create the "illusion of objective reality" rather than surrealistic fantasy, as one might expect. Edenbaum claims that it is absurd to call Homer the central character, as some have done, because Homer is incapable of judging himself or his world. Too, unlike the other critics, Edenbaum finds Tod involved in the action to an extent; and, he is the one character who truly judges. Finally, Edenbaum sees the dreams of the characters as defense mechanisms, and since the tale is told after the fact, the machine is proven functional. "The idea is not a new one, but West's conception of the conditioned response acting as a defense against a mechanized world is a brilliant irony: it turns Pavlov into Christ" (p. 210).

282. Fadiman, Clifton. "Books." *The New Yorker,* 15 (20 May 1939), 78-80. Fadiman says that West--"about the ablest of our surrealist authors" (p. 79)--has written an "unpleasant, thoroughly original book" (p. 80) in *The Day of the Locust.*

112. Fiedler, Leslie A. *The Return of the Vanishing American.* New York: Stein and Day, 1968, pp. 147-149. Fiedler discusses *The Day of*

the Locust as a parody of the Western, focussing on Earl Shoop--"last obscene descendant of Natty Bumpo" (p. 149). In the novel, "Everybody plays himself badly" (p. 148).

113. Fiedler, Leslie A. *Waiting For the End*. New York: Dell Publishing Company, 1964, pp. 37, 45-46, 48-52, 63-64, 83, 108, 143, 226. Fiedler says that the Hollywood novel--such as *The Day of the Locust*--was the great literary form of the thirties, not the proletarian novel, as so many assert.

288. Friedman, Robert. "Nathaniel [*sic*] West's 'Day of the Locust'." *Daily Worker* (23 November 1950), p. 11. In a review of the novel based on Marxist criticism, Friedman says that it is a powerful book, but its emphasis on the lower rungs of life fails to uncover the evils of capitalist society as a whole. West rejects the people, not the society.

290. Galloway, David D. "Nathanael West's Dream Dump." *Critique: Studies in Modern Fiction*, 6, no. 3 (Winter 1963-64), 46-64. "He found in Hollywood both an instant symbolism and a microcosm of his favorite subjects: the ignoble lie, the world of illusion, the surrealistic incongruities of the American experience" (p. 47).

294. Gehman, Richard B. "My Favorite Forgotten Book." *Tomorrow*, 8, no. 7 (March 1949), 61-62. Gehman discusses what he finds to be "the key to the whole book [*The Day of the Locust*]: that life is a tragic masquerade, a pitiful comic opera. . . . West seems to be saying that Hollywood is the synthesis of modern materialistic civilization" (p. 62).

295. Gehman, Richard B. "Nathanael West: A Novelist Apart." *The Atlantic Monthly*, 186, no. 3 (September 1950), 69-72. Of *The Day of the Locust* Gehman observes, "If it was less perfect in form and structure than *Miss Lonelyhearts*, it was also more ambitious and showed marked progress in West's thinking." Here West lets the scenes and characters make their own points without authorial intrusion. This places West above the dogmatism of his contemporaries.

315. Hollis, C. Carroll. "Nathanael West: Diagnostician of the Lonely Crowd." *Fresco*, 8, no. 1 (1957), 5-21. Hollis claims that *The Day of the Locust* was unpopular because it was so far ahead of its time.

2. Hyman, Stanley Edgar. *Nathanael West*. Pamphlets on American Writers, No. 21. Minneapolis: University of Minnesota, 1962. Hyman says that-- like the characters in *Miss Lonelyhearts*, those in *The Day of the Locust* tend to be symbolic abstractions, but here with a loss of "human reality" (p. 33). He sees Faye as a symbol for nature, but here nature is deceptive, invulnerable. He feels that the image of Homer's hands is a beautiful one, but West lets it go to waste, with the violence of the final scene not making use of Homer's hands. Hyman concludes that the novel fails ultimately because of a lack of dramatic unity and because, in comparison to *Miss Lonelyhearts*, "It has no moral core" (p. 45).

147. Ketterer, David. *New Worlds For Old: The Apocalyptic Imagination, Science Fiction, and American Literature*. Garden City, New York: Anchor Books, 1974, p. 4. Ketterer calls *The Day of the Locust* the most

obvious example of apocalypse in American fiction.

328. Light, James F. "Nathanael West." *Prairie Schooner*, 31, no. 3 (Fall 1957), 279-283. *The Day of the Locust* examines the dream factory-- Hollywood. Man is caught between the animal and the spiritual world, and all attempts to satisfy emotional needs fail.

3. Light, James F. *Nathanael West: An Interpretative Study*. 2nd ed. Evanston: Northwestern University Press, 1971. Light says of *The Day of the Locust*, "The half-world can be divided into spectators (the cheated whose emotional needs demand satisfaction) and performers (the cheaters who are attempting to satisfy the emotional needs of others). The roles, however, occasionally shift, for in the world of grotesquerie all men are both performers and spectators" (p. 173). Light observes that the images of violence in the novel fulfills "in West's terms the artist's duty: to use Freud as Bullfinch in presenting pictorially, symbolically, the mythology of our day. The particular mythology that West was concerned with in *The Day* [*sic*] . . . is a drama about man's emotional needs, the frustration of those needs, and the need for a scapegoat to vent one's rage upon" (p. 183).

334. Lokke, V. L. "A Side Glance at Medusa: Hollywood, the Literature Boys, and Nathanael West." *Southwest Review*, 46, no. 1 (Winter 1961), 35-45. Lokke finds that *The Day of the Locust* emphasizes themes seen in earlier novels. Here America pits its spiritual hopes on mechanical manifestations. Lokke examines in particular Faye (the dream America is selling) and Homer (who represents the middle class system). "The point of West's allegory is apparent. The studied, mechanical, and commercialized sexuality of Faye Greener invited not love and compassion, but violence, insanity, and death" (p. 44). Lokke maintains that the success of the novel lies not in its direct assault on Hollywood, as Edmund Wilson maintained (see [59]). "West's novel is important not so much because he knew the scene intimately or because he possessed any brash courage, but rather because he had developed a technique, a point of view, and a general theory of popular culture which permitted analysis of Hollywood as a symbol rather than as a peculiar institution, industry, or city" (pp. 35-36). West examines not the stars and directors as most Hollywood novels did, but the periphery. Too, unlike other Jeremiads, West "makes no plea for high culture" or hope of religion, solutions which were offered and rejected in previous works. Lokke concludes that West's vision is totally bleak.

39. Malin, Irving. *Nathanael West's Novels*. Carbondale and Edwardsville: Southern Illinois University Press; London and Amsterdam: Feffer and Simons, Incorporated, 1972. Malin agrees with many that *The Day of the Locust* lacks focus, Tod Hackett getting lost in the confusion--shifting from actor to spectator and back--but he maintains that this does not really bother the reader. "We are troubled by these sudden loses of identity, but once we realize that he surrenders to Hollywood, we do not mind his absence. We understand that it is perfectly appropriate" (p. 117).

339. Markfield, Wallace. "From the Underbelly." *The New Leader*, 33 (27 November 1950), 25. In a review of *The Day of the Locust* Markfield

summarizes the typical Hollywood novel, then comments, "But *The Day of the Locust* is concerned with types never seen before in Hollywood fiction, characters who, like Faulkner's creations, horrify us because we know so little of their origin, freaks and grotesqueries whose actions have no visible morality behind them, governed only by hallucinatory logic" (p. 25).

64. Martin, Jay. *Nathanael West: The Art of His Life*. New York: Farrar, Straus and Giroux, 1970. Martin observes that *The Day of the Locust* "is a satire which shows to the full the rule of chaos over both past and present by hinting at an alternative state of man, with his illusions revealed, returning to what Pope termed his 'lawful callings'. West refused to turn his vision, romantically and nostalgically, backward; in the best sense his vision was classical, stoical, and reserved; what beliefs he had were held without hope" (p. 315). Martin's observations on Tod Hacket's involvement in the novel may serve as partial answer to those who feel that the novel is flawed because Tod is merely an observer. "Tod's story, then, mirrors the rest of the novel. On the one hand, he moves from desire to frustration to frenzy and at last personal dissolution; on the other, aesthetically, toward experience, vision, prophecy, and finally art" (p. 317).

344. McLaughlin, Richard. "West of Hollywood." *Theatre Arts*, 35 (August 1951), 46-47, 93. Mclaughlin claims that *The Day of the Locust* tells only the "grimmer half" (p. 93) of Hollywood, not "its whole fantastic story." Of West McLaughlin comments, "He was a canny assayer of dreams, the most treacherous commodity sold in the cold stone market place" (p. 93).

345. Milburn, George. "The Hollywood Nobody Knows." *The Saturday Review of Literature*, 20, no. 4 (20 May 1939), 14-15. Milburn finds the worst fault of *The Day of the Locust* to be its "choppy, episodic technique of a movie scenario" (p. 14); still, its scenic power saves the novel.

176. Millgate, Michael. *American Social Fiction: James to Cozzens*. Edinburgh and London: Oliver and Boyd, 1964, pp. 154-156. Millgate contends that in *The Day of the Locust* West was less concerned with picturing Hollywood realistically than with "defining the meaning of Hollywood in relation to American society as a whole" (p. 154). He concludes that West felt that movies had no relationship to art.

180. Murray, Edward. "Nathanael West--The Pictorial Eye in Locust-Land." *The Cinematic Imagination: Writers and the Motion Pictures*. New York: Frederick Ungar Publishing Company, 1972, pp. 206-216. Murray finds that *The Day of the Locust* is more cinematic in nature than West's earlier novels. It employs a roving, panoramic technique. The novel is weaker than *Miss Lonelyhearts*, not because of this cinematic technique, but because of a flaw in point of view. He concludes that West took Hollywood and the art of the movies more seriously than many suggest.

185. O'Connor, William Van. *The Grotesque: An American Genre and Other Essays*. Carbondale: Southern Illinois University Press, 1962, pp. 18, 56. O'Connor finds that *The Day of the Locust* is more objective, therefore more successful, than West's earlier fiction. He sees Hollywood

as the stage setting for the novel and concludes, "In West . . . one finds grotesques, the comedy and pathos of the misfit" (p. 56).

186. Olsen, Bruce. "Nathanael West: The Use of Cynicism." *Minor American Novelists*, ed. Charles Alva Hoyt. Carbondale and Edwardsville: Southern Illinois Unversity Press; London and Amsterdam: Feffer and Simons, Incorporated, 1970, pp. 81-94. Olsen finds that the problem with *The Day of the Locust* concerns the narrator; Tod Hackett has no stake in the action, and Homer Simpson is not perceptive enough to "express or even realize the unconscious forces pushing him" (p. 89). Not only is the shift in narrators a flaw, but the dogma is too explicit; the reader realizes the emptiness of Hollywood long before it has any effect on Tod.

353. Peden, William. "Nathanael West." *The Virginia Quarterly Review*, 33, no. 3 (Summer 1957), 468-472. Peden calls *The Day of the Locust* the best novel to date about Hollywood.

360. Pisk, George M. "The Graveyard of Dreams: A Study of Nathanael West's Last Novel, *The Day of the Locust.*" *The South Central Bulletin*, 27, no. 4 (Winter 1967), 64-72. Pisk places Homer Simpson in West's 'holy fool' tradition and finds his spiritual brother to be Benjamin Compson. He examines in some detail animal imagery, the use of music to create mood, violence, and the articiality of the dream as opposed to reality in the novel. He concludes that it lacks the swift pace of earlier novels but makes up for it by a compassion not found in the rest of West's work.

191. Pritchett, V. S. *"Miss Lonelyhearts."* *The Living Novel and Later Appreciations.* New York: Random House, 1968, pp. 276-282. Says Pritchett, *"The Day of the Locust* has the defect of insufficient ambition. It calls for a larger treatment and we have a slight suspicion that the painter-observer is shunning. But West had not the breadth for full-length works" (p. 281).

66. Reid, Randall. *The Fiction of Nathanael West: No Redeemer, No Promised Land.* Chicago and London: University of Chicago Press, 1967. States Reid, *"The Day of the Locust* can be read as a statement of what must follow the failure of the Christ dream. In this novel, even the pseudo-savior is missing" (p. 116). An interesting discussion is Reid's examination of the shift in descriptive patterns from *Miss Lonelyhearts* to *The Day of the Locust.* The earlier novel's form followed the comic strip, but the latter follows the motion picture. Too, Reid examines the performer/audience theme of the novel. "In West, the interaction between performer and audience is compulsive and mutually degrading, like mechanical stimulation. It is also the paradigm for all interactions--demagogue and mob, redeemer and sufferer, seducer and victim" (p. 120). Reid denies the charge that Tod Hackett's non-involvement is a flaw; what the novel loses in intensity it makes up for in "range and veracity" (p. 150).

194. Ross, Alan. "The Dead Center: An Introduction to Nathanael West." *The Complete Works of Nathanael West.* New York: Farrar, Straus, and Cudahy, 1957, pp. vii-xxii. Ross feels that *The Day of the Locust*'s

weaknesses come from the slowness in momentum of plot and subplots that
are never clearly integrated. Of Hollywood, Ross comments, "More than
anything it is made up of significant boredom, of etiolated ennui: the
whole canvas on which the motiveless actions take place acquires a
Breughel-like stillness, as if all the monstrous things going on where
part of a very ordinary pattern" (p. xxii).

197. [Ross, Alan]. "West, Nathanael." *The Concise Encyclopedia of
Modern World Literature*, ed. Geoffrey Grigson. New York: Hawthorne
Books, Incorporated, 1963, p. 483. In *The Day of the Locust*, Tod Hackett
remains "never absorbed into the world he lives in because he retains
his critical sense" (p. 483).

372. Salomon, Louis B. "California Grotesque." *The Nation*, 149 (15 July
1939), 78-79. Salomon says that *The Day of the Locust* could have been
even better if it were less sketchy. "It needs more thorough characterization, more documentation" (p. 79).

376. Schneider, Cyril M. "The Individuality of Nathanael West." *The
Western Review*, 20, no. 1 (Autumn 1955), 7-28. Schneider finds *The Day
of the Locust* trenchent satire, but the plot is choppy, "suggesting a
movie montage technique" (p. 21).

380. Schulberg, Budd Wilson. "Literature of the Film: The Hollywood
Novel." *Films*, 1, no. 2 (Spring 1940), 68-78. In a review of *The
Day of the Locust*, Schulberg is particularly taken with the incipient
violence of the mobs who feel betrayed by the Hollywood dream. However,
he feels that West's vision is limited to the lunatic fringe.

203. Schulz, Max F. *Radical Sophistication: Studies in Contemporary
Jewish-American Novelists*. Athens: Ohio University Press, 1969, pp.
178-179. Schulz comments that "the Westian novel is concerned at its
center with the instability of existence" derived from our contemporary
belief in a world of flux. Hollywood (*The Day of the Locust*) is the best
example of mindless flux. However, he feels that West's "angry despair"
is an "easy solution" (pp. 178-179).

67. Scott, Nathan A., Jr. *Nathanael West: A Critical Essay*. Contemporary
Writers in Christian Perspective. Grand Rapids, Michigan: William B.
Eerdmans, 1971. Scott observes that the common complaint about *The Day
of the Locust* and West in general--limited vision and theme--could be
made about almost all writers save the very greatest--Dante, Shakespeare,
or Tolstoy.

169. See, Carolyn. "The Hollywood Novel: The American Dream Cheat."
Tough Guy Writers of the Thirties, ed. David Madden. Carbondale and
Edwardsville: Southern Illinois University Press; London and Amsterdam:
Feffer and Simon, Incorporated, 1968, pp. 199, 216. See mentions *The
Day of the Locust* in discussing the Hollywood Novel as a type (p. 119),
and discusses Claude Estee in the novel as emblematic of the "hardboiled"
attitude many characters assume in order to deal with "Hollywood's
dehumanizing artificiality" (p. 216).

382. Seymour-Smith, Martin. "Prophet of Black Humor." *Spectator*, 221 (19 July 1968), 94-95. Seymour-Smith believes that *The Day of the Locust* is West's best work, one of the best short novels of the century.

384. Simonson, Harold P. "California, Nathanael West, and the Journey's End." *The Closed Frontier: Studies in American Literary Tragedy*. New York [*etc*]: Holt, Rinehart, and Winston, Incorporated, 1970, pp. 99-124. Of *The Day of the Locust* Simonson concludes, "What West sees is the collapsing American myth of the open frontier, the tragedy of a society too proud to accept the disparity between promises and realities" (p. 124).

386. Smith, Roger H. "Complete Works of Nathanael West." *The Saturday Review of Literature*, 40 (11 May 1957), 13-14. Smith calls *The Day of the Locust* "unquestionably the best novel ever written about Hollywood" (p. 13).

210. Symons, Julian. *Critical Occasions*. London: Hamish Hamilton, 1966, pp. 99-105. Symons says that *The Day of the Locust* has a certain "brittle brilliance" but it lacks energy and power.

392. Tibbetts, A. M. "The Strange Half-World of Nathanael West." *Prairie Schooner*, 34, no. 1 (Spring 1960), 8-14. Tibbetts cites the poor structure of *The Day of the Locust*. "Each event in *The Day of the Locust* is exactly like the one that preceded. The book never reaches a climax" (p. 14).

394. Van Gelder, Robert. "A Tragic Chorus." *The New York Times Book Review*, 44 (21 May 1939), 6-7. In a review of *The Day of the Locust*, Van Gelder praises the novel, but offers little new insight.

218. Wells, Walter. *Tycoons and Locusts: A Regional Look at Hollywood Fiction of the 1930's*. Carbondale and Edwardsville: Southern Illinois University Press; London and Amsterdam: Feffer and Simons, 1973, pp. 11, 39, 49-73, 80, 84, 87, 94-95, 100-101, 107, 109-110, 117-119, 125, 56, 62, 103, 122. Wells sees the central theme in *The Day of the Locust* as the corruption of love and sex. He finds a strong regional basis to the novel: "It would be hard, in fact, to find a closer relationship between prose narrative and place than that between West's *Day* [*sic*] and the Hollywood-Southland" (p. 49). There follows an in-depth discussion of the theme of the "ongoing breakdown of human values, purpose, and dreams, with nothing but sordid emptiness left in their wake" (p. 49). The whole process of breakdown is symbolized by Faye and her relationship to the other characters. Identity, communication, and art all break down, and a willingness to destroy is a common characteristic of the Hollywood people. Too, deception, role playing, and sex and violence are major motifs in the novel. Wells concludes that West is a bleak moralist.

224. Widmer, Kingsley. "The Sweet Savage Prophecies of Nathanael West." *The Thirties: Fiction, Poetry, Drama*, ed. Warren French. Deland, Florida: Everett/Edwards, Incorporated, 1967, pp. 97-106. One of the key issues missed by many critics of *The Day of the Locust*, Widmer feels, is West's concern with "the essence of mass-technological society" (p. 105). This results in mechanical responses, a loss of vitality and selfhood.

226. Williams, William Carlos. *The Autobiography of William Carlos Williams*. New York: A New Directions Book, 1967, pp. 301-302. Says Williams, "His book *The Day of the Locust* is the only piece about Hollywood that can be ranked, as far as I know, as *belles lettres*" (p. 302).

58. Williams, William Carols. *"The Day of the Locust." Nathanael West: A Collection of Critical Essays*, ed. Jay Martin. Englewood Cliffs, New Jersey: Prentice-Hall, Incorporated, 1971, pp. 138-139. Williams finds *The Day of the Locust* "a most beautiful and tenderly conceived portrait of the eternal bitch" (p. 138). Of West he remarks, "Had he gone on there would have unfolded, I think, the finest prose talent of our age" (p. 138).

59. Wilson, Edmund. "The Boys in the Back Room." *Nathanael West: A Collection of Critical Essays*, ed. Jay Martin. Englewood Cliffs, New Jersey: Prentice-Hall, Incorporated, 1971, pp. 140-143. Of *The Day of the Locust* Wilson comments, "Mr. West has caught the emptiness of Hollywood; and he is, as far as I know, the first writer to make this emptiness horrible" (p. 141). Concludes Wilson, "The America of murder and rapes which fill the Los Angeles papers is only the obverse side of the America of the inanities of the movies . . . [but the novel suffers] from the lack of a center in the community with which it deals" (p. 142).

Appendix--West's Works

A) West's Novels

Note. Below I have listed West's novels, plus their English language
editions and translations with introductions that might be useful to
scholars. However, I have not personally examined all of these editions.
Most of my titles come from the various Library of Congress listings,
C.B.I., the *British Museum Catalogue of Printed Books*, the French *Biblio*,
and *Deutsche Bibliographie*. I have provided whatever information is
available in those sources. For formal bibliographical descriptions
of most of the editions and reprints, plus a complete listing of translations, see William White's *Nathanael West: A Comprehensive Bibliography*.

1. *The Dream Life of Balso Snell*. New York, Paris: Contact Editions,
1931, 95 pp.

2. *Miss Lonelyhearts*. New York: Liveright, Incorporated, Publishers,
1933, 213 pp.

   a. *Miss Lonelyhearts*. New York: Greenberg, Publisher, 1934,
   213 pp.

   b. *Miss Lonelyhearts*. New York: New Directions (The New Classics
   Series), 1946, 213 pp. Introduction by Robert M. Coates.

   c. *Miss Lonelyhearts*. London: The Grey Walls Press, 1949, 116 pp.
   Introduction by Alan Ross.

   d. *Miss Lonelyhearts*. New York: Avon Publications, Incorporated,
   1955, 95 pp.

   e. *Miss Lonelyhearts*. New York: Avon Publications, Incorporated,
   1959, 96 pp. Introduction by Malcolm Cowley.

   f. *Miss Lonelyhearts*. New York: An Avon Book, 1964, 128 pp.
   Introduction by Stanley Edgar Hyman. The same novel was published
   as "An Avon Library Book" in 1965, with an afterward by Hyman.

   g. *Mademoiselle Coeur-Brisé (Miss Lonelyhearts)*. Roman. Tr.
   par Marcelle Sibon. Preface de Phillipe Soupalt. Paris: Le
   Sagittaire, 1946, 152 pp.

   h. *Schreiben Sie Miss Lonelyhearts*. Ein Roman. (Aus. d. Amerikan
   ubertragen von Fritz Guttinger. Mit einer Einfuhrung von Alan Ross.)
   Zurich: Diogenes Verlag, 1961, 138 pp.

   i. *Schreiben Sie Miss Lonelyhearts*. Ein Roman. (Aus d. Amerikan.
   ins Dt. ubertr. von Fritz Guttinger. Mit e. Einf. von Alan Ross.)
   Frankfurt a. M. und Hamburg: Fischer Bucherei, 1963, 141 pp.

j. *Froken Hjertesukk*. Oversatt av Gunnel Malmstrom. Oslo: H. Aschehoug & Co., 1965, 113 pp. Introduction by Alan Ross.

k. *Vastaathan kirjeeseeni*. Helsinki: Werner Soderstrom Osakeyhtio, 1966, 117 pp. Introduction by Antero Tiusanen, the translator.

3. *A Cool Million. The Dismantling of Lemuel Pitkin*. New York: Covici, Friede, Publishers, 1934, 229 pp.

    a. *A Cool Million. The Dismantling of Lemuel Pitkin*. London: Neville Spearman, 1954, 139 pp.

    b. *Miss Lonelyhearts* and *A Cool Million*. Harmondsworth, Middlesex: Penguin Books, 1961, 176 pp.

    c. *A Cool Million*. New York: The Berkley Publishing Corporation (A Berkley Medallion Book), 1961, 142 pp.

    d. *The Dream Life of Balso Snell* and *A Cool Million*. New York: Noonday Press, 1963, 184 pp.

    e. *A Cool Million* and *The Dream Life of Balso Snell*. New York: An Avon Library Book, 1965, 158 pp.

4. *The Day of the Locust*. New York: Random House, 1939, 238 pp.

    a. *The Day of the Locust*. New York: New Directions (New Classics Series), 1950, 167 pp. Introduction by Richard B. Gehman.

    b. *The Day of the Locust*. London: The Grey Walls Press, 1951, 208 pp.

    c. *The Day of the Locust*. New York: Bantom Books, 1953, 144 pp. Introduction by Richard B. Gehman.

    d. *Miss Lonelyhearts & The Day of the Locust*. New York: A New Directions Paperback, 1962, 247 pp.

    e. *The Day of the Locust*. New York: Time Incorporated (Time Reading Program Special Edition), 1965, 167 pp. Introduction by Budd Schulberg.

    f. *Grashopporna*. Stockholm: Christofers Bokforlag, 1959, 201 pp. Translated with an introduction by Reider Ekner.

5. *The Complete Works of Nathanael West*. New York: Farrar, Straus and Cudahy, 1957, 421 pp. Introduction by Alan Ross.

    a. *The Complete Works of Nathanael West*. London: Secker and Warburg, 1957, 421 pp. Introduction by Alan Ross.

    b. *Romans*. Trad. par Marcelle Sibon. Avant-pro-pos de Monique Nathan. Paris: Editions du Seuil, 1961, 352 pp.

B) Other Works by West Published
During His Lifetime

1. "Rondeau." *The Brown Jug*, 2 (December 1922), 24.

2. "Euripides--A Playwright." *Casements*, 1 (July 1923).

3. "Death." *Casements*, 2 (May 1924), 15.

4. "A Barefaced Lie." *Overland Monthly*, 87 (July 1929), 210, 219. See [321], [419], and [319] for a dispute over the attribution of this story.

5. "Book Marks for Today." *New York World Telegram* (20 October 1931), 23. A letter to the editor written with Julian L. Shapiro.

6. "Miss Lonelyhearts and the Lamb." *Contact*, 1 (February 1932), 80-85.

7. "Miss Lonelyhearts and the Dead Pan" and "Miss Lonelyhearts and the Clean Old Man." *Contact* 1 (May 1932), 13-27.

8. "Miss Lonelyhearts in the Dismal Swamp." *Contempo*, 2 (5 July 1932), 1, 2.

9. "Miss Lonelyhearts on a Field Trip." *Contact*, 1 (October 1932), 50-57.

10. "Some Notes on Violence." *Contact*, 1 (October 1932), 132-133.

11. "Christmass Poem." *Contempo*, 3 (21 February 1933), 4.

12. "Some Notes on *Miss L.*" *Contempo*, 3 (15 May 1933), 1-2.

13. "Business Deal." *Americana*, 1 (October 1933), 14-15.

14. "Soft Soap for the Barber." *The New Republic*, 81 (14 November 1934), 23. Review.

15. "Bird and Bottle." *Pacific Weekly*, 5 (10 November 1936), 329-331.

C) Movie Scripts by West

Note. The following movie scripts are discussed by Jay Martin in *Nathanael West: The Art of His Life*, pp. 401-406, and in various places in the text of his biography. I will first list those movies which were eventually produced and then those which were not.

1. *Ticket to Paradise*. Republic Productions, 1936. With Jack Natteford.

2. *Follow Your Heart*. Republic Productions, 1936. With Lester Cole and Samuel Ornitz.

3. *The President's Mystery*. Republic Productions, 1936. With Lester Cole.

4. *Gangs of New York*. Republic Productions, 1936-37.

5. *Jim Hanvey--Detective*. Republic Productions, 1936.

6. *Rhythm in the Clouds*. Republic Productions, 1937.

7. *Ladies in Distress*. Republic Productions, 1938. West's version was revised.

8. *Born to Be Wild*. Republic Productions, 1937.

9. *It Could Happen to You*. Republic Productions, 1937.

10. *Orphans of the Street*. Republic Productions, 1937-38.

11. *Five Came Back*. RKO Pictures, 1938. With Jerry Cady and Dalton Trumbo.

12. *Before the Fact*. RKO Pictures, 1939. With Boris Ingster. Released as *Suspicion*.

13. *Men Against the Sky*. RKO Pictures, 1940.

14. *Let's Make Music*. RKO Pictures, 1940.

15. *Strangers on the Third Floor*. RKO Pictures, 1940.

16. *The Spirit of Culver*. Universal Corporation, 1939. With Whitney Bolton.

17. *I Stole a Million*. Universal Corporation, 1939.

18. *The Victoria Docks at Eight*. Universal Corporation, 1939.

*The following movie scripts by West were never produced:

19. *Beauty Parlor*. Columbia Studios, 1933.

20. *Return to the Soil*. Columbia Studios, 1933.

21. [A race-horse story]. Columbia Studios, 1936.

22. *Bachelor Girl*. Republic Productions, 1937.

23. *Stormy Weather*. Republic Productions, 1937-38.

24. *Osceola*. 1935?

26. *Broadway Bible*. 1938.

27. *The Squealor*. Columbia Studios, 1938.

156

28. *Flight South*. MGM, 1938. With Gordon Kahn and Wells Root.

29. *A Cool Million: A Screen Story*. Columbia Studios, 1940. With Boris Ingster.

30. *Amateur Angel*. Columbia Pictures, 1940. With Boris Ingster.

D) Plays by West

1. *Good Hunting: A Satire in Three Acts*. With Joseph Schrank. This play was produced by Jerome Mayer and Leonard S. Field and had a brief run in New York, 1938. It was never published. For a discussion of the play, see Jay Martin's *Nathanael West: The Art of His Life*, pp. 289, 290 ff.q., 298 ff.q., 314, 317, 349, 359, 363.

2. *Even Stephen*. With S. J. Perelman, 1934. Never published or produced. For a discussion of this play, see Jay Martin's *Nathanael West: The Art of His Life*, pp. 250-51 q., 255, 261, 295.

E) West's Unpublished Writings

Note. All of the following are discussed in Jay Martin's *Nathanael West: The Art of His Life*. Page numbers refer to Martin's study.

1. "The Adventurer," pp. 35-6 q., 50-1 q., 166 ff., 183. Note also that Martin quotes a previously unpublished extract of this story in his foreward to this work.

2. "American Chauve Souris," **pp. 248-9 q.**, 261.

3. "Burn the Cities," pp. 185, 329 ff. q.

4. "The Imposter," pp. 88-9 q., 126, 172.

5. "Mr. Potts of Pottstown," pp. 168 ff. q., 183.

6. "St. Pamphile: A Novelette," pp. 109, 251.

7. "The Sun, the Lady and the Gas Station," pp. 171-2 q.

8. "Three Eskimos," p. 213 q.

9. "Tibetan Night," pp. 170-71 q.

10. "Western Union Boy," pp. 41-2 q., 55, 172, 268n, 269 n. q.

F) Miscellany

1. *Through the Hole in the Mundane Millstone*, a four page advertisement for *The Dream Life of Balso Snell*. West's text is reprinted in Jay Martin's *Nathanael West: A Collection of Critical Essays* (see [43]).

2. "Makers of Mass Neuroses," a speech given by West to a San Francisco writers' convention. As far as I have been able to determine, the text of this speech has not survived.

G) Some Information on Manuscripts

Note. I am indebted to Professor J. Albert Robbins and Professor Jay Martin for the following information.

1. UCLA has a typescript with ink corrections of *A Cool Million* in Special Collections; L1.

2. New York Public Library has a copy of *The Spirit of Culver*.

3. Yale University Library, L12.

4. University of Delaware, L1.

5. Morris Library, Southern Illinois University, Carbondale, L12, C2.

6. Lockwood Memorial Library, SUNY, Buffalo, L3.

7. Princeton Theological Seminary, Princeton, N.J., L1.

8. Princeton University, (significant holdings without specific count).

10. All movie scripts and treatments listed in Jay Martin's *Nathanael West: The Art of His Life* (see pp. 401-406) are in the files of the various studios.

11. S. J. Perelman has a good deal of material, including one ms. of *The Day of the Locust*, a ts. with ink corrections of one chapter of *Miss Lonelyhearts*, and several letters.

12. Jay Martin possesses zeroxes of all the stories, plus some movie scripts, and also has some unpublished letters West wrote to Jo Conway.

The Complete Works of

Farrar, Straus and Cudahy : New York

Index

162

165